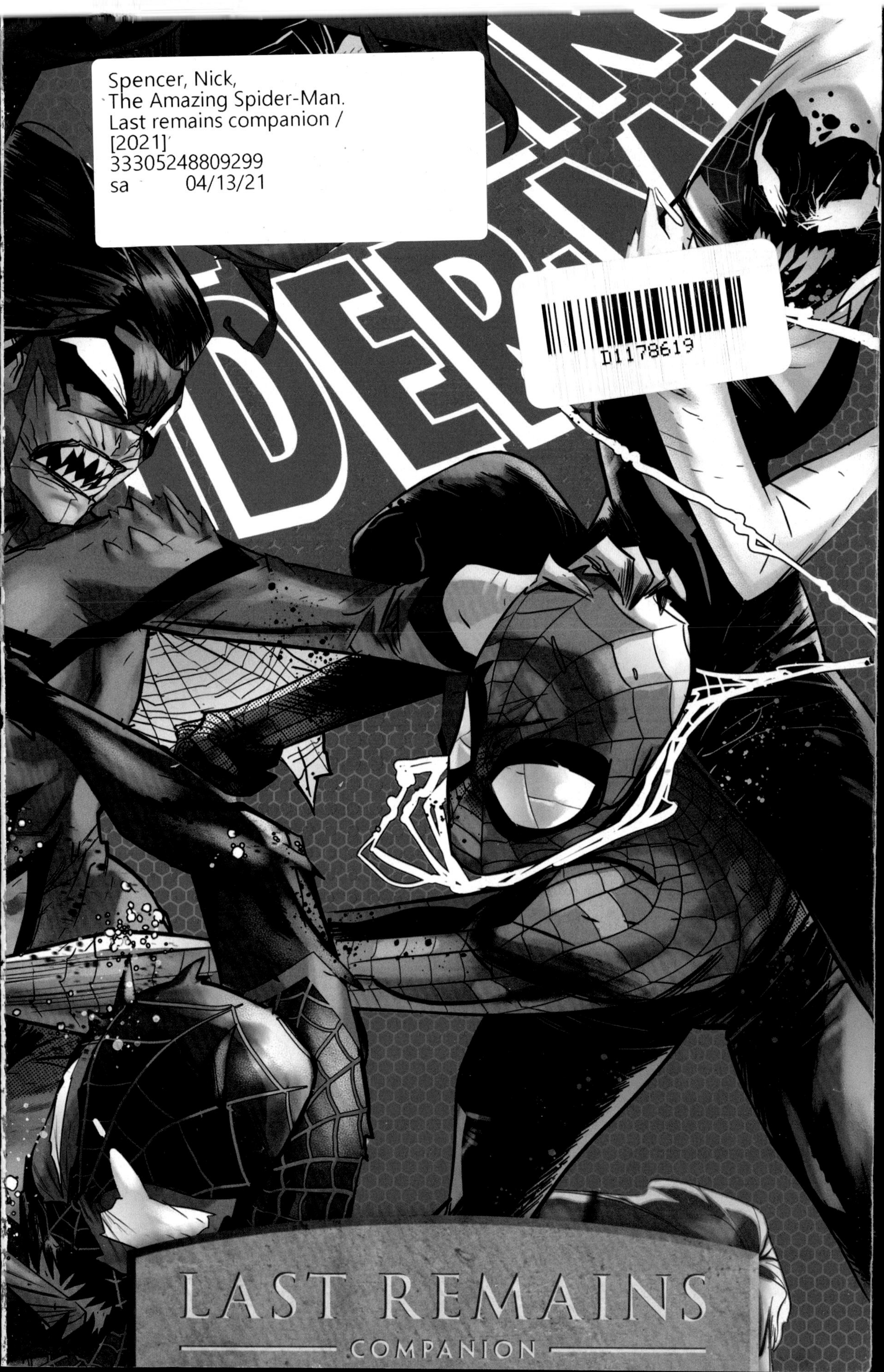
LAST REMAINS
COMPANION

Norman Osborn, formerly the Green Goblin, went from inmate to administrator at Ravencroft Institute, until the Sin-Eater cleansed him of his sins. Now he has to face everything he's done. He claims that the true threat behind the Sin-Eater — the mysterious villain Kindred — is really his son, Harry.

Meanwhile, Peter's Spider-Friends are in trouble. Known as the Order of the Web, they were helping Peter against the Sin-Eater when they were consumed by all the sins cleansed by the Sin-Eater and turned into demonic versions of themselves. Now they are Kindred's puppets with which he plans to wreak havoc on Spider-Man and the rest of New York City...

SPIDER-MAN CREATED BY STAN LEE & STEVE DITKO

COLLECTION EDITOR JENNIFER GRÜNWALD
ASSISTANT EDITOR DANIEL KIRCHHOFFER ✦ ASSISTANT MANAGING EDITOR MAIA LOY
ASSISTANT MANAGING EDITOR LISA MONTALBANO ✦ VP PRODUCTION & SPECIAL PROJECTS JEFF YOUNGQUIST
BOOK DESIGNERS ADAM DEL RE WITH JAY BOWEN
SVP PRINT, SALES & MARKETING DAVID GABRIEL ✦ EDITOR IN CHIEF C.B. CEBULSKI

AMAZING SPIDER-MAN: LAST REMAINS COMPANION. Contains material originally published in magazine form as AMAZING SPIDER-MAN (2020) #50.LR-54.LR. First printing 2021. ISBN 978-1-302-92779-0. Published by MARVEL WORLDWIDE, INC., a subsidiary of MARVEL ENTERTAINMENT, LLC. OFFICE OF PUBLICATION: 1290 Avenue of the Americas, New York, NY. 10104. © 2021 MARVEL. No similarity between any of the names, characters, persons, and/or institutions in this magazine with those of any living or dead person or institution is intended, and any such similarity which may exist is purely coincidental. Printed in Canada. KEVIN FEIGE, Chief Creative Officer; DAN BUCKLEY, President, Marvel Entertainment; JOE QUESADA, EVP & Creative Director; DAVID BOGART, Associate Publisher & SVP of Talent Affairs; TOM BREVOORT, VP, Executive Editor; NICK LOWE, Executive Editor, VP of Content, Digital Publishing; DAVID GABRIEL, VP of Print & Digital Publishing; JEFF YOUNGQUIST, VP of Production & Special Projects; ALEX MORALES, Director of Publishing Operations; DAN EDINGTON, Managing Editor; RICKEY PURDIN, Director of Talent Relations; JENNIFER GRÜNWALD, Senior Editor, Special Projects; SUSAN CRESPI, Production Manager; STAN LEE, Chairman Emeritus. For information regarding advertising in Marvel Comics or on Marvel.com, please contact Vit DeBellis, Custom Solutions & Integrated Advertising Manager, at vdebellis@marvel.com. For Marvel subscription inquiries, please call 888-511-5480. Manufactured between 1/15/2021 and 2/16/2021 by SOLISCO PRINTERS, SCOTT, QC, CANADA.

10 9 8 7 6 5 4 3 2 1

the AMAZING SPIDER-MAN

LAST REMAINS COMPANION

WRITERS   **NICK SPENCER** & **MATTHEW ROSENBERG**

AMAZING SPIDER-MAN #50.LR-52.LR

ARTIST   **FEDERICO VICENTINI**

COLOR ARTISTS   **MARCIO MENYZ** WITH **ERICK ARCINIEGA** (#52.LR)

AMAZING SPIDER-MAN #53.LR-54.LR

PENCILERS   **FEDERICO VICENTINI** & **TAKESHI MIYAZAWA**

INKERS   **FEDERICO VICENTINI** & **TAKESHI MIYAZAWA** WITH **SCOTT HANNA**

COLOR ARTISTS   **MARCIO MENYZ** (#53.LR) & **ERICK ARCINIEGA** (#53.LR-54.LR)

LETTERERS   **VC's JOE CARAMAGNA** (#50.LR) & **ARIANA MAHER** (#51.LR-54.LR)

COVER ART   **SARA PICHELLI** & **RACHELLE ROSENBERG** (#50.LR) **MARCELO FERREIRA** & **DAVID CURIEL** (#51.LR-54.LR)

ASSISTANT EDITORS   **TOM GRONEMAN** & **LINDSEY COHICK**
ASSOCIATE EDITOR   **KATHLEEN WISNESKI**
EDITOR   **NICK LOWE**

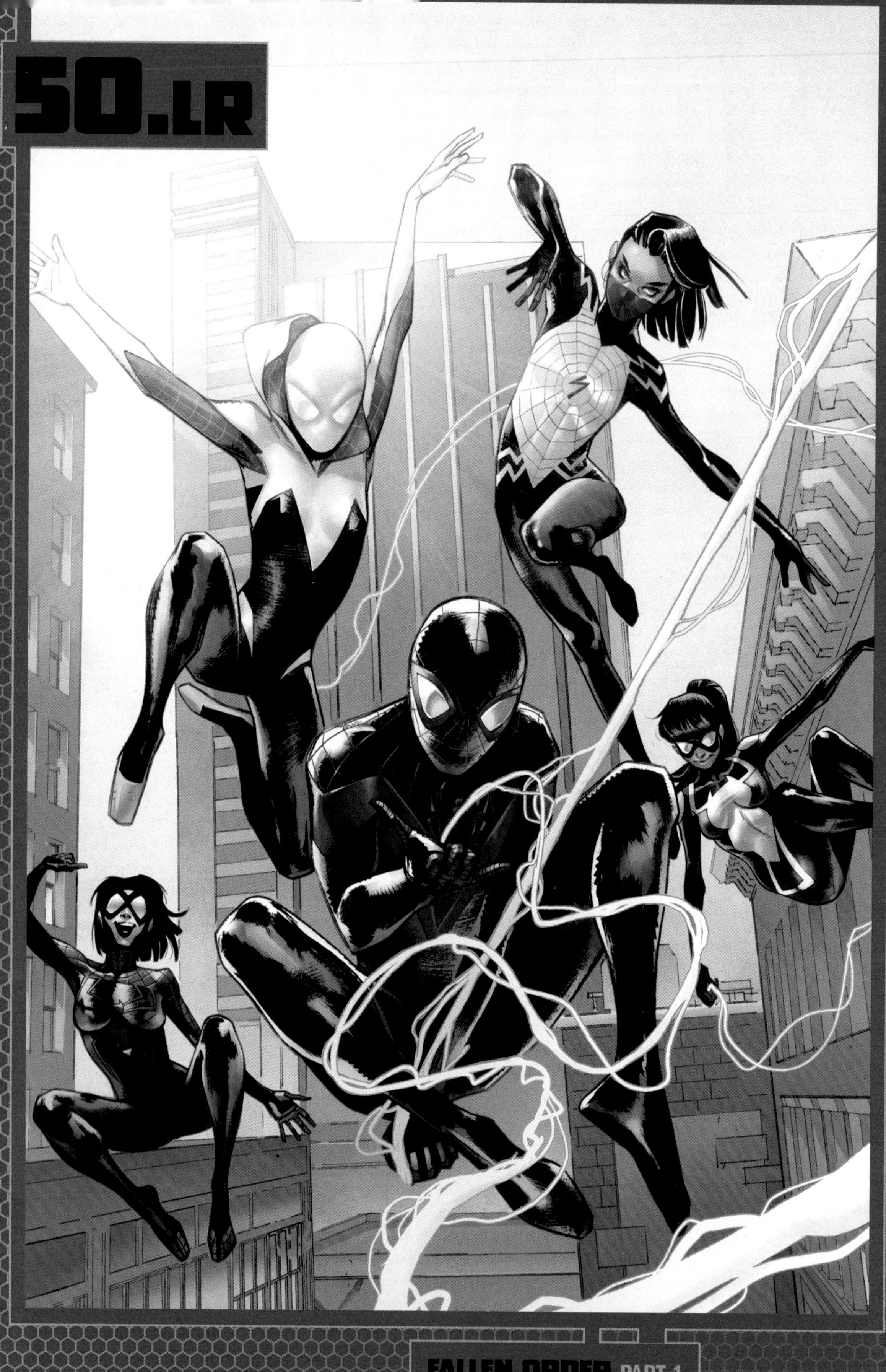
50.LR

FALLEN ORDER PART 1

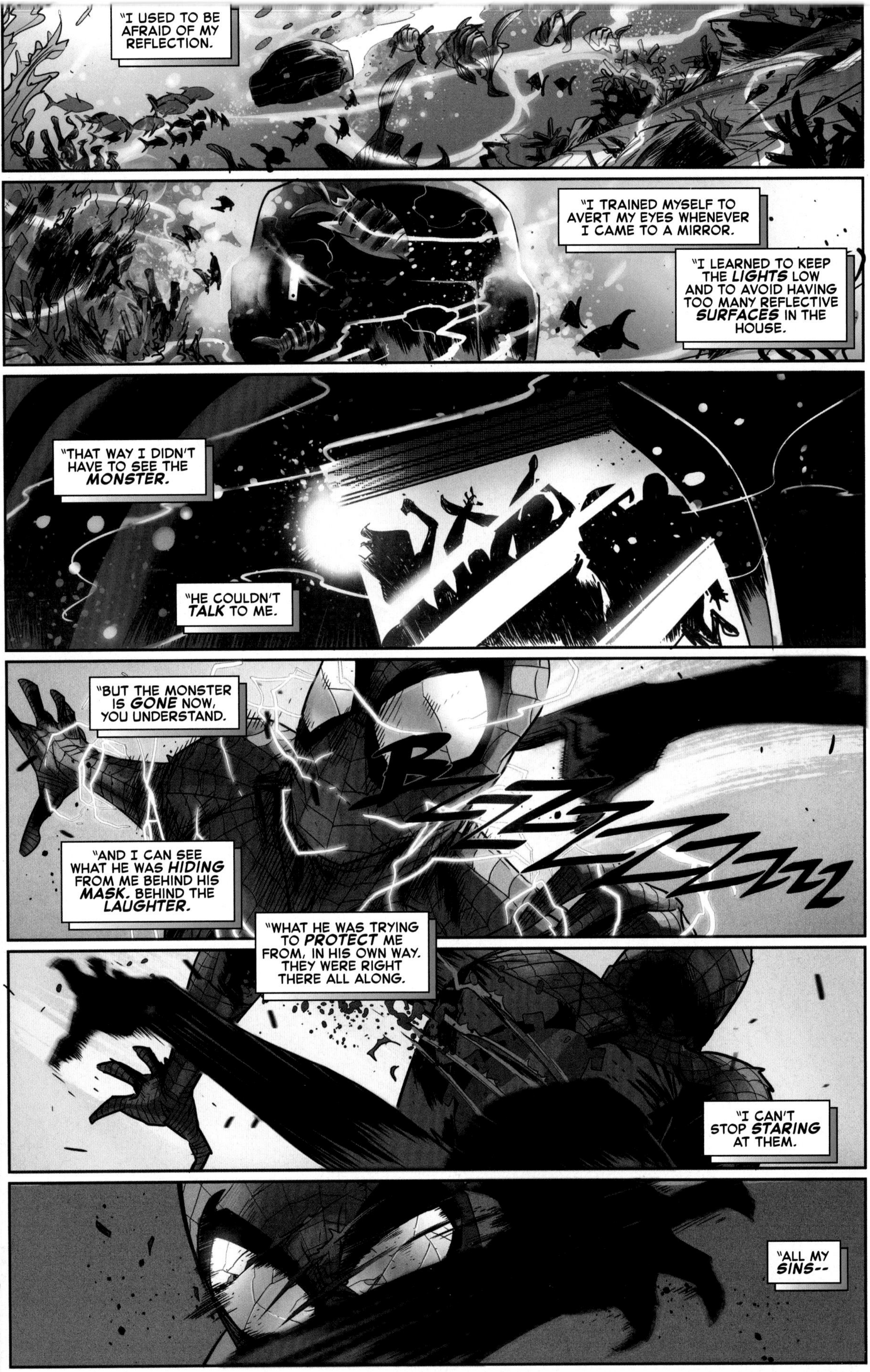
"I USED TO BE AFRAID OF MY REFLECTION.
"I TRAINED MYSELF TO AVERT MY EYES WHENEVER I CAME TO A MIRROR.
"I LEARNED TO KEEP THE LIGHTS LOW AND TO AVOID HAVING TOO MANY REFLECTIVE SURFACES IN THE HOUSE.
"THAT WAY I DIDN'T HAVE TO SEE THE MONSTER.
"HE COULDN'T TALK TO ME.
"BUT THE MONSTER IS GONE NOW, YOU UNDERSTAND.
BZZZZZZZZZ
"AND I CAN SEE WHAT HE WAS HIDING FROM ME BEHIND HIS MASK. BEHIND THE LAUGHTER.
"WHAT HE WAS TRYING TO PROTECT ME FROM, IN HIS OWN WAY. THEY WERE RIGHT THERE ALL ALONG.
"I CAN'T STOP STARING AT THEM.
"ALL MY SINS--

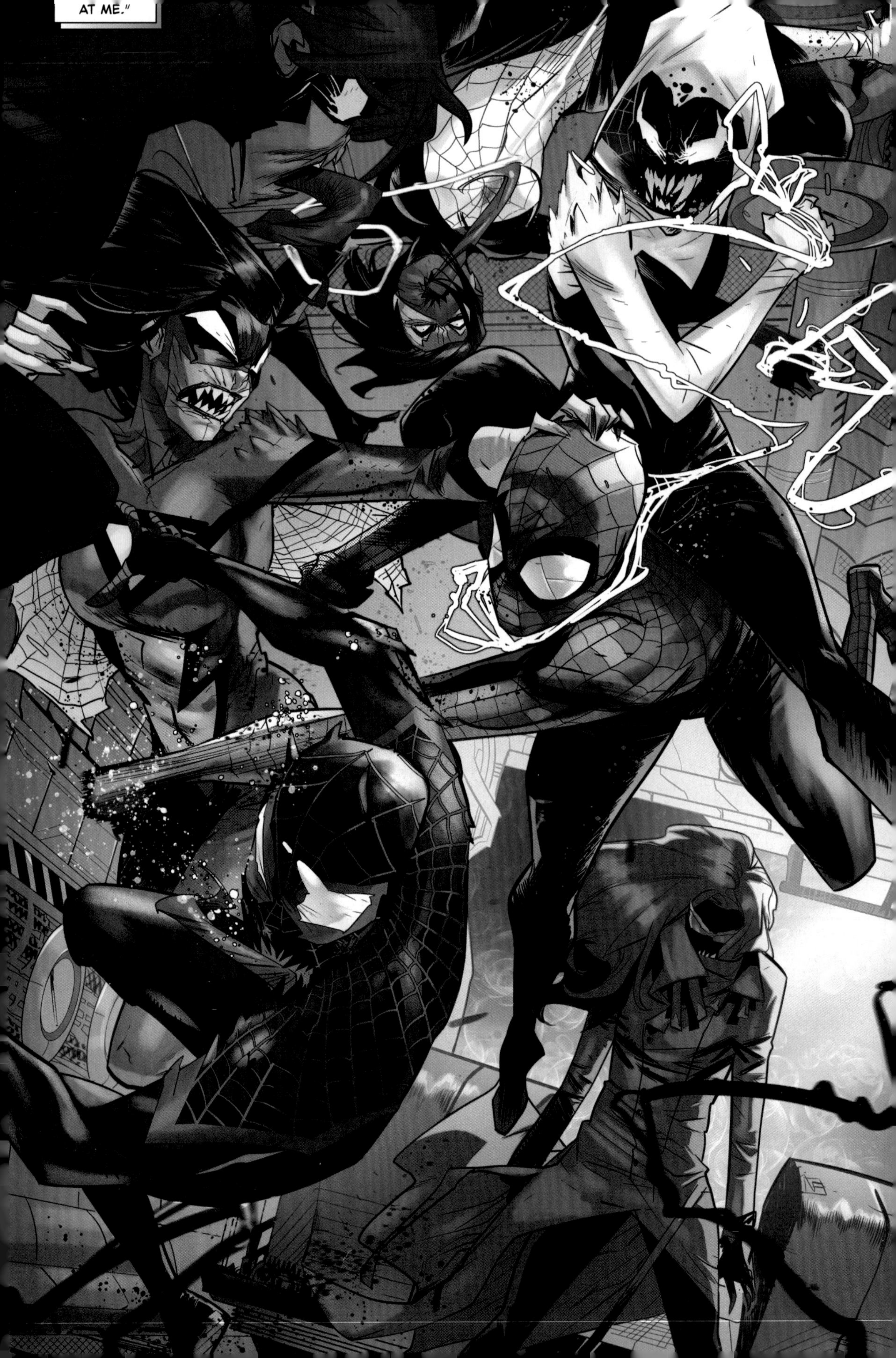
AT ME."

UNDERSTAND NOW.

I SOLD MY SOUL TO A *DEMON.*

...I LET IT TURN ME INTO A MONSTER THAT DESTROYED *COUNTLESS* LIVES. AND ALL I ASKED FOR IN EXCHANGE--

--WAS TO BE FREE OF THE *GUILT.*

OH, COME ON, NORMAN--

--YOU'RE HARDLY THE FIRST TO BLAME A *DIVINE POWER* FOR YOUR OWN SHORTCOMINGS. AND YOU'RE CERTAINLY AMONG THE LEAST CONVINCING.

I CAME BACK TO RAVENCROFT AND TRIED TO GIVE YOU A CHANCE. I THOUGHT PERHAPS WE COULD DO SOME *GOOD* TOGETHER.

BUT NOW I SEE YOU HAVEN'T CHANGED AT *ALL.* WHATEVER IT IS YOU WERE PLANNING DOWN IN THOSE HIDDEN SUBLEVELS, I'M SURE THE AUTHORITIES WOULD LIKE TO HEAR ABOUT IT.

THE ONLY REASON I HAVEN'T REPORTED IT YET IS YOUR INSISTENCE THAT LIVES ARE AT *IMMEDIATE RISK.* BUT I WON'T SIT HERE AND LISTEN TO YOU TRY TO PASS THE BLAME FOR--

YOU *MISUNDERSTAND* ME, DOCTOR KAFKA...

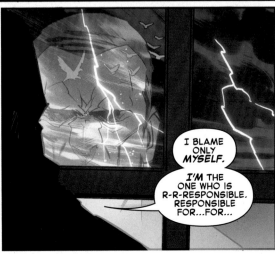

I BLAME ONLY *MYSELF.*

I'M THE ONE WHO IS R-R-RESPONSIBLE. RESPONSIBLE FOR...FOR...

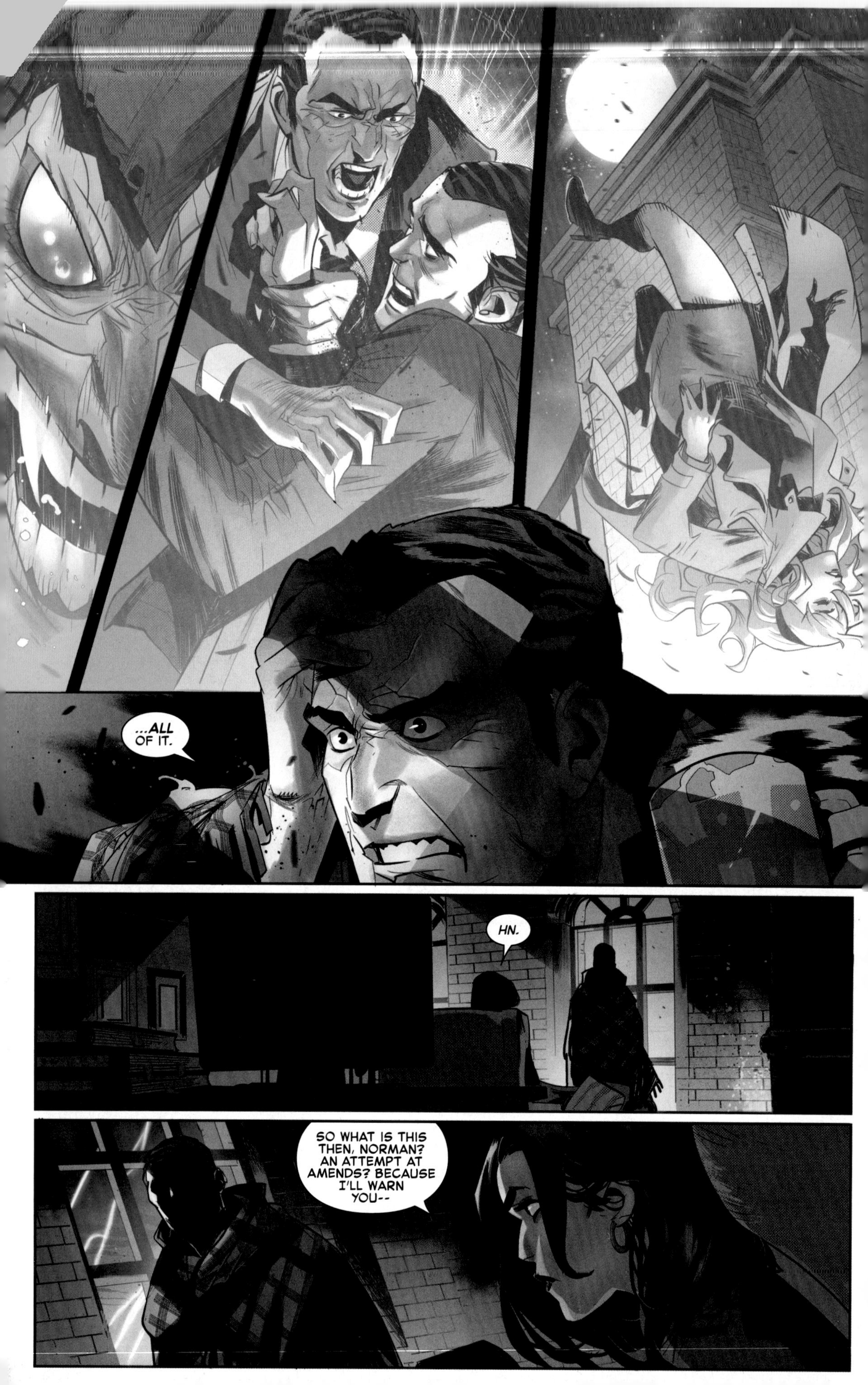
...ALL OF IT.
HN.
SO WHAT IS THIS THEN, NORMAN? AN ATTEMPT AT AMENDS? BECAUSE I'LL WARN YOU--

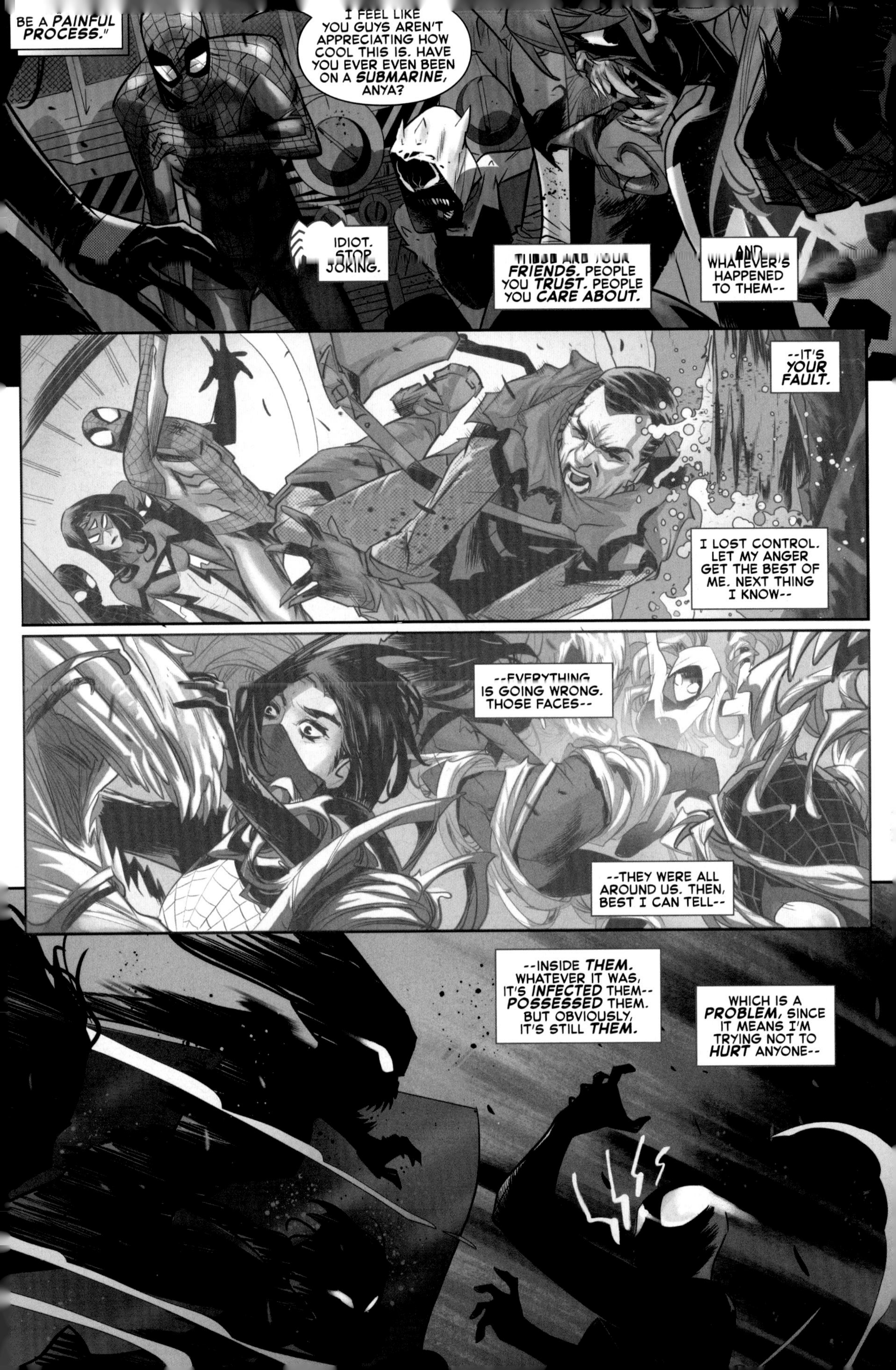

BE A *PAINFUL PROCESS.*"
I FEEL LIKE YOU GUYS AREN'T APPRECIATING HOW COOL THIS IS. HAVE YOU EVER EVEN BEEN ON A *SUBMARINE,* ANYA?
IDIOT. STOP JOKING.
FRIENDS. PEOPLE YOU *TRUST.* PEOPLE YOU *CARE ABOUT.*
AND WHATEVER'S HAPPENED TO THEM--
--IT'S *YOUR FAULT.*
I LOST CONTROL. LET MY ANGER GET THE BEST OF ME. NEXT THING I KNOW--
--EVERYTHING IS GOING WRONG. THOSE FACES--
--THEY WERE ALL AROUND US. THEN, BEST I CAN TELL--
--INSIDE *THEM.* WHATEVER IT WAS, IT'S *INFECTED* THEM-- *POSSESSED* THEM. BUT OBVIOUSLY, IT'S STILL *THEM.*
WHICH IS A *PROBLEM,* SINCE IT MEANS I'M TRYING NOT TO *HURT* ANYONE--

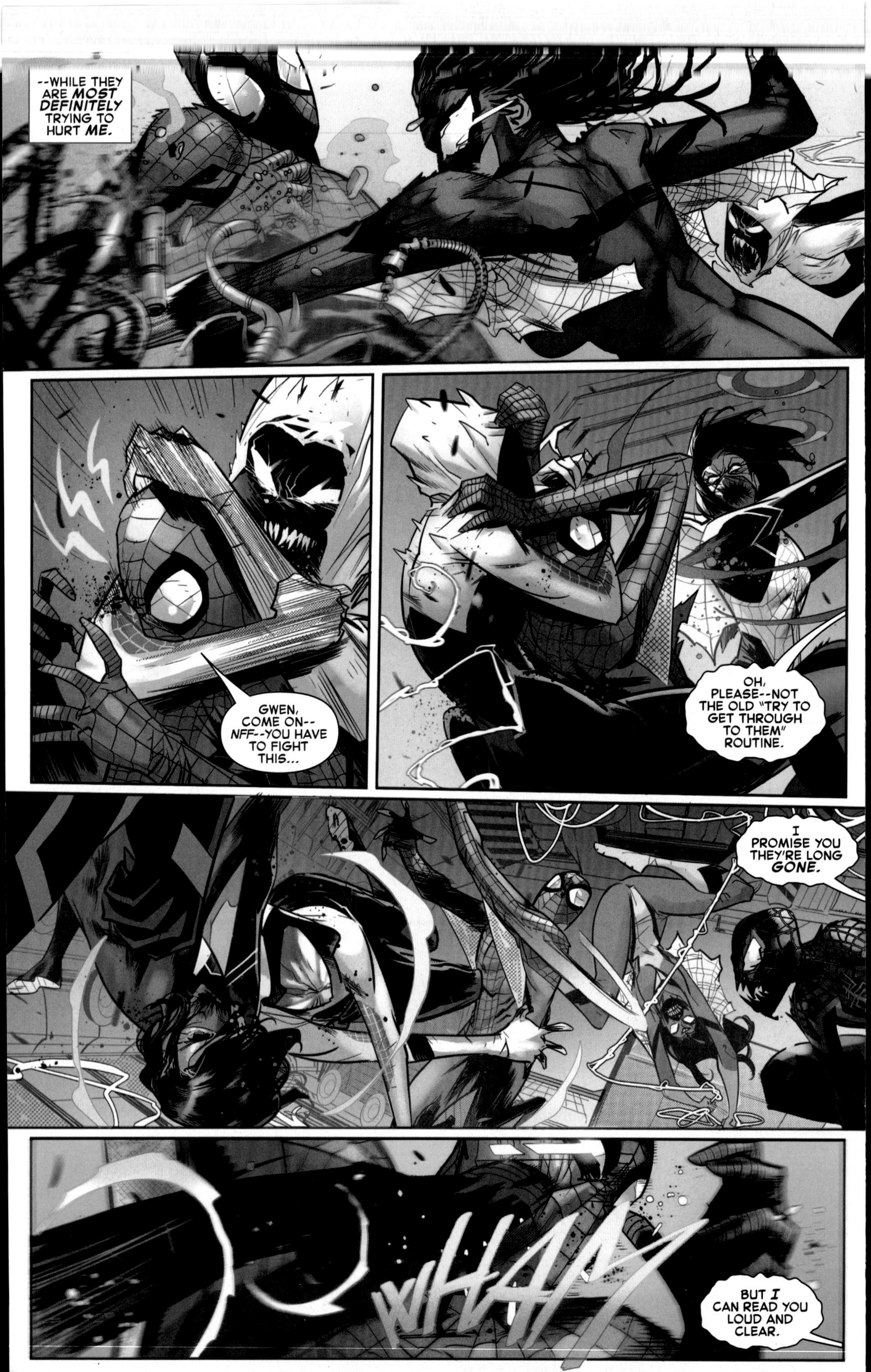
--WHILE THEY ARE *MOST DEFINITELY* TRYING TO HURT *ME.*
GWEN, COME ON-- *NFF*--YOU HAVE TO FIGHT THIS...
OH, PLEASE--NOT THE OLD "TRY TO GET THROUGH TO THEM" ROUTINE.
I PROMISE YOU THEY'RE LONG *GONE.*
WHAM
BUT *I* CAN READ YOU LOUD AND CLEAR.

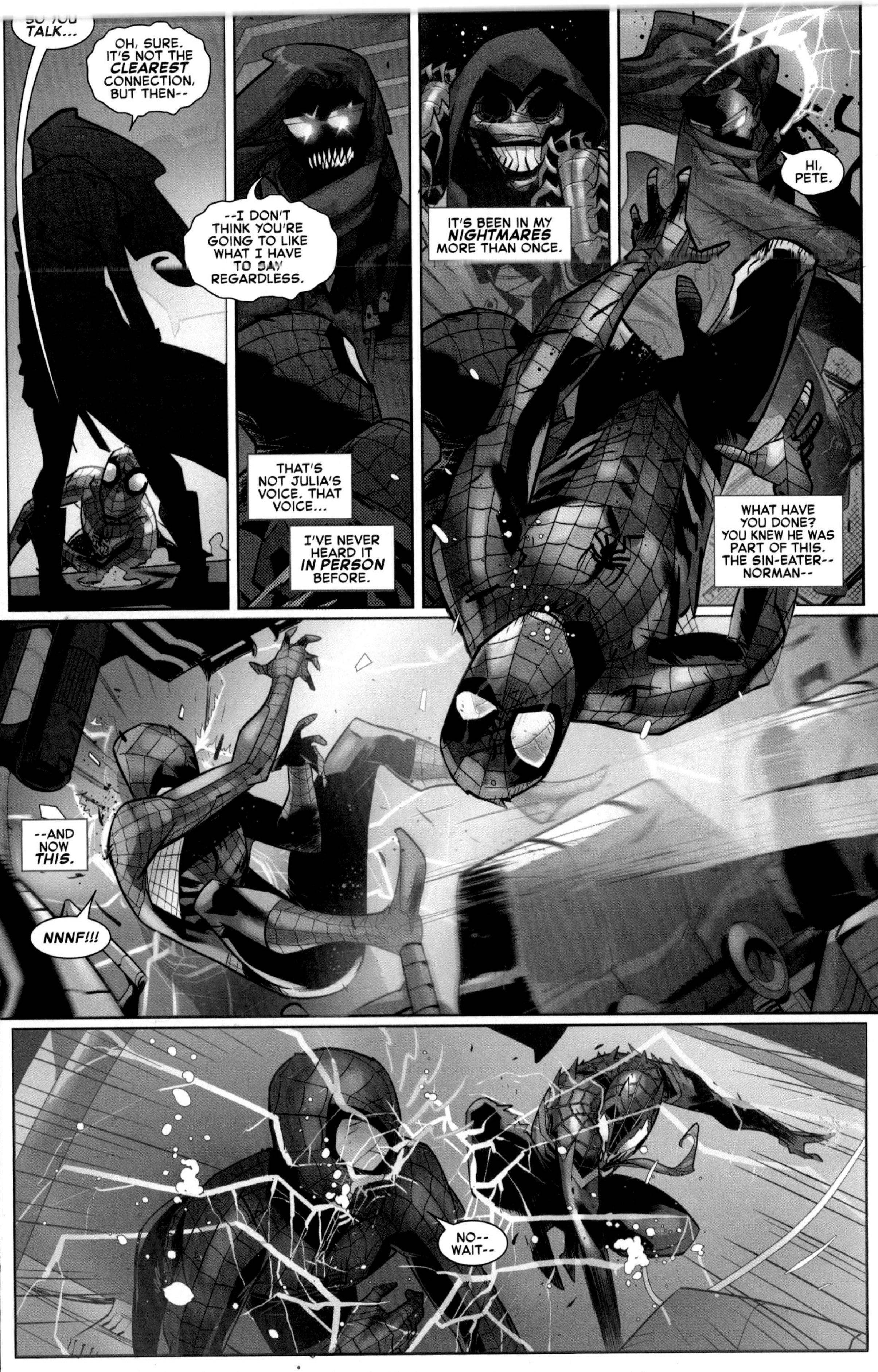

SO YOU TALK...
OH, SURE. IT'S NOT THE CLEAREST CONNECTION, BUT THEN--
--I DON'T THINK YOU'RE GOING TO LIKE WHAT I HAVE TO SAY REGARDLESS.
THAT'S NOT JULIA'S VOICE. THAT VOICE...
I'VE NEVER HEARD IT IN PERSON BEFORE.
IT'S BEEN IN MY NIGHTMARES MORE THAN ONCE.
HI, PETE.
WHAT HAVE YOU DONE? YOU KNEW HE WAS PART OF THIS. THE SIN-EATER-- NORMAN--
--AND NOW THIS.
NNNF!!!
NO-- WAIT--

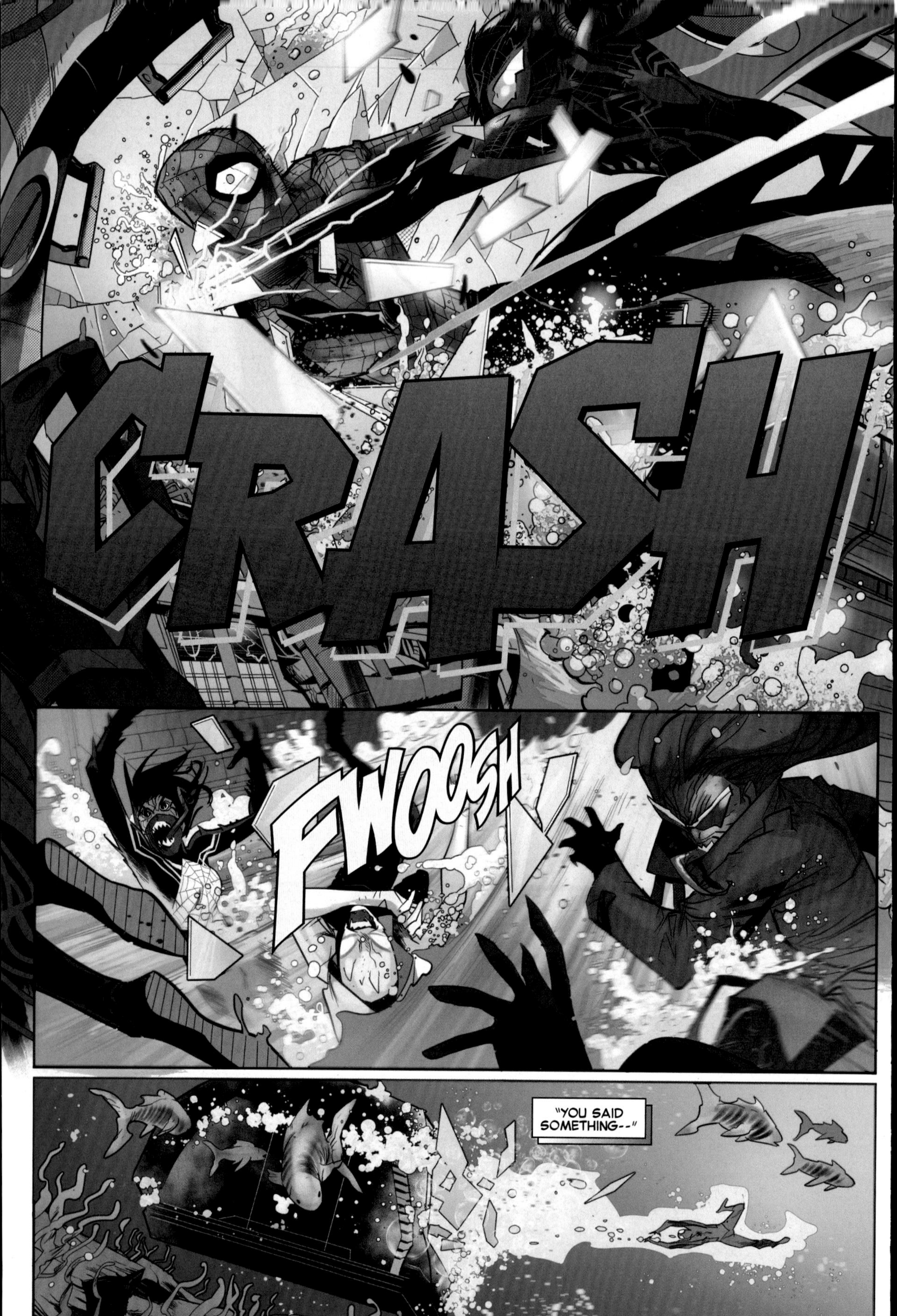
CRASH
FWOOSH
"YOU SAID SOMETHING--"

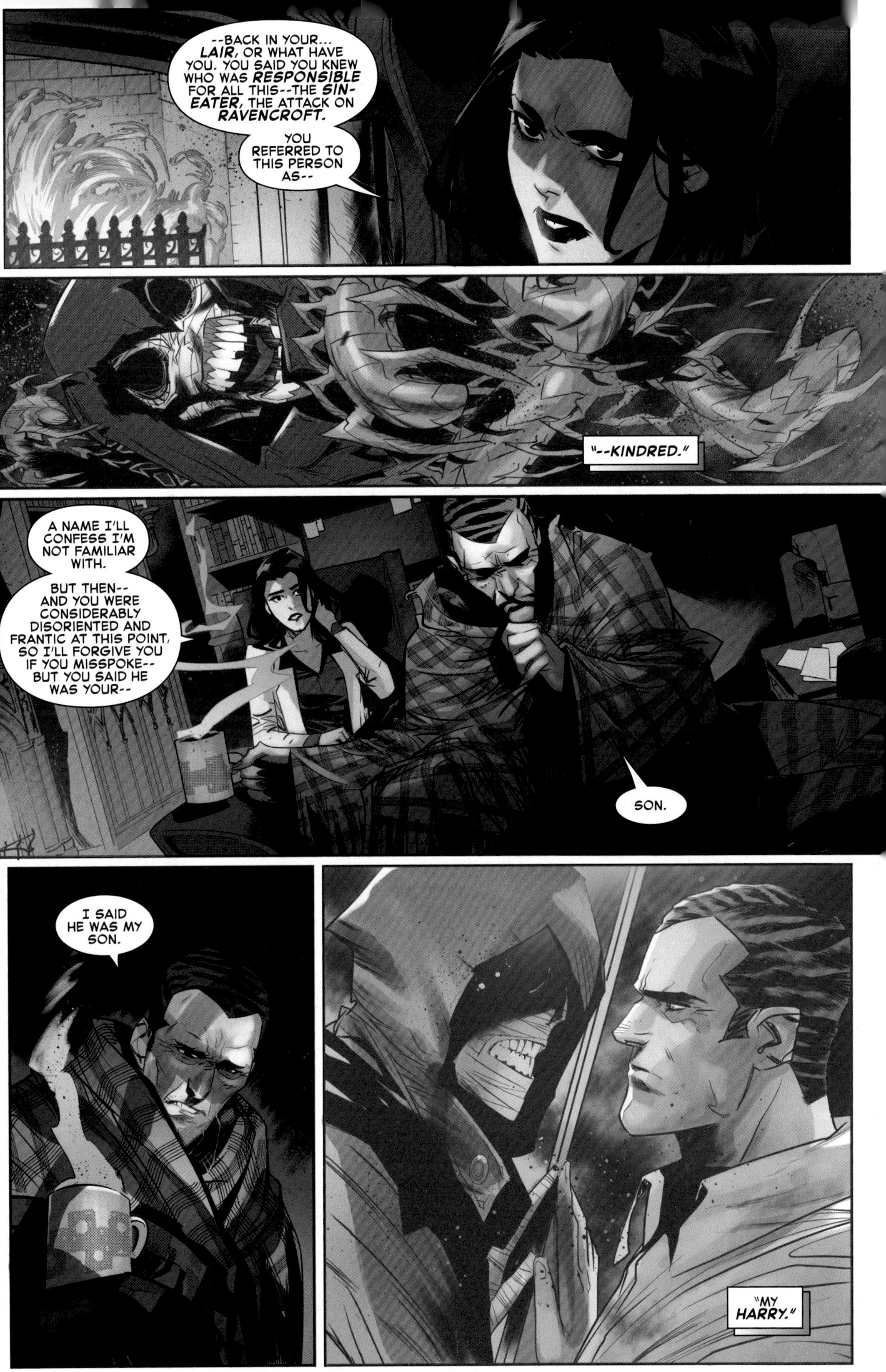
--BACK IN YOUR... LAIR, OR WHAT HAVE YOU. YOU SAID YOU KNEW WHO WAS RESPONSIBLE FOR ALL THIS--THE SIN-EATER, THE ATTACK ON RAVENCROFT.
YOU REFERRED TO THIS PERSON AS--
"--KINDRED."
A NAME I'LL CONFESS I'M NOT FAMILIAR WITH.
BUT THEN--AND YOU WERE CONSIDERABLY DISORIENTED AND FRANTIC AT THIS POINT, SO I'LL FORGIVE YOU IF YOU MISSPOKE--BUT YOU SAID HE WAS YOUR--
SON.
I SAID HE WAS MY SON.
"MY HARRY."

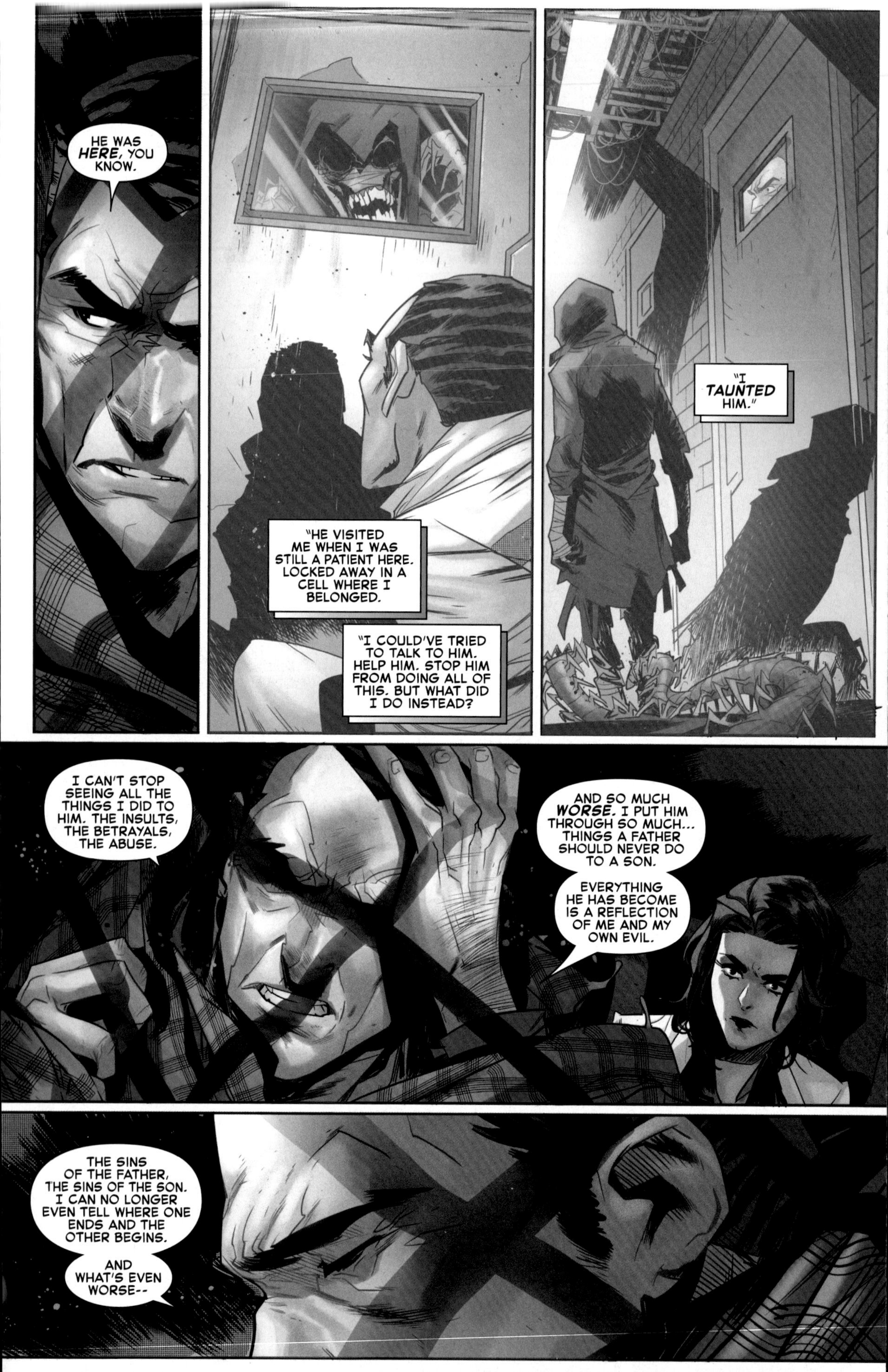
HE WAS HERE, YOU KNOW.
"HE VISITED ME WHEN I WAS STILL A PATIENT HERE. LOCKED AWAY IN A CELL WHERE I BELONGED.
"I COULD'VE TRIED TO TALK TO HIM. HELP HIM. STOP HIM FROM DOING ALL OF THIS. BUT WHAT DID I DO INSTEAD?
"I TAUNTED HIM."
I CAN'T STOP SEEING ALL THE THINGS I DID TO HIM. THE INSULTS, THE BETRAYALS, THE ABUSE.
AND SO MUCH WORSE. I PUT HIM THROUGH SO MUCH... THINGS A FATHER SHOULD NEVER DO TO A SON.
EVERYTHING HE HAS BECOME IS A REFLECTION OF ME AND MY OWN EVIL.
THE SINS OF THE FATHER, THE SINS OF THE SON. I CAN NO LONGER EVEN TELL WHERE ONE ENDS AND THE OTHER BEGINS.
AND WHAT'S EVEN WORSE--

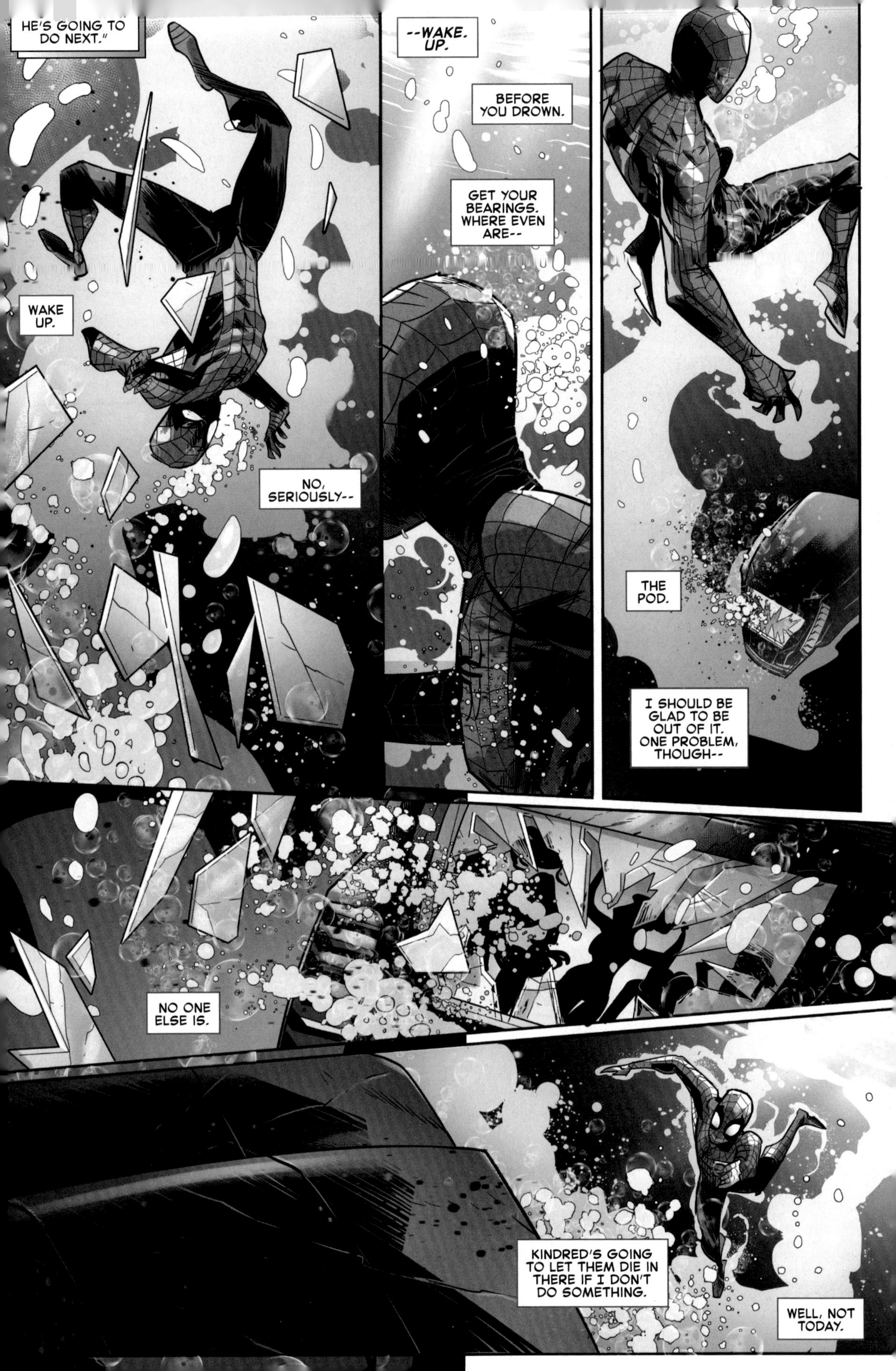
HE'S GOING TO DO NEXT."
WAKE UP.
NO, SERIOUSLY--
--WAKE. UP.
BEFORE YOU DROWN.
GET YOUR BEARINGS. WHERE EVEN ARE--
THE POD.
I SHOULD BE GLAD TO BE OUT OF IT. ONE PROBLEM, THOUGH--
NO ONE ELSE IS.
KINDRED'S GOING TO LET THEM DIE IN THERE IF I DON'T DO SOMETHING.
WELL, NOT TODAY.

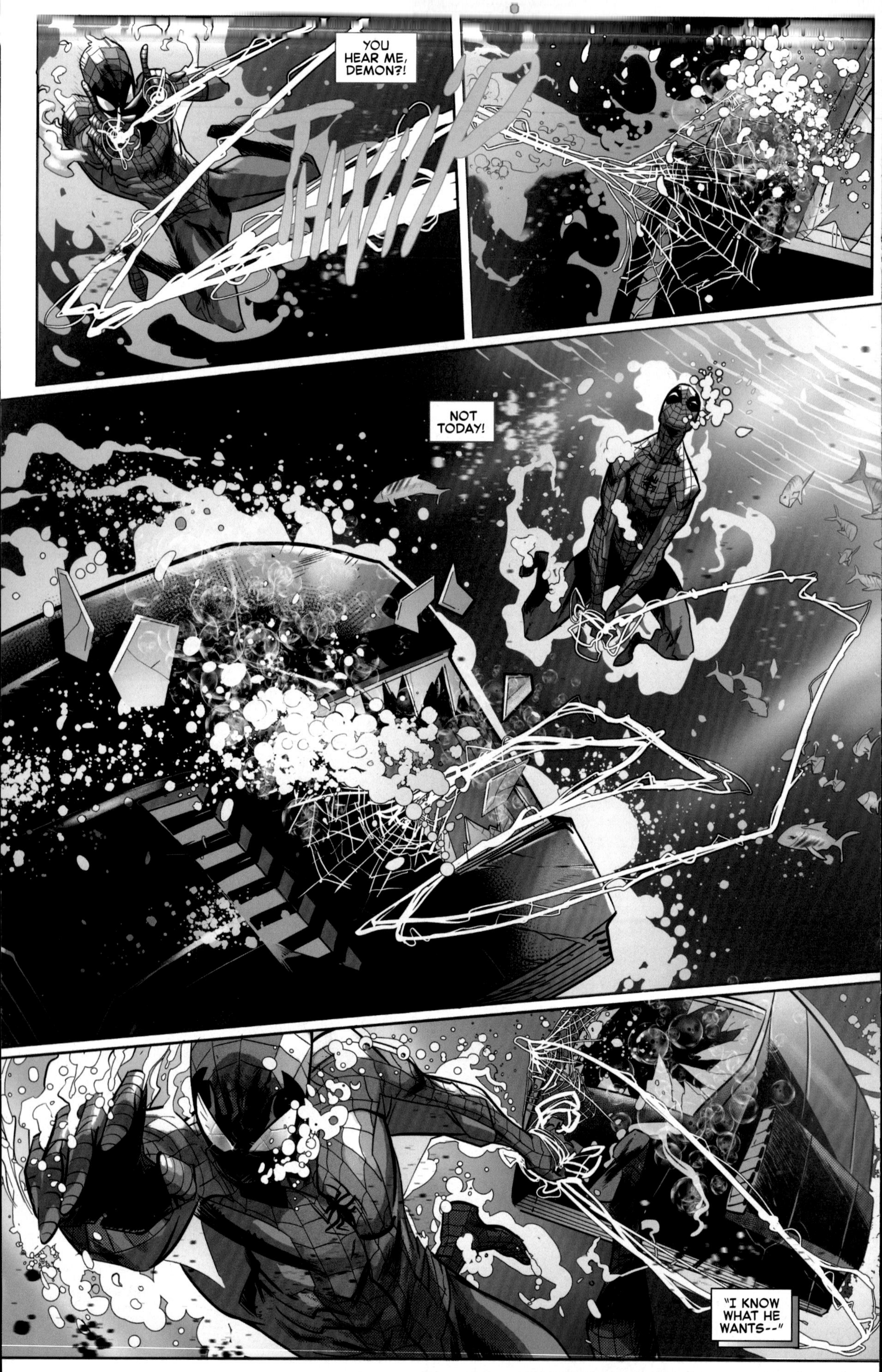
YOU HEAR ME, DEMON?!
THWIP
NOT TODAY!
"I KNOW WHAT HE WANTS--"

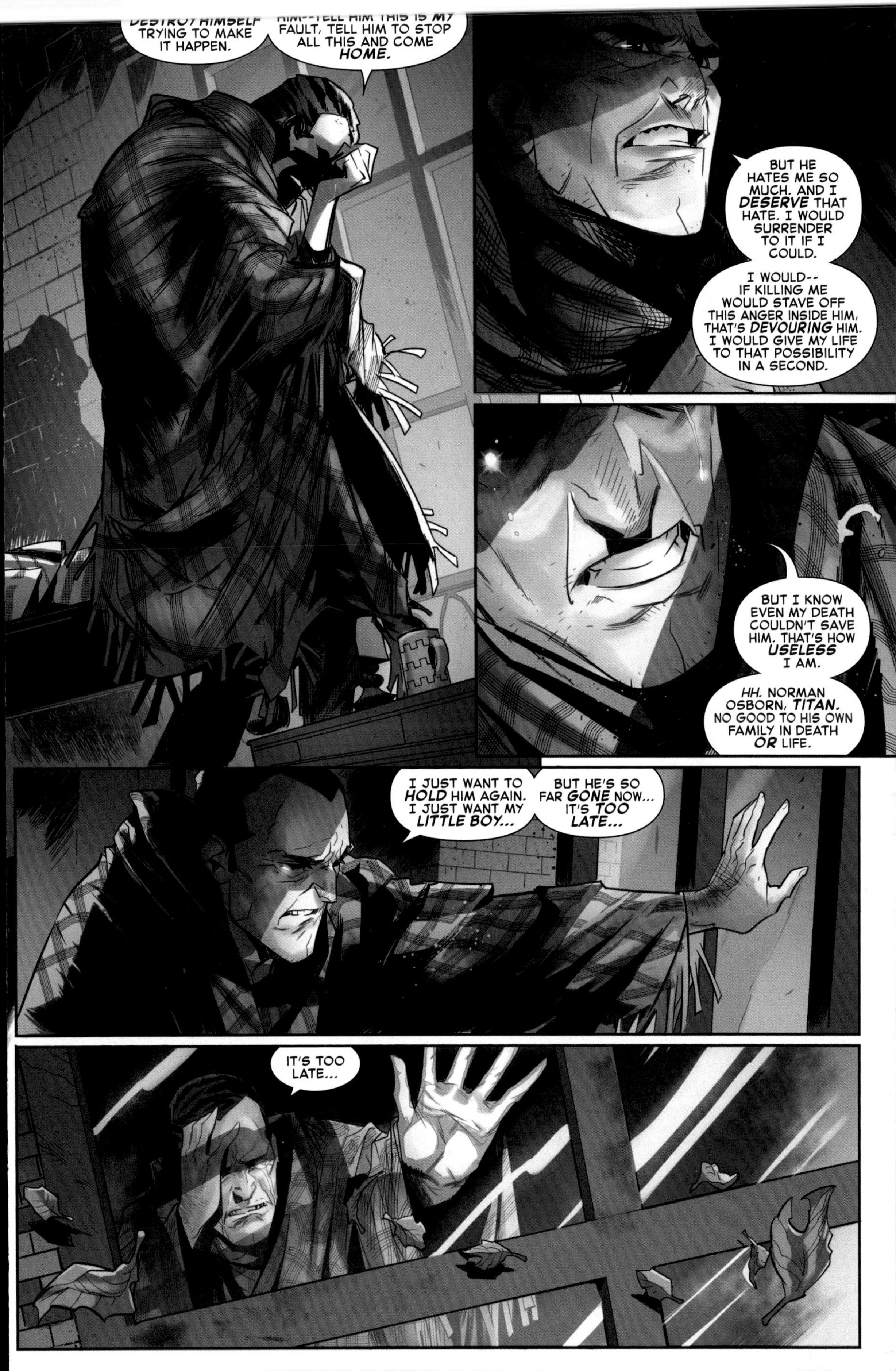
DESTROY HIMSELF TRYING TO MAKE IT HAPPEN.
HIM--TELL HIM THIS IS MY FAULT, TELL HIM TO STOP ALL THIS AND COME HOME.
BUT HE HATES ME SO MUCH. AND I DESERVE THAT HATE. I WOULD SURRENDER TO IT IF I COULD.
I WOULD-- IF KILLING ME WOULD STAVE OFF THIS ANGER INSIDE HIM, THAT'S DEVOURING HIM. I WOULD GIVE MY LIFE TO THAT POSSIBILITY IN A SECOND.
BUT I KNOW EVEN MY DEATH COULDN'T SAVE HIM. THAT'S HOW USELESS I AM.
HH. NORMAN OSBORN, TITAN. NO GOOD TO HIS OWN FAMILY IN DEATH OR LIFE.
I JUST WANT TO HOLD HIM AGAIN. I JUST WANT MY LITTLE BOY...
BUT HE'S SO FAR GONE NOW... IT'S TOO LATE...
IT'S TOO LATE...

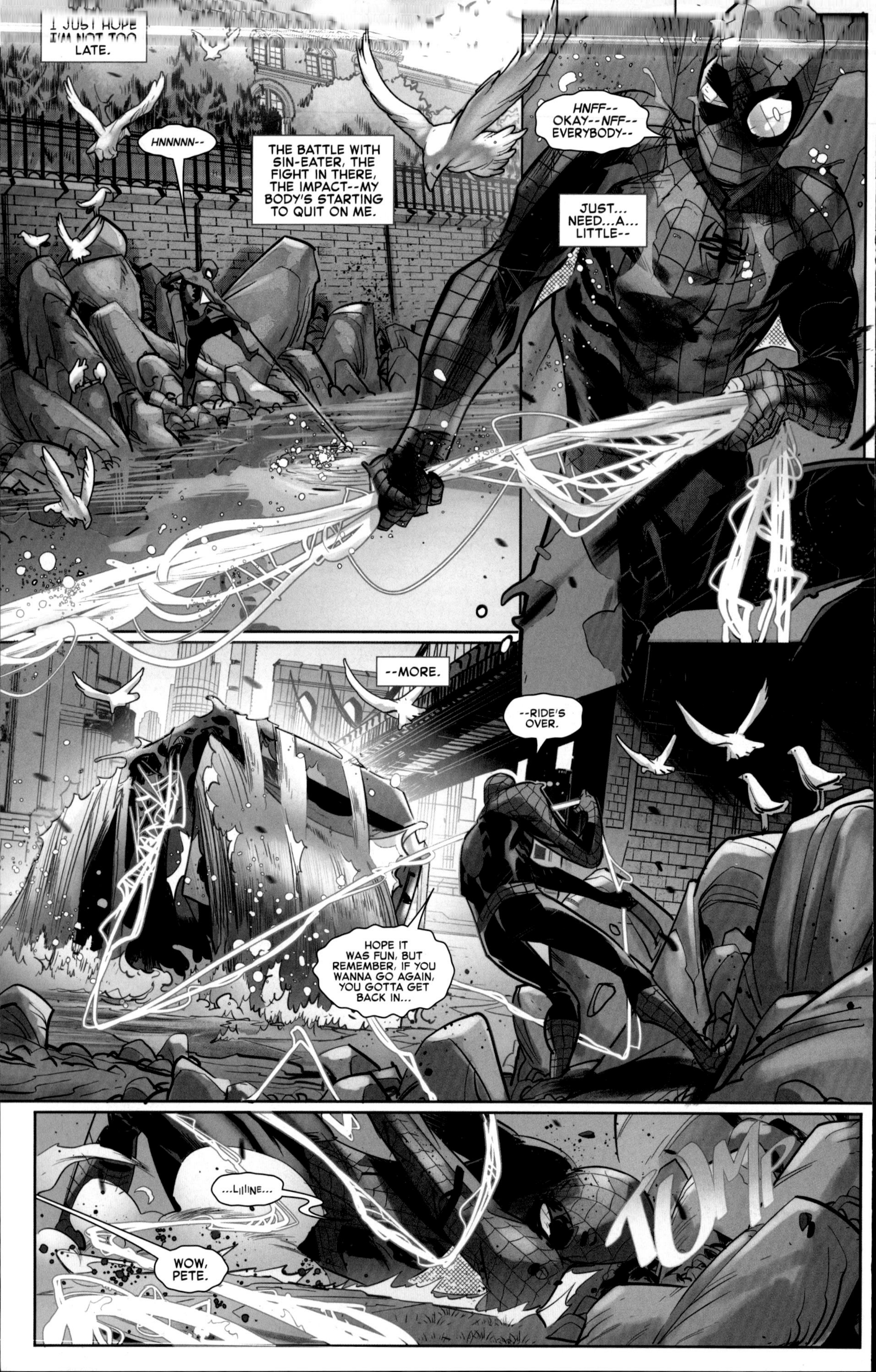
I JUST HOPE I'M NOT TOO LATE.
HNNNNN--
THE BATTLE WITH SIN-EATER, THE FIGHT IN THERE, THE IMPACT--MY BODY'S STARTING TO QUIT ON ME.
HNFF-- OKAY--NFF-- EVERYBODY--
JUST... NEED...A... LITTLE--
--MORE.
--RIDE'S OVER.
HOPE IT WAS FUN, BUT REMEMBER, IF YOU WANNA GO AGAIN, YOU GOTTA GET BACK IN...
...LIIIINE...
WOW, PETE.
TOMP

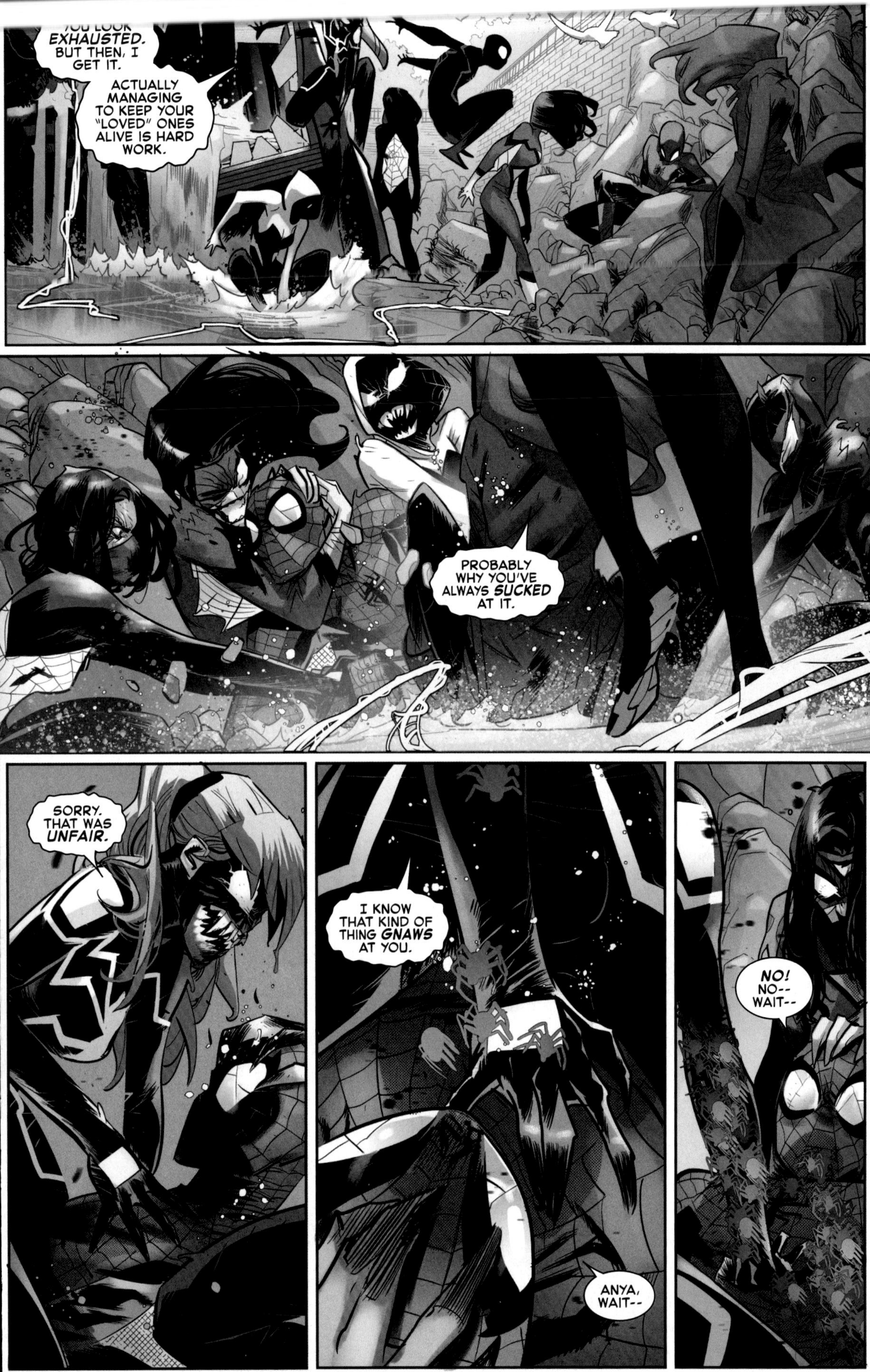
YOU LOOK EXHAUSTED. BUT THEN, I GET IT.
ACTUALLY MANAGING TO KEEP YOUR "LOVED" ONES ALIVE IS HARD WORK.
PROBABLY WHY YOU'VE ALWAYS SUCKED AT IT.
SORRY. THAT WAS UNFAIR.
I KNOW THAT KIND OF THING GNAWS AT YOU.
ANYA, WAIT--
NO! NO-- WAIT--

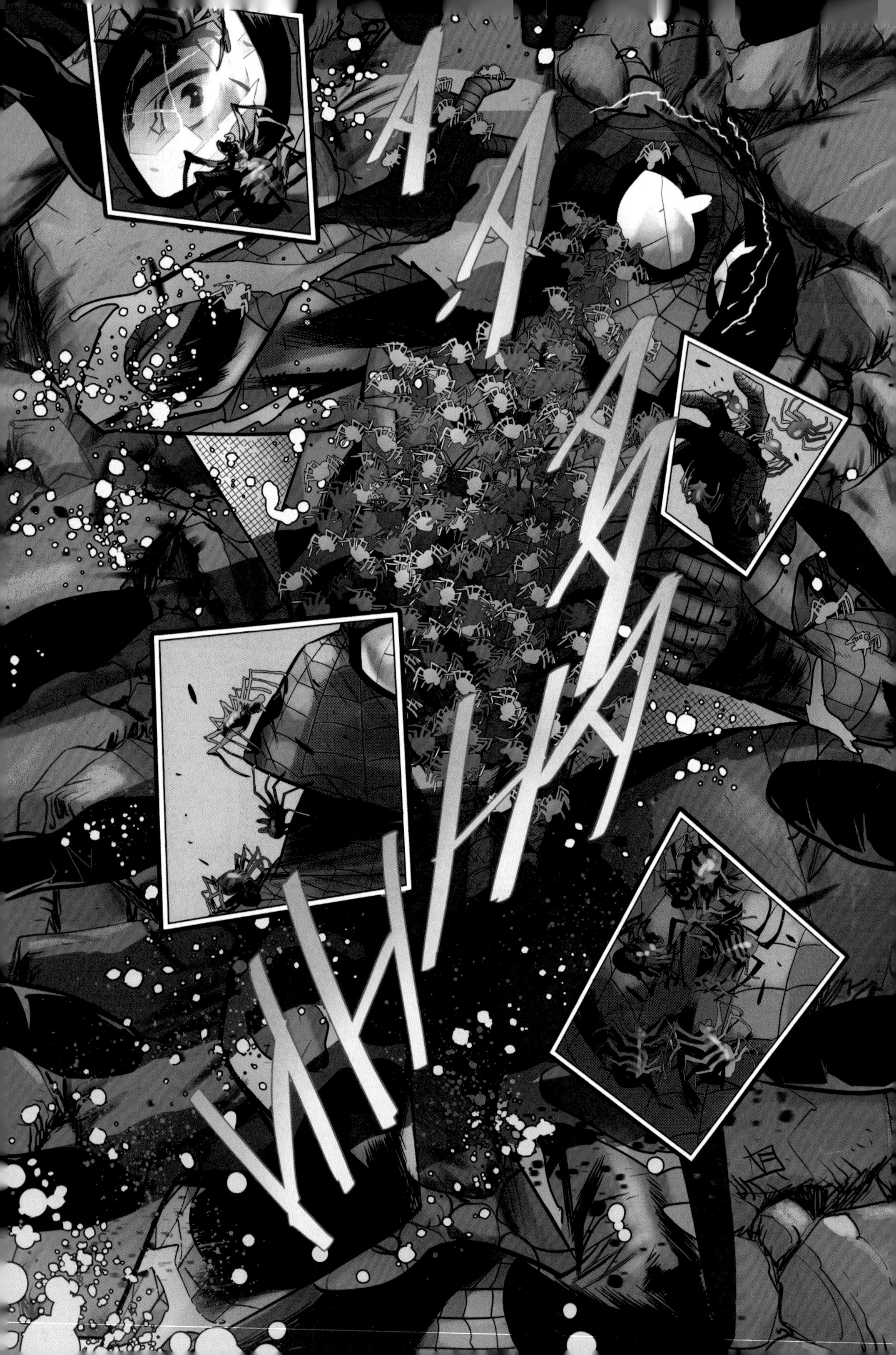
AAAAAAHHH

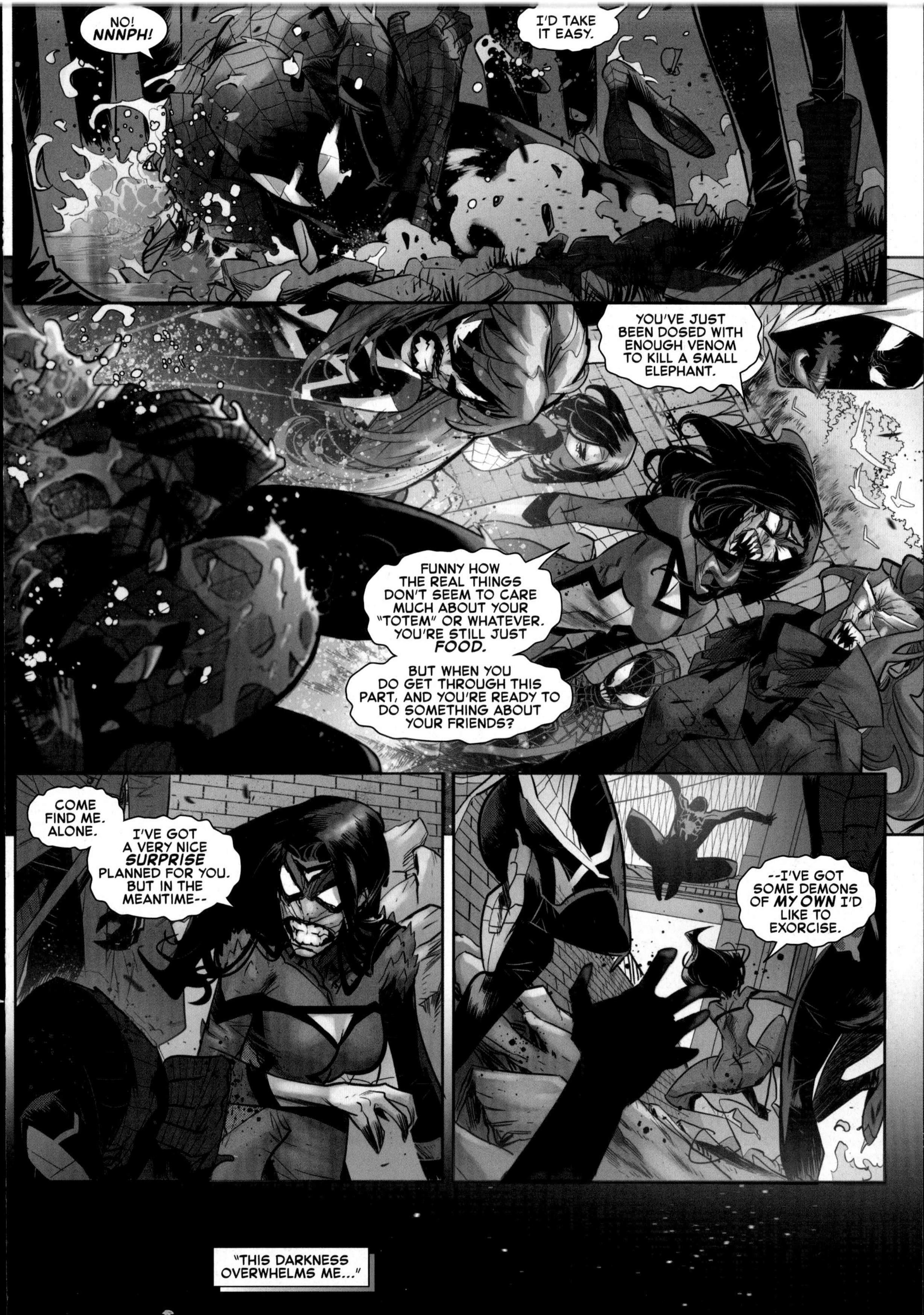
NO! NNNPH!
I'D TAKE IT EASY.
YOU'VE JUST BEEN DOSED WITH ENOUGH VENOM TO KILL A SMALL ELEPHANT.
FUNNY HOW THE REAL THINGS DON'T SEEM TO CARE MUCH ABOUT YOUR "TOTEM" OR WHATEVER. YOU'RE STILL JUST FOOD.
BUT WHEN YOU DO GET THROUGH THIS PART, AND YOU'RE READY TO DO SOMETHING ABOUT YOUR FRIENDS?
COME FIND ME. ALONE.
I'VE GOT A VERY NICE SURPRISE PLANNED FOR YOU. BUT IN THE MEANTIME--
--I'VE GOT SOME DEMONS OF MY OWN I'D LIKE TO EXORCISE.
"THIS DARKNESS OVERWHELMS ME..."

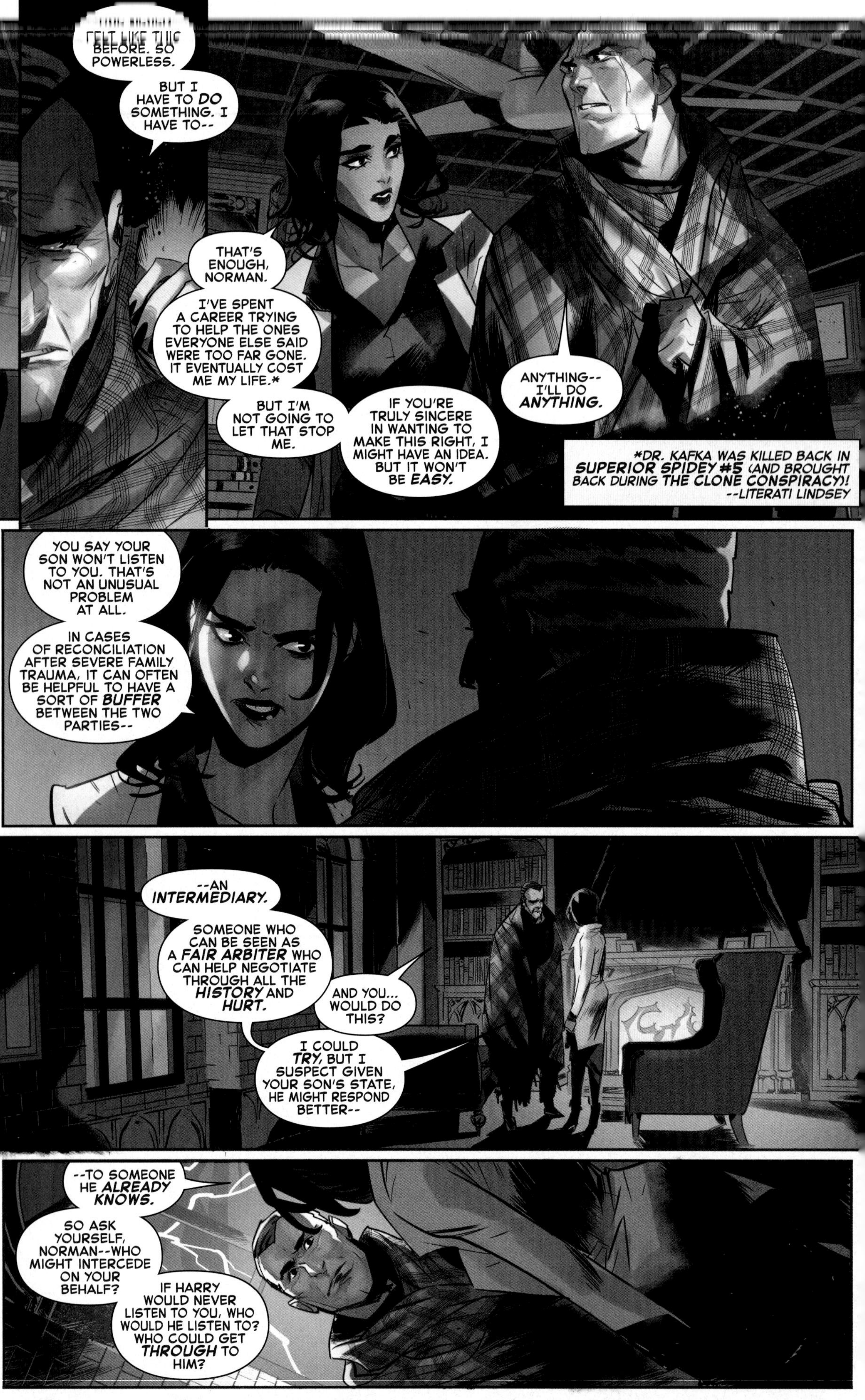
FELT LIKE THIS BEFORE. SO POWERLESS.
BUT I HAVE TO DO SOMETHING. I HAVE TO--
THAT'S ENOUGH, NORMAN.
I'VE SPENT A CAREER TRYING TO HELP THE ONES EVERYONE ELSE SAID WERE TOO FAR GONE. IT EVENTUALLY COST ME MY LIFE.*
BUT I'M NOT GOING TO LET THAT STOP ME.
IF YOU'RE TRULY SINCERE IN WANTING TO MAKE THIS RIGHT, I MIGHT HAVE AN IDEA. BUT IT WON'T BE EASY.
ANYTHING-- I'LL DO ANYTHING.
*DR. KAFKA WAS KILLED BACK IN SUPERIOR SPIDEY #5 (AND BROUGHT BACK DURING THE CLONE CONSPIRACY)! --LITERATI LINDSEY
YOU SAY YOUR SON WON'T LISTEN TO YOU. THAT'S NOT AN UNUSUAL PROBLEM AT ALL.
IN CASES OF RECONCILIATION AFTER SEVERE FAMILY TRAUMA, IT CAN OFTEN BE HELPFUL TO HAVE A SORT OF BUFFER BETWEEN THE TWO PARTIES--
--AN INTERMEDIARY.
SOMEONE WHO CAN BE SEEN AS A FAIR ARBITER WHO CAN HELP NEGOTIATE THROUGH ALL THE HISTORY AND HURT.
AND YOU... WOULD DO THIS?
I COULD TRY, BUT I SUSPECT GIVEN YOUR SON'S STATE, HE MIGHT RESPOND BETTER--
--TO SOMEONE HE ALREADY KNOWS.
SO ASK YOURSELF, NORMAN--WHO MIGHT INTERCEDE ON YOUR BEHALF?
IF HARRY WOULD NEVER LISTEN TO YOU, WHO WOULD HE LISTEN TO? WHO COULD GET THROUGH TO HIM?

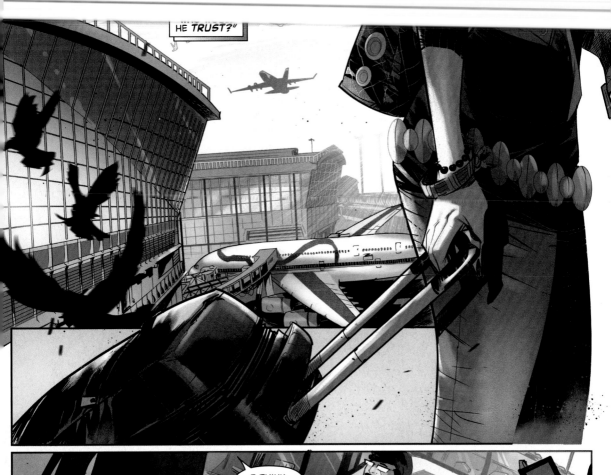

HE *TRUST?*"

I THINK YOU'RE HERE FOR ME.

YES, MA'AM-- LET ME GET THAT BAG FOR YOU.

COMING HOME OR JUST VISITING?

WELL, THIS IS HOME, BUT JUST VISITING.

AH. I HOPE YOU AT LEAST GET TO STAY A WHILE THEN?

NOT AS LONG AS I'D *LIKE*, SADLY. BUT STILL--

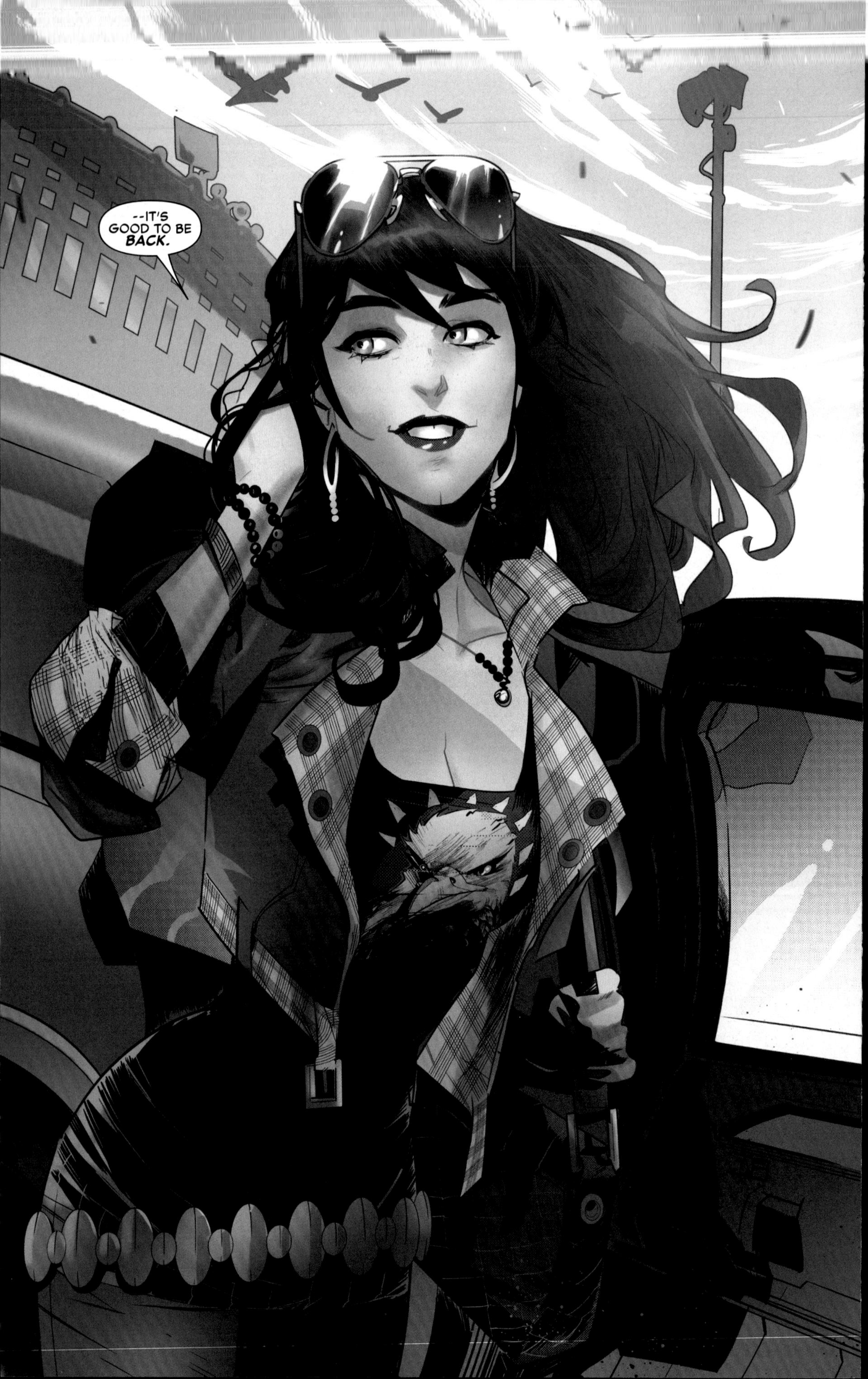
--IT'S GOOD TO BE BACK.

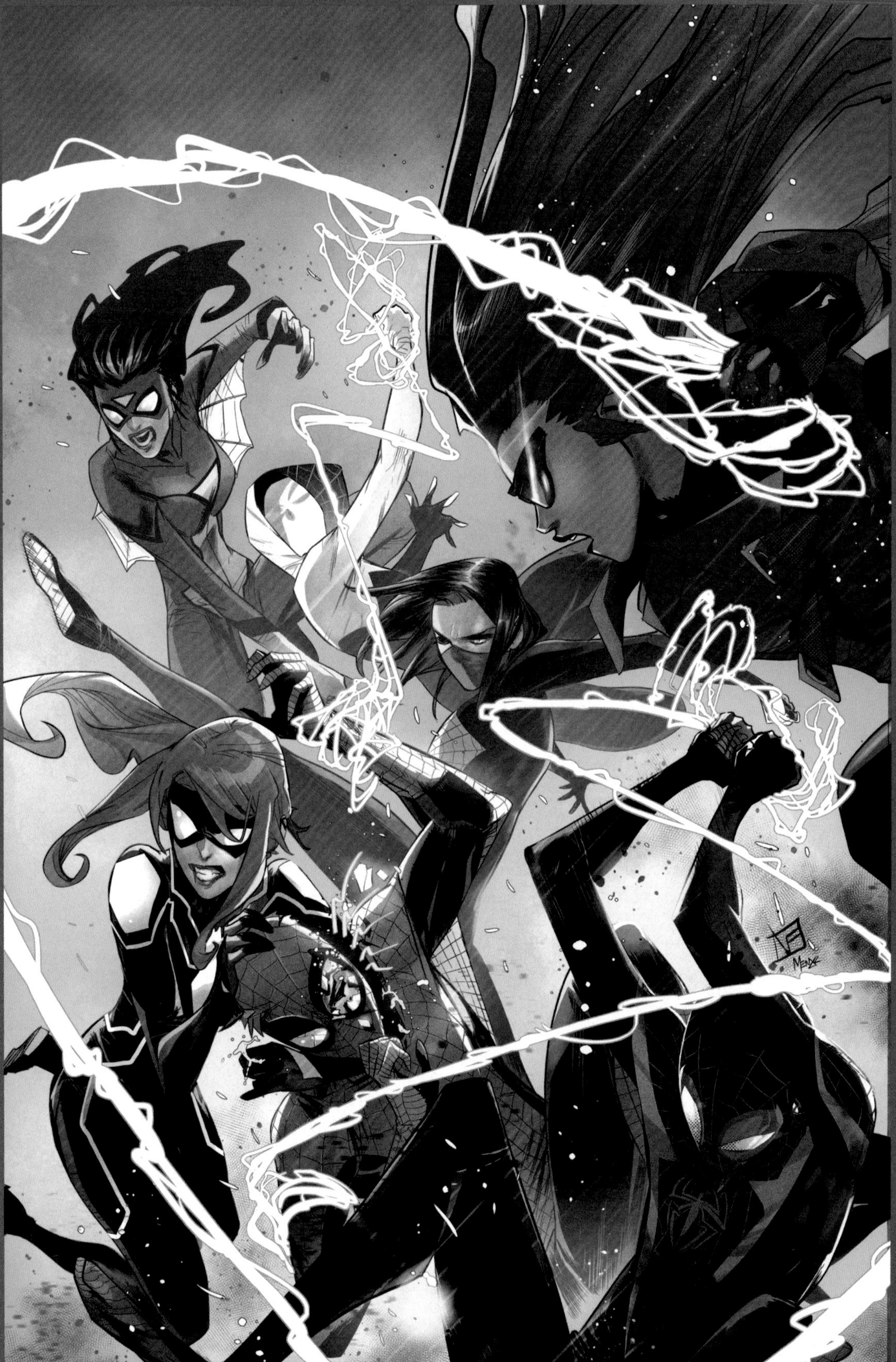
MENYZ

#50.LR VARIANT BY FEDERICO VICENTINI & MARCIO MENYZ

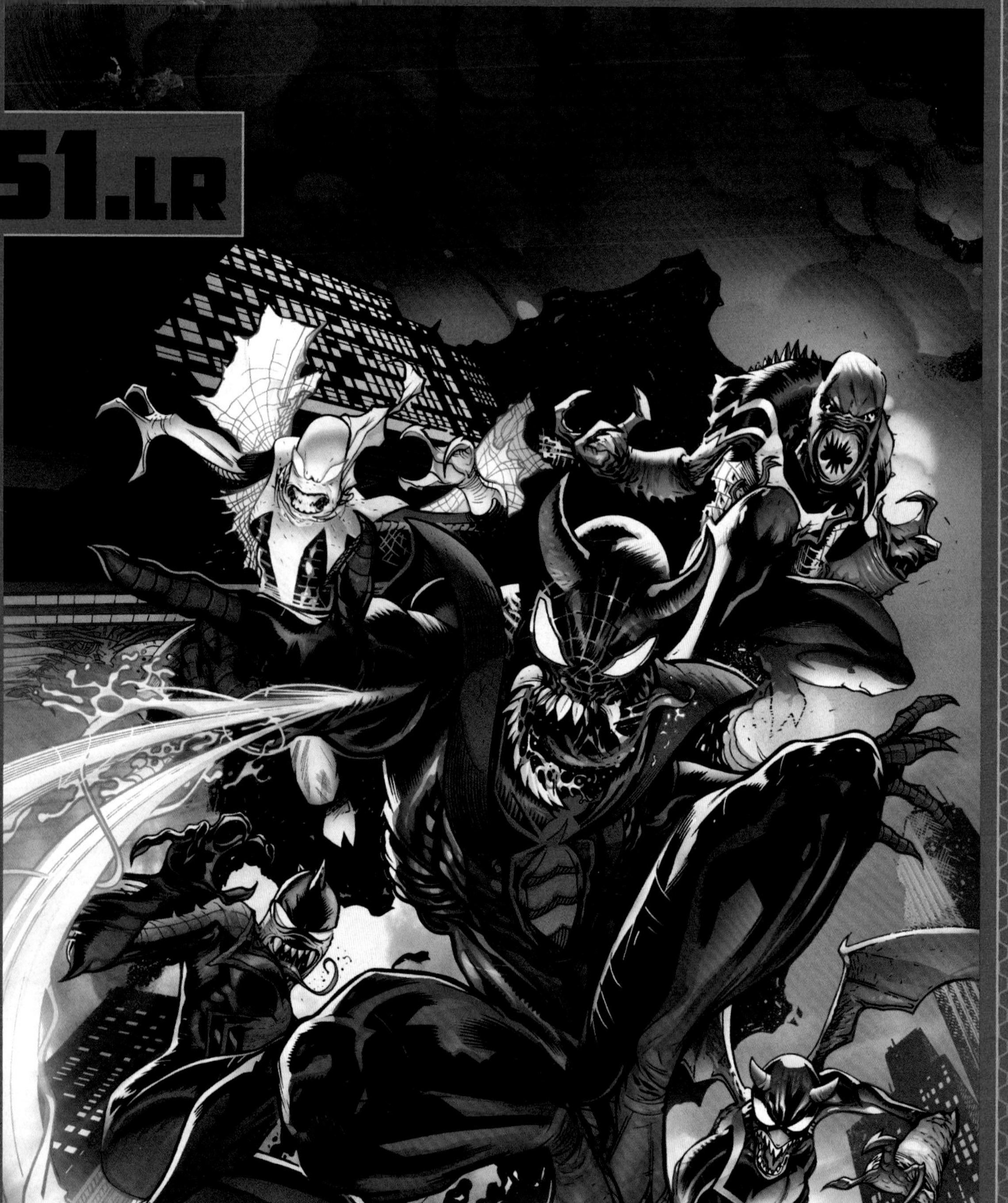
51.LR

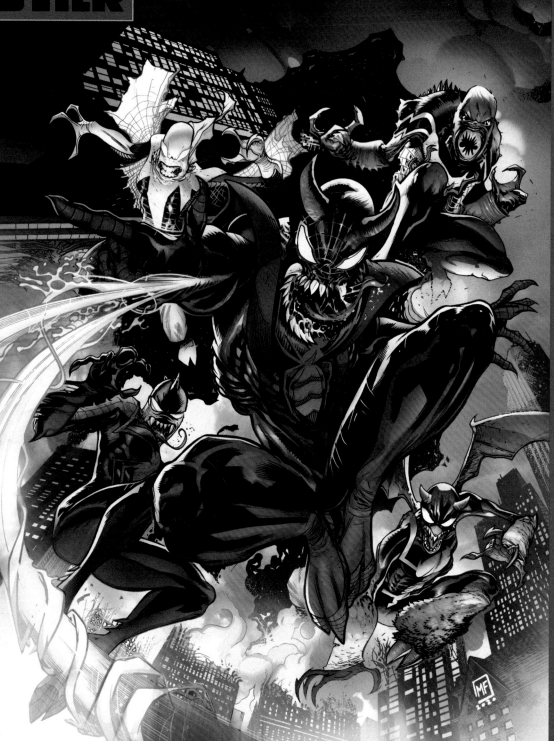

FALLEN ORDER PART 2

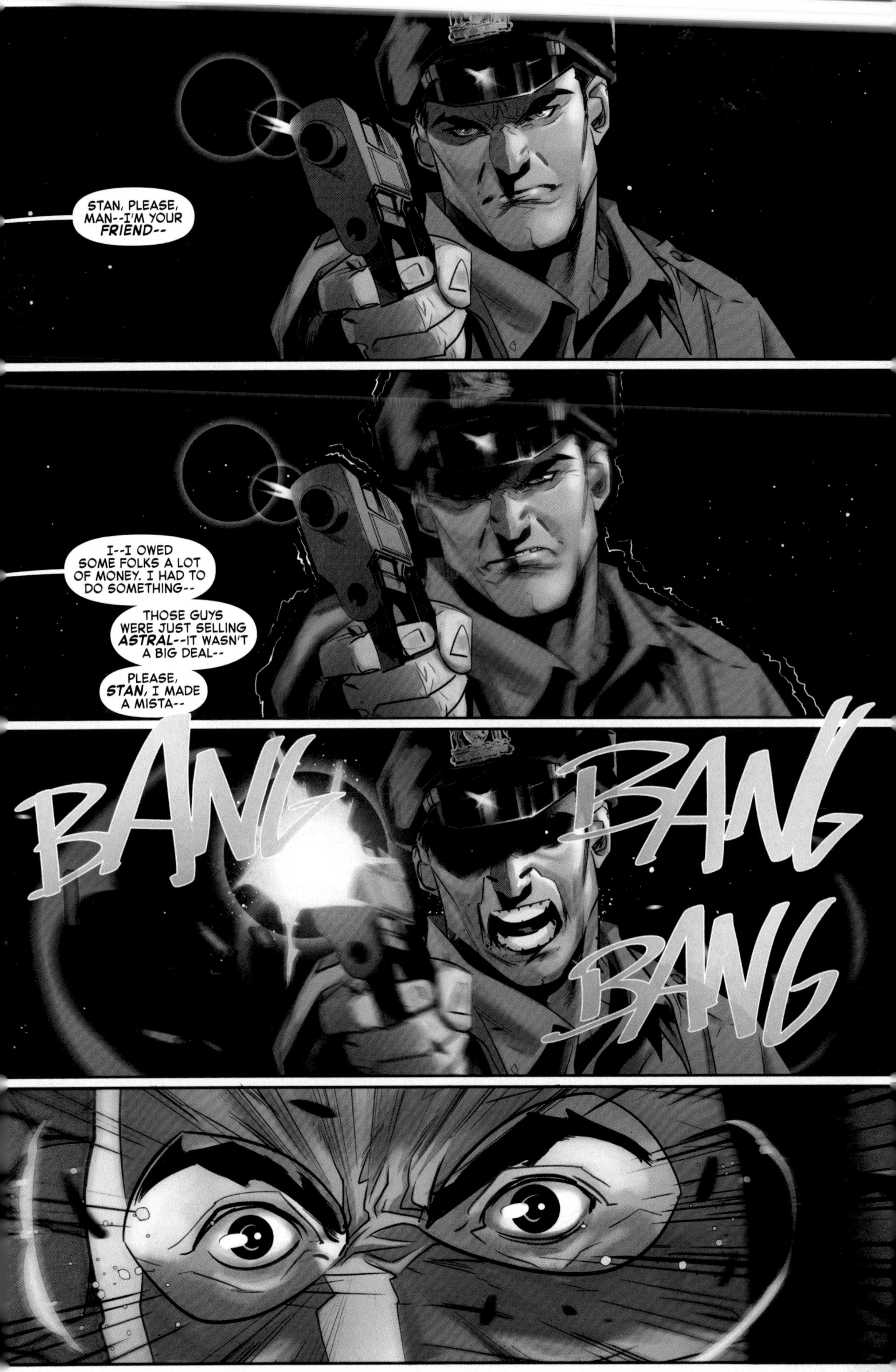

STAN, PLEASE, MAN--I'M YOUR FRIEND--
I--I OWED SOME FOLKS A LOT OF MONEY. I HAD TO DO SOMETHING--
THOSE GUYS WERE JUST SELLING ASTRAL--IT WASN'T A BIG DEAL--
PLEASE, STAN, I MADE A MISTA--
BANG
BANG
BANG

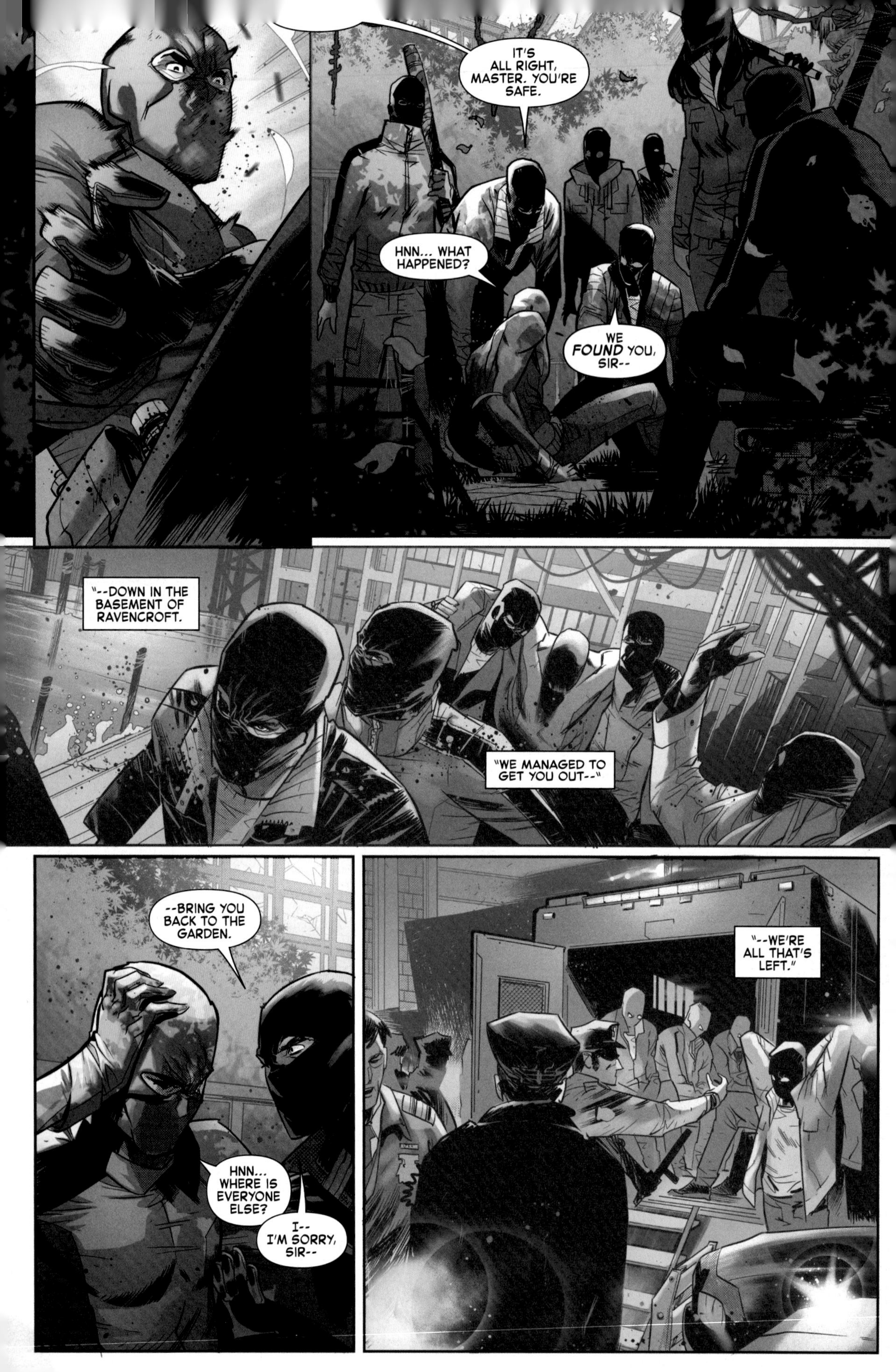
IT'S ALL RIGHT, MASTER. YOU'RE SAFE.
HNN... WHAT HAPPENED?
WE FOUND YOU, SIR--
"--DOWN IN THE BASEMENT OF RAVENCROFT.
"WE MANAGED TO GET YOU OUT--"
--BRING YOU BACK TO THE GARDEN.
HNN... WHERE IS EVERYONE ELSE?
I-- I'M SORRY, SIR--
"--WE'RE ALL THAT'S LEFT."

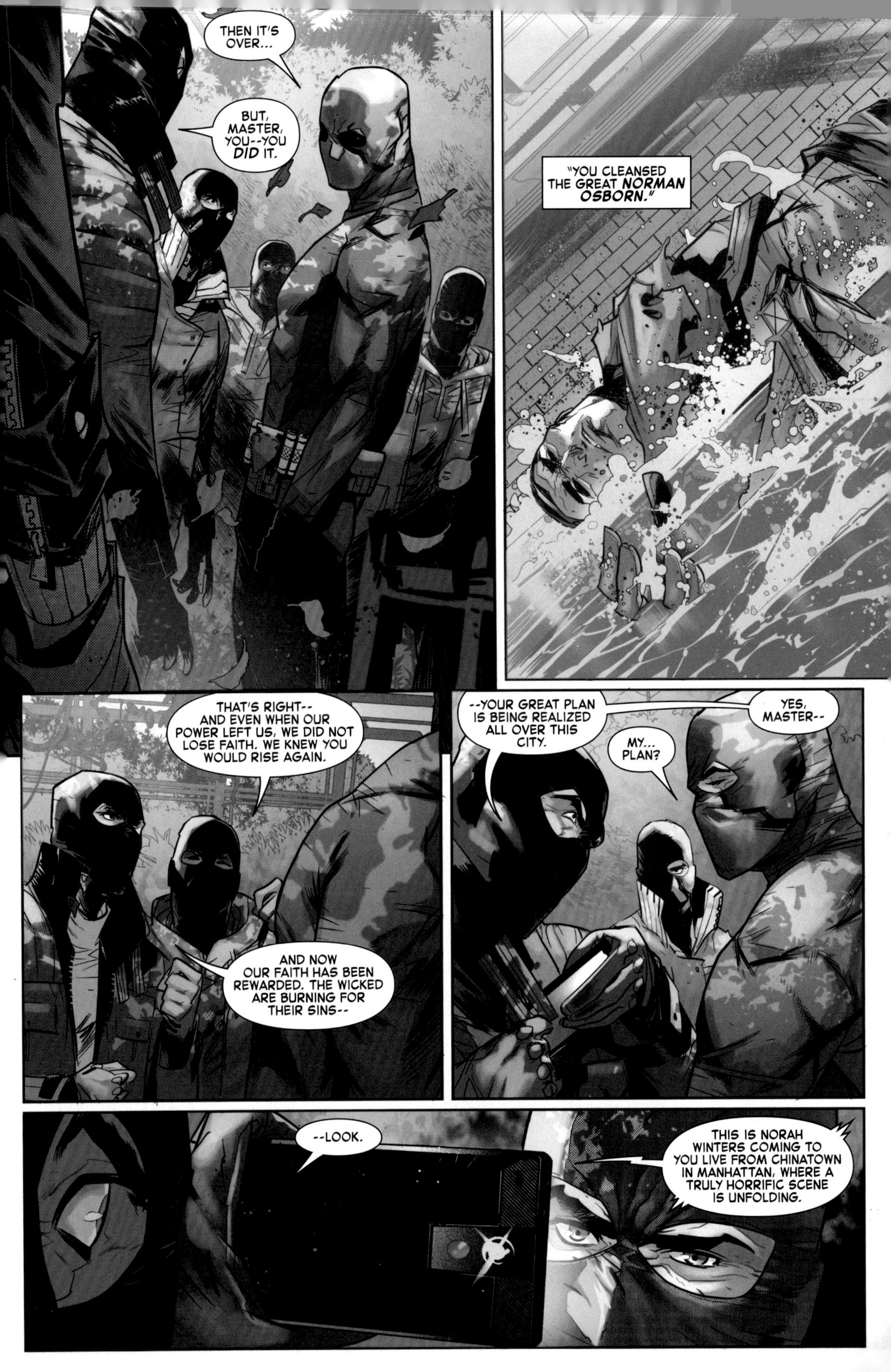
THEN IT'S OVER...
BUT, MASTER, YOU--YOU DID IT.
"YOU CLEANSED THE GREAT NORMAN OSBORN."
THAT'S RIGHT-- AND EVEN WHEN OUR POWER LEFT US, WE DID NOT LOSE FAITH. WE KNEW YOU WOULD RISE AGAIN.
AND NOW OUR FAITH HAS BEEN REWARDED. THE WICKED ARE BURNING FOR THEIR SINS--
--YOUR GREAT PLAN IS BEING REALIZED ALL OVER THIS CITY.
YES, MASTER--
MY... PLAN?
--LOOK.
THIS IS NORAH WINTERS COMING TO YOU LIVE FROM CHINATOWN IN MANHATTAN, WHERE A TRULY HORRIFIC SCENE IS UNFOLDING.

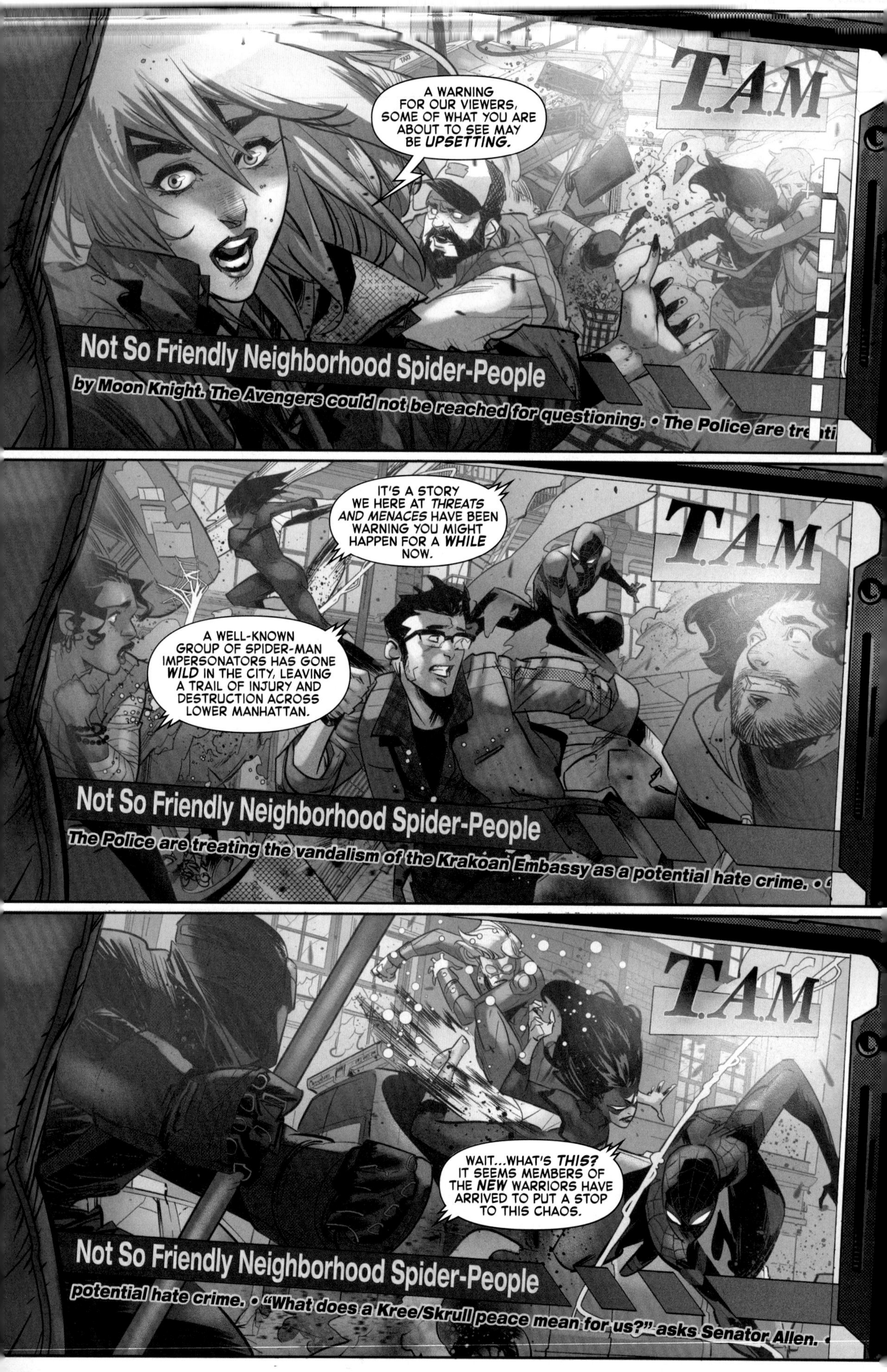
T.A.M
A WARNING FOR OUR VIEWERS, SOME OF WHAT YOU ARE ABOUT TO SEE MAY BE UPSETTING.
Not So Friendly Neighborhood Spider-People
by Moon Knight. The Avengers could not be reached for questioning. • The Police are tre
T.A.M
IT'S A STORY WE HERE AT THREATS AND MENACES HAVE BEEN WARNING YOU MIGHT HAPPEN FOR A WHILE NOW.
A WELL-KNOWN GROUP OF SPIDER-MAN IMPERSONATORS HAS GONE WILD IN THE CITY, LEAVING A TRAIL OF INJURY AND DESTRUCTION ACROSS LOWER MANHATTAN.
Not So Friendly Neighborhood Spider-People
The Police are treating the vandalism of the Krakoan Embassy as a potential hate crime. •
T.A.M
WAIT...WHAT'S THIS? IT SEEMS MEMBERS OF THE NEW WARRIORS HAVE ARRIVED TO PUT A STOP TO THIS CHAOS.
Not So Friendly Neighborhood Spider-People
potential hate crime. • "What does a Kree/Skrull peace mean for us?" asks Senator Allen. •

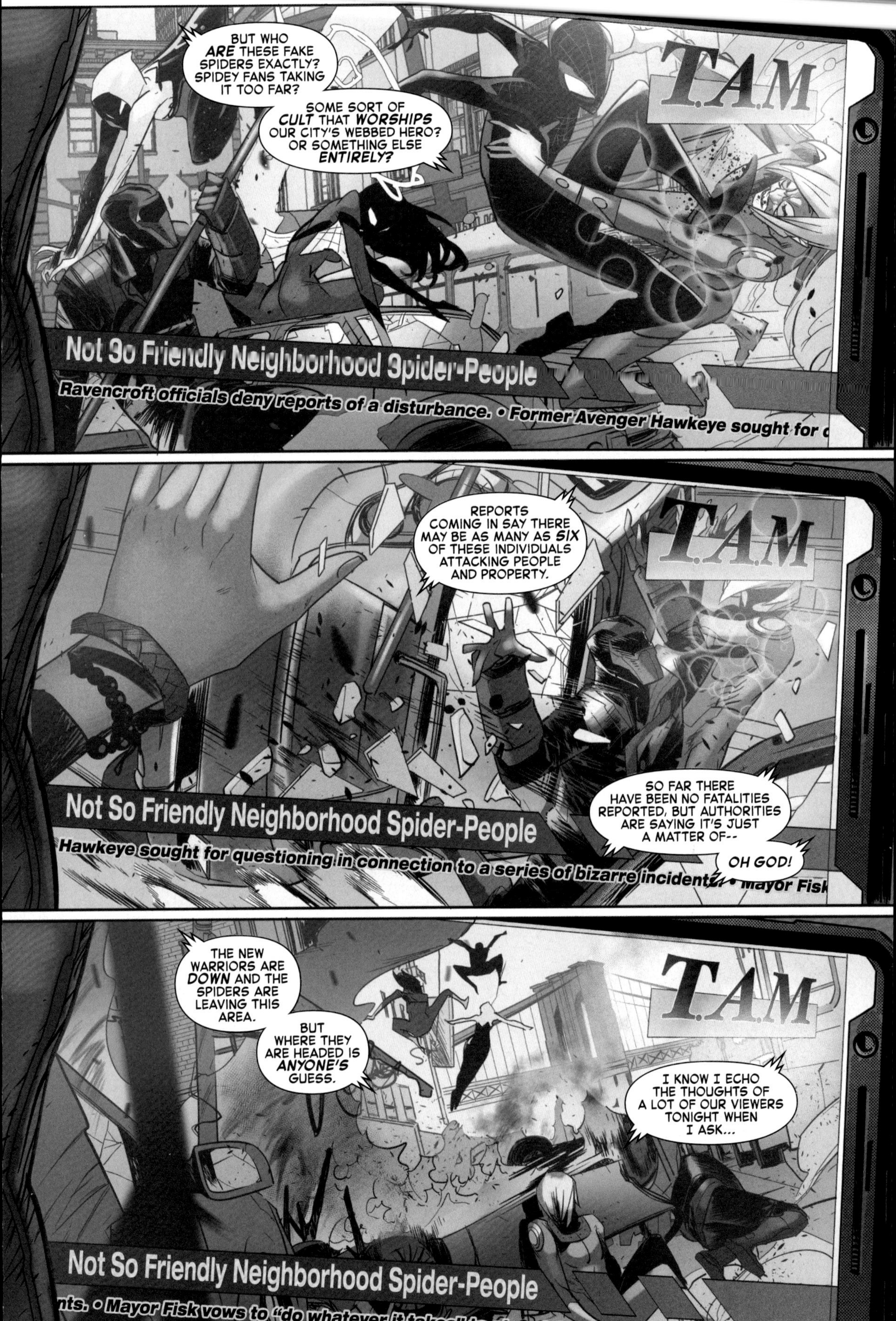

BUT WHO ARE THESE FAKE SPIDERS EXACTLY? SPIDEY FANS TAKING IT TOO FAR?
SOME SORT OF CULT THAT WORSHIPS OUR CITY'S WEBBED HERO? OR SOMETHING ELSE ENTIRELY?
T.A.M
Not So Friendly Neighborhood Spider-People
Ravencroft officials deny reports of a disturbance. • Former Avenger Hawkeye sought for
REPORTS COMING IN SAY THERE MAY BE AS MANY AS SIX OF THESE INDIVIDUALS ATTACKING PEOPLE AND PROPERTY.
T.A.M
Not So Friendly Neighborhood Spider-People
Hawkeye sought for questioning in connection to a series of bizarre incidents. • Mayor Fisk
SO FAR THERE HAVE BEEN NO FATALITIES REPORTED, BUT AUTHORITIES ARE SAYING IT'S JUST A MATTER OF--
OH GOD!
THE NEW WARRIORS ARE DOWN AND THE SPIDERS ARE LEAVING THIS AREA.
BUT WHERE THEY ARE HEADED IS ANYONE'S GUESS.
T.A.M
I KNOW I ECHO THE THOUGHTS OF A LOT OF OUR VIEWERS TONIGHT WHEN I ASK...
Not So Friendly Neighborhood Spider-People
nts. • Mayor Fisk vows to "do whatever it takes" to stop rising crime rates in Hell's Kitchen.

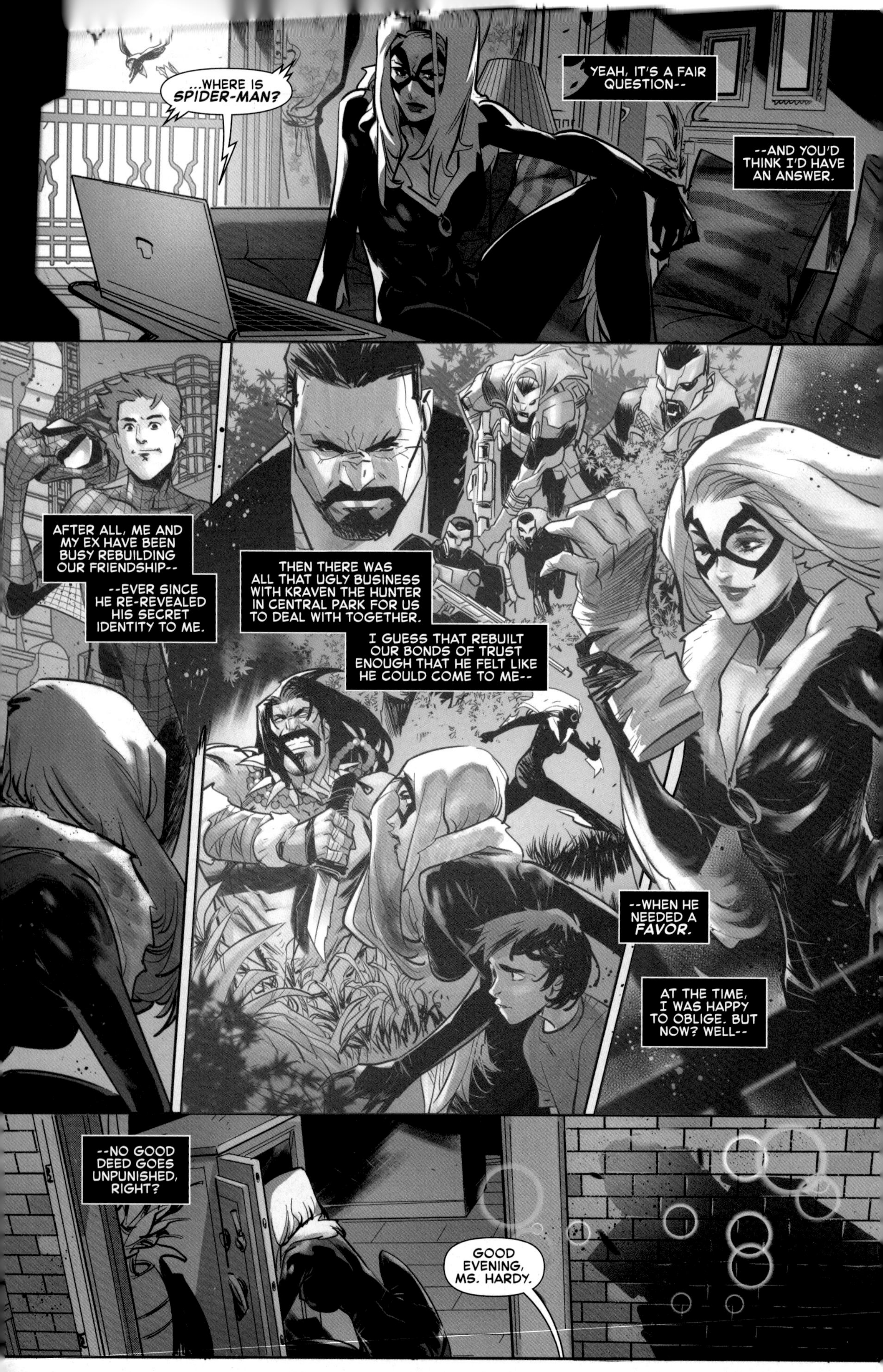
...WHERE IS SPIDER-MAN?
YEAH, IT'S A FAIR QUESTION--
--AND YOU'D THINK I'D HAVE AN ANSWER.
AFTER ALL, ME AND MY EX HAVE BEEN BUSY REBUILDING OUR FRIENDSHIP--
--EVER SINCE HE RE-REVEALED HIS SECRET IDENTITY TO ME.
THEN THERE WAS ALL THAT UGLY BUSINESS WITH KRAVEN THE HUNTER IN CENTRAL PARK FOR US TO DEAL WITH TOGETHER.
I GUESS THAT REBUILT OUR BONDS OF TRUST ENOUGH THAT HE FELT LIKE HE COULD COME TO ME--
--WHEN HE NEEDED A FAVOR.
AT THE TIME, I WAS HAPPY TO OBLIGE. BUT NOW? WELL--
--NO GOOD DEED GOES UNPUNISHED, RIGHT?
GOOD EVENING, MS. HARDY.

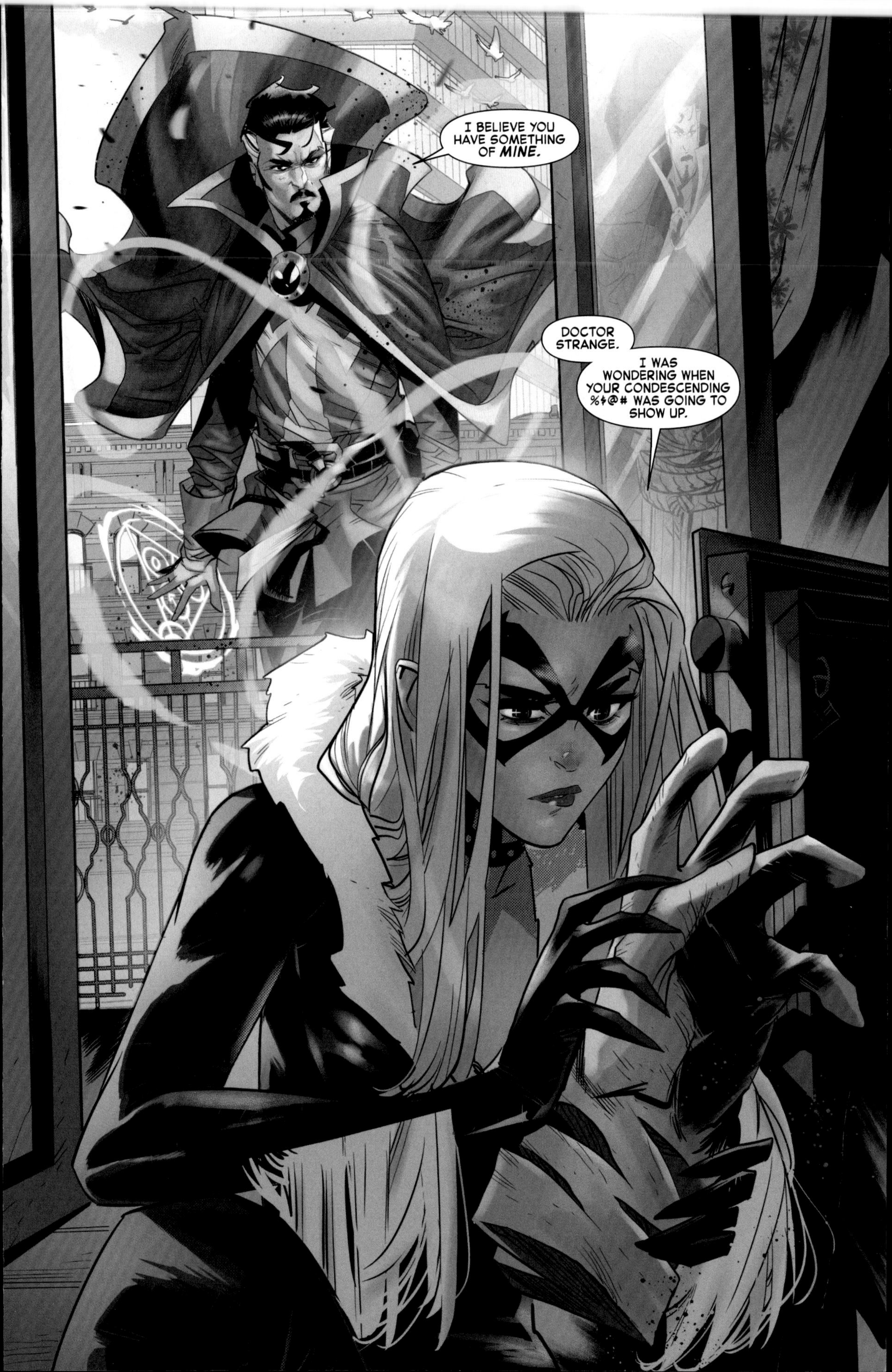
I BELIEVE YOU HAVE SOMETHING OF *MINE.*
DOCTOR STRANGE.
I WAS WONDERING WHEN YOUR CONDESCENDING %$@# WAS GOING TO SHOW UP.

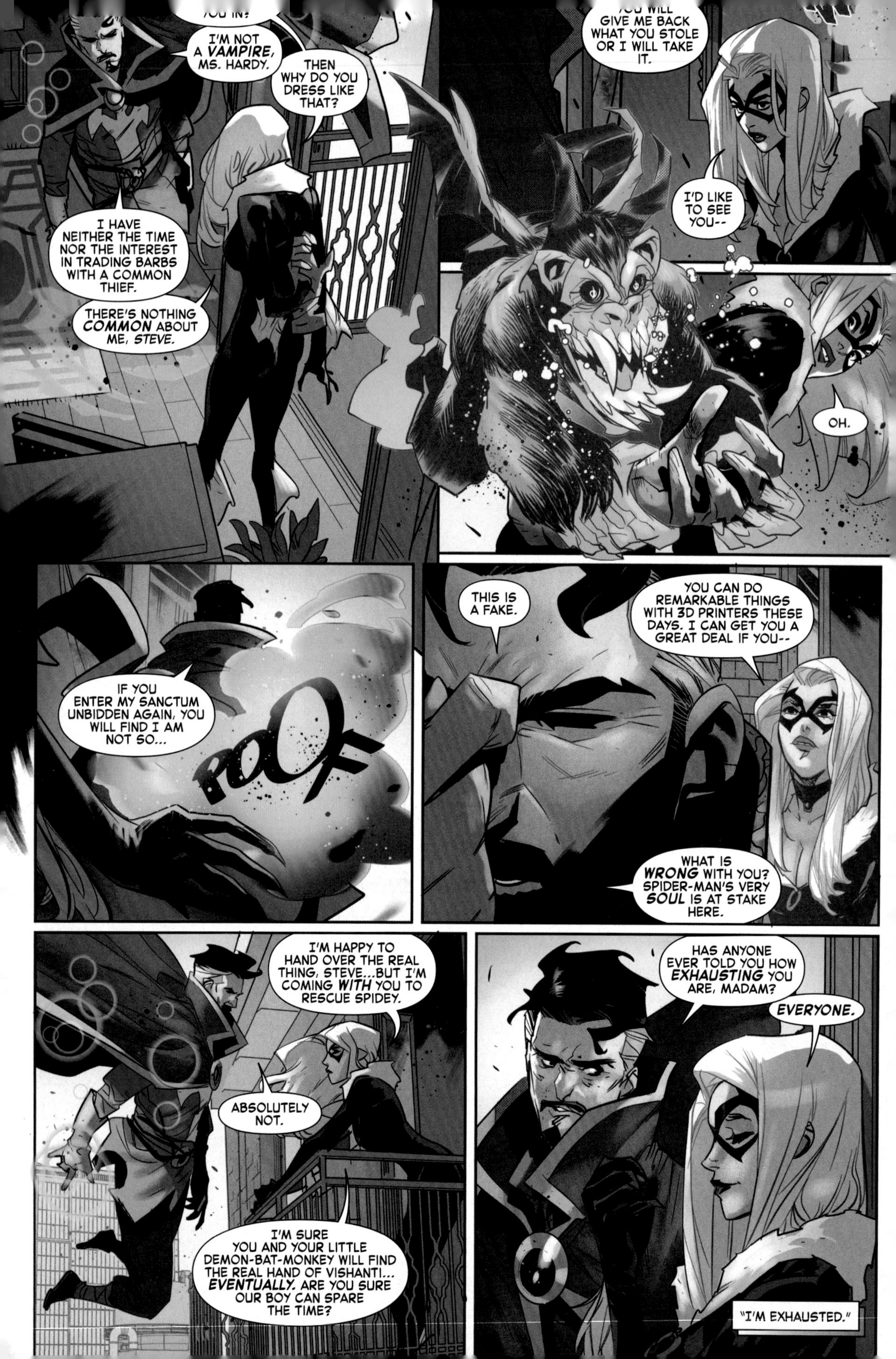
I'M NOT A VAMPIRE, MS. HARDY.
THEN WHY DO YOU DRESS LIKE THAT?
I HAVE NEITHER THE TIME NOR THE INTEREST IN TRADING BARBS WITH A COMMON THIEF.
THERE'S NOTHING COMMON ABOUT ME, STEVE.
GIVE ME BACK WHAT YOU STOLE OR I WILL TAKE IT.
I'D LIKE TO SEE YOU--
OH.
IF YOU ENTER MY SANCTUM UNBIDDEN AGAIN, YOU WILL FIND I AM NOT SO...
POOF
THIS IS A FAKE.
YOU CAN DO REMARKABLE THINGS WITH 3D PRINTERS THESE DAYS. I CAN GET YOU A GREAT DEAL IF YOU--
WHAT IS WRONG WITH YOU? SPIDER-MAN'S VERY SOUL IS AT STAKE HERE.
I'M HAPPY TO HAND OVER THE REAL THING, STEVE...BUT I'M COMING WITH YOU TO RESCUE SPIDEY.
ABSOLUTELY NOT.
I'M SURE YOU AND YOUR LITTLE DEMON-BAT-MONKEY WILL FIND THE REAL HAND OF VISHANTI... EVENTUALLY. ARE YOU SURE OUR BOY CAN SPARE THE TIME?
HAS ANYONE EVER TOLD YOU HOW EXHAUSTING YOU ARE, MADAM?
EVERYONE.
"I'M EXHAUSTED."

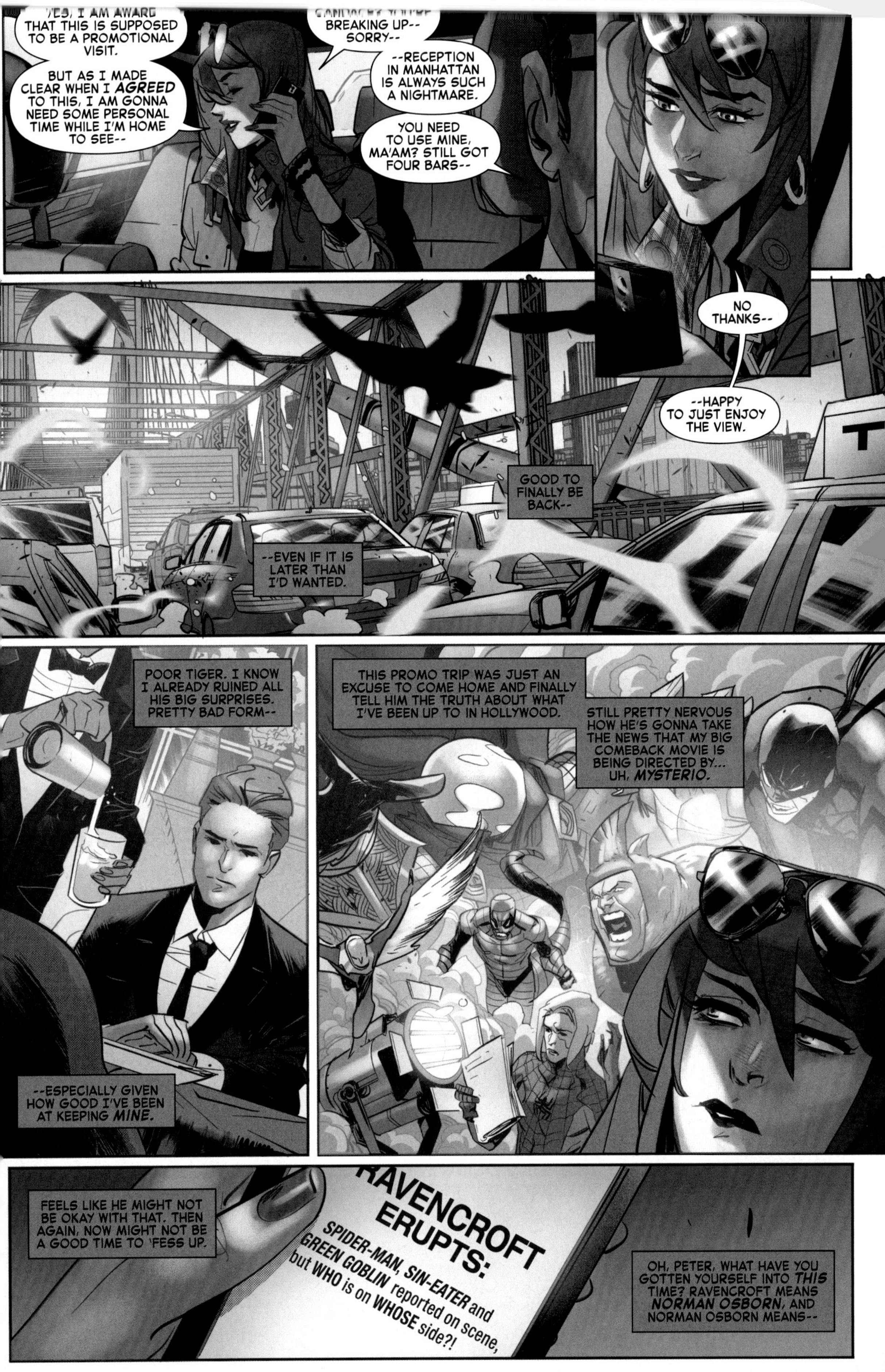
YES, I AM AWARE THAT THIS IS SUPPOSED TO BE A PROMOTIONAL VISIT.
BUT AS I MADE CLEAR WHEN I AGREED TO THIS, I AM GONNA NEED SOME PERSONAL TIME WHILE I'M HOME TO SEE--
BREAKING UP-- SORRY--
--RECEPTION IN MANHATTAN IS ALWAYS SUCH A NIGHTMARE.
YOU NEED TO USE MINE, MA'AM? STILL GOT FOUR BARS--
NO THANKS--
--HAPPY TO JUST ENJOY THE VIEW.
GOOD TO FINALLY BE BACK--
--EVEN IF IT IS LATER THAN I'D WANTED.
POOR TIGER. I KNOW I ALREADY RUINED ALL HIS BIG SURPRISES. PRETTY BAD FORM--
--ESPECIALLY GIVEN HOW GOOD I'VE BEEN AT KEEPING MINE.
THIS PROMO TRIP WAS JUST AN EXCUSE TO COME HOME AND FINALLY TELL HIM THE TRUTH ABOUT WHAT I'VE BEEN UP TO IN HOLLYWOOD.
STILL PRETTY NERVOUS HOW HE'S GONNA TAKE THE NEWS THAT MY BIG COMEBACK MOVIE IS BEING DIRECTED BY... UH, MYSTERIO.
FEELS LIKE HE MIGHT NOT BE OKAY WITH THAT. THEN AGAIN, NOW MIGHT NOT BE A GOOD TIME TO 'FESS UP.
RAVENCROFT ERUPTS:
SPIDER-MAN, SIN-EATER and GREEN GOBLIN reported on scene, but WHO is on WHOSE side?!
OH, PETER, WHAT HAVE YOU GOTTEN YOURSELF INTO THIS TIME? RAVENCROFT MEANS NORMAN OSBORN, AND NORMAN OSBORN MEANS--

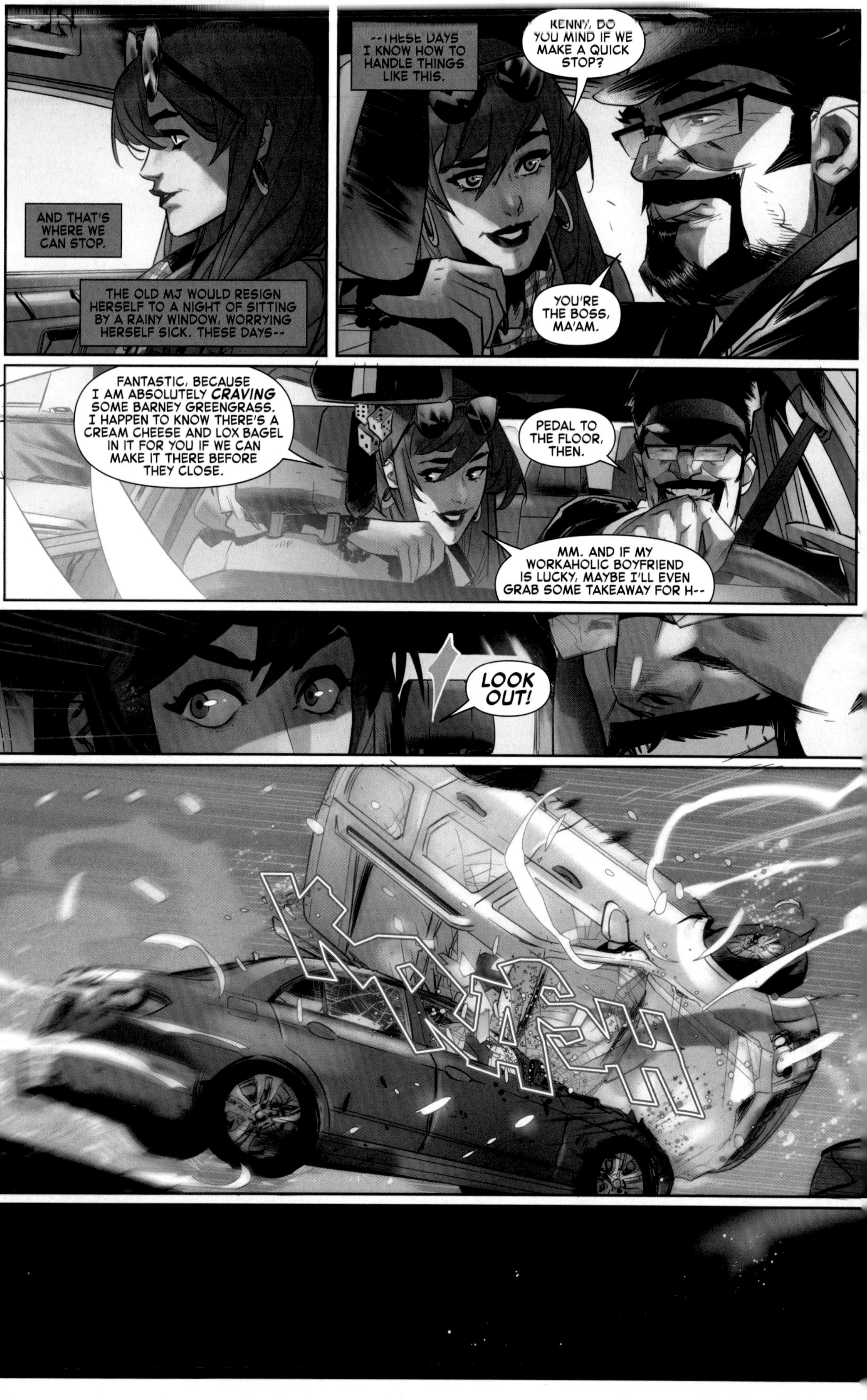
AND THAT'S WHERE WE CAN STOP.
THE OLD MJ WOULD RESIGN HERSELF TO A NIGHT OF SITTING BY A RAINY WINDOW, WORRYING HERSELF SICK. THESE DAYS--
--THESE DAYS I KNOW HOW TO HANDLE THINGS LIKE THIS.
KENNY, DO YOU MIND IF WE MAKE A QUICK STOP?
YOU'RE THE BOSS, MA'AM.
FANTASTIC, BECAUSE I AM ABSOLUTELY CRAVING SOME BARNEY GREENGRASS. I HAPPEN TO KNOW THERE'S A CREAM CHEESE AND LOX BAGEL IN IT FOR YOU IF WE CAN MAKE IT THERE BEFORE THEY CLOSE.
PEDAL TO THE FLOOR, THEN.
MM. AND IF MY WORKAHOLIC BOYFRIEND IS LUCKY, MAYBE I'LL EVEN GRAB SOME TAKEAWAY FOR H--
LOOK OUT!
KRASH

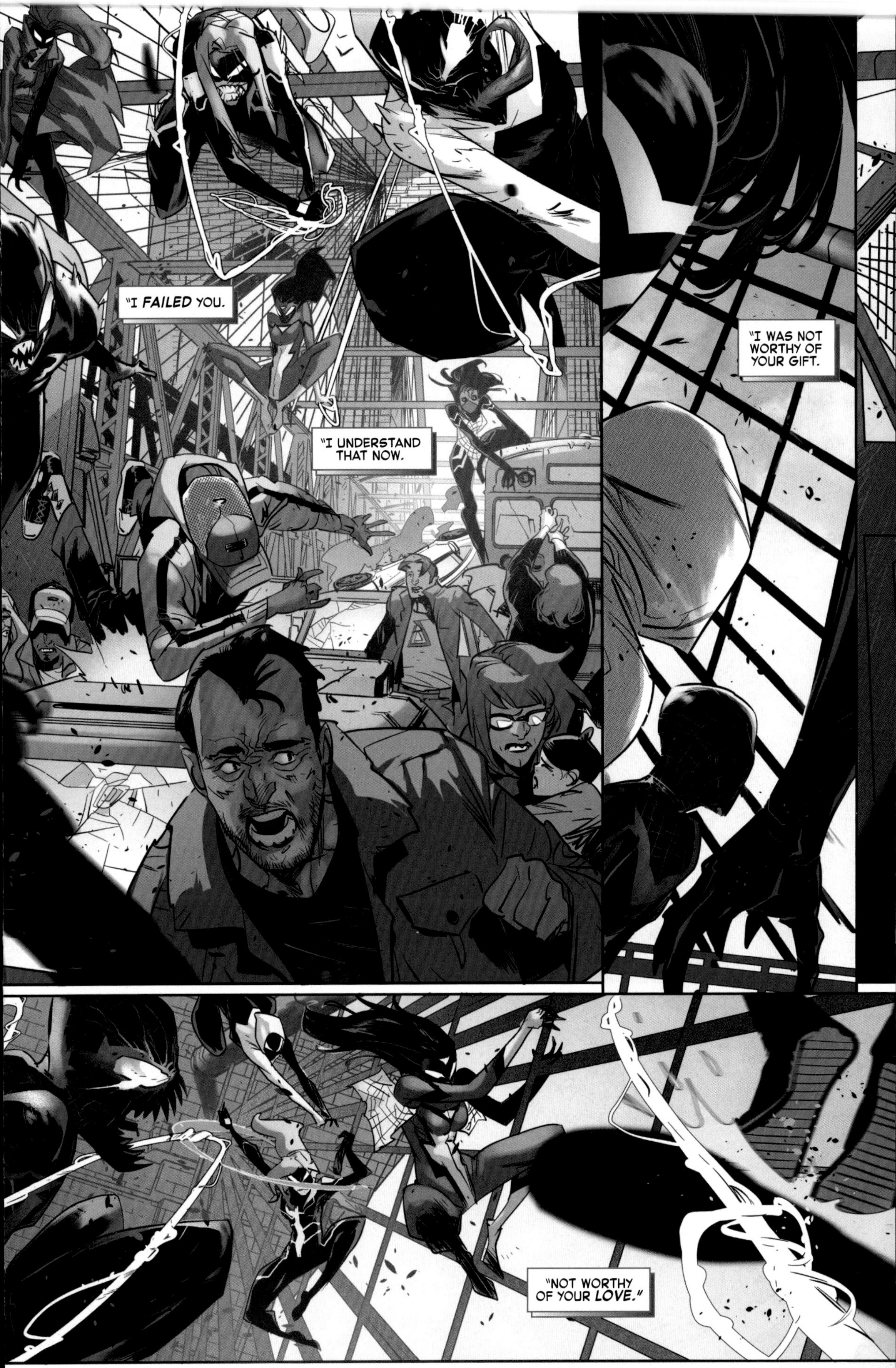
"I FAILED YOU.
"I UNDERSTAND THAT NOW.
"I WAS NOT WORTHY OF YOUR GIFT.
"NOT WORTHY OF YOUR LOVE."

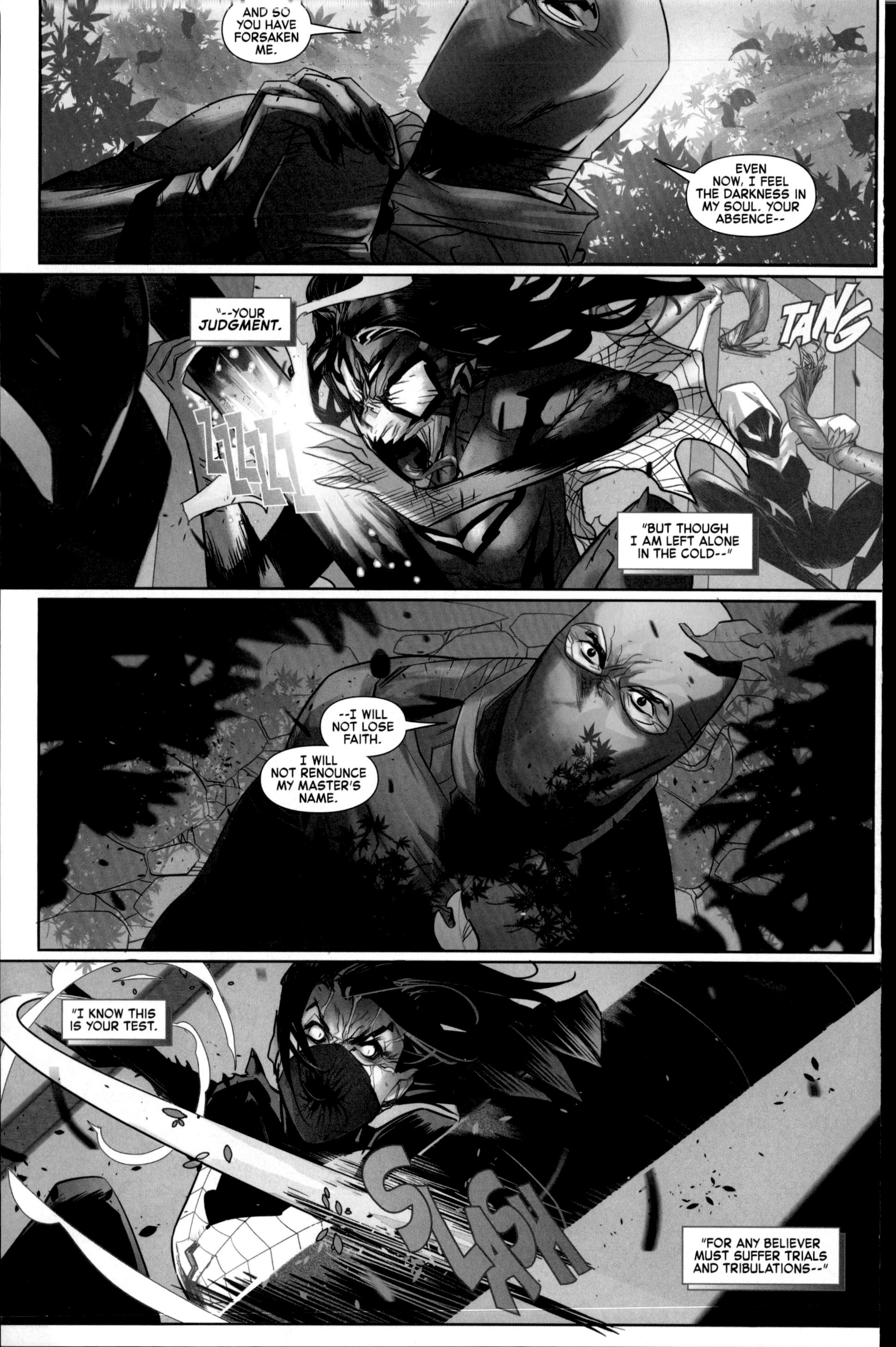
AND SO YOU HAVE FORSAKEN ME.
EVEN NOW, I FEEL THE DARKNESS IN MY SOUL. YOUR ABSENCE--
"--YOUR JUDGMENT.
TANG
ZZZZZT
"BUT THOUGH I AM LEFT ALONE IN THE COLD--"
--I WILL NOT LOSE FAITH.
I WILL NOT RENOUNCE MY MASTER'S NAME.
"I KNOW THIS IS YOUR TEST.
SLASH
"FOR ANY BELIEVER MUST SUFFER TRIALS AND TRIBULATIONS--"

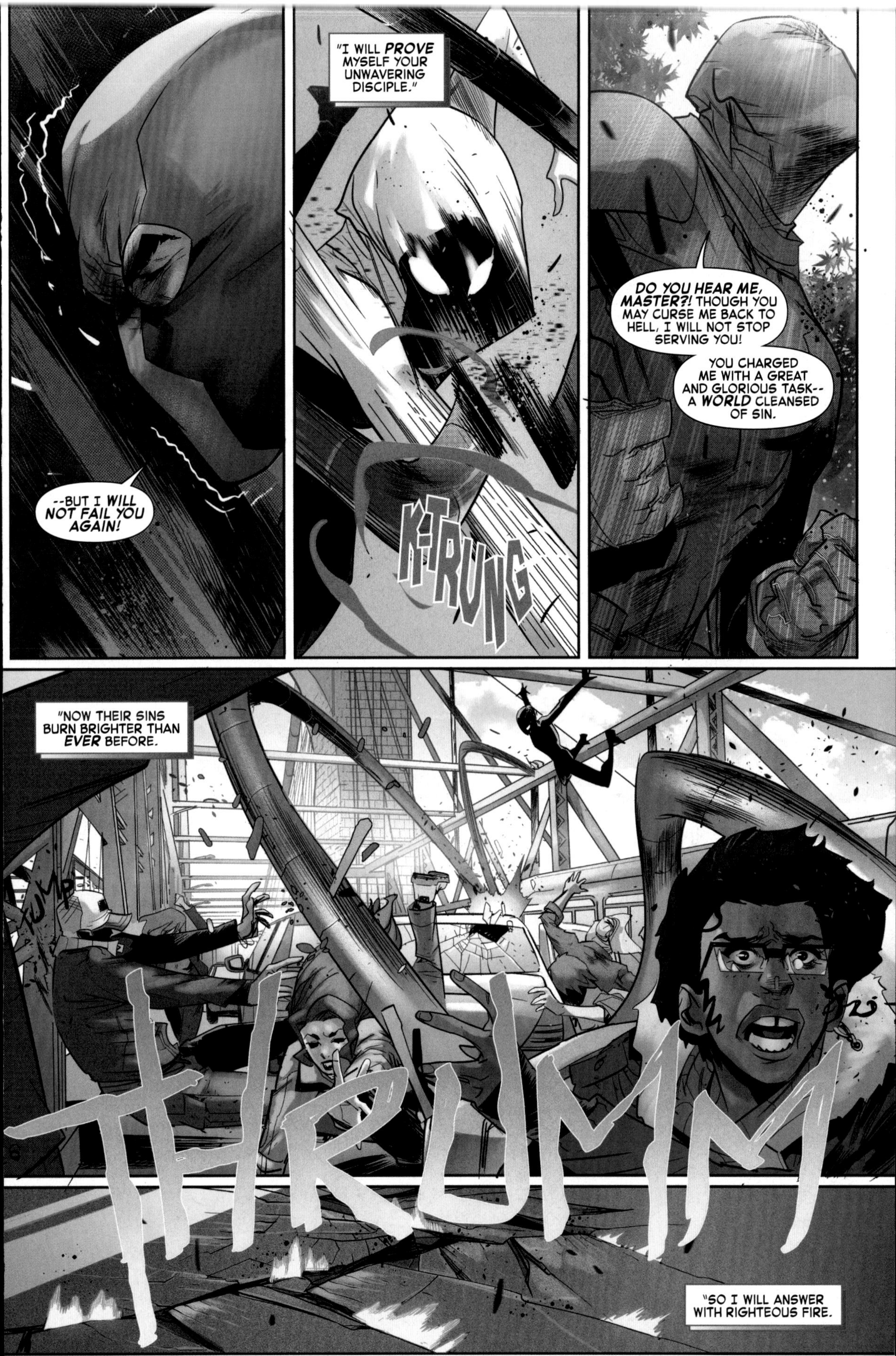
--BUT I WILL NOT FAIL YOU AGAIN!
"I WILL PROVE MYSELF YOUR UNWAVERING DISCIPLE."
K-TRUNG
DO YOU HEAR ME, MASTER?! THOUGH YOU MAY CURSE ME BACK TO HELL, I WILL NOT STOP SERVING YOU!
YOU CHARGED ME WITH A GREAT AND GLORIOUS TASK-- A WORLD CLEANSED OF SIN.
"NOW THEIR SINS BURN BRIGHTER THAN EVER BEFORE.
THRUMM
"SO I WILL ANSWER WITH RIGHTEOUS FIRE.

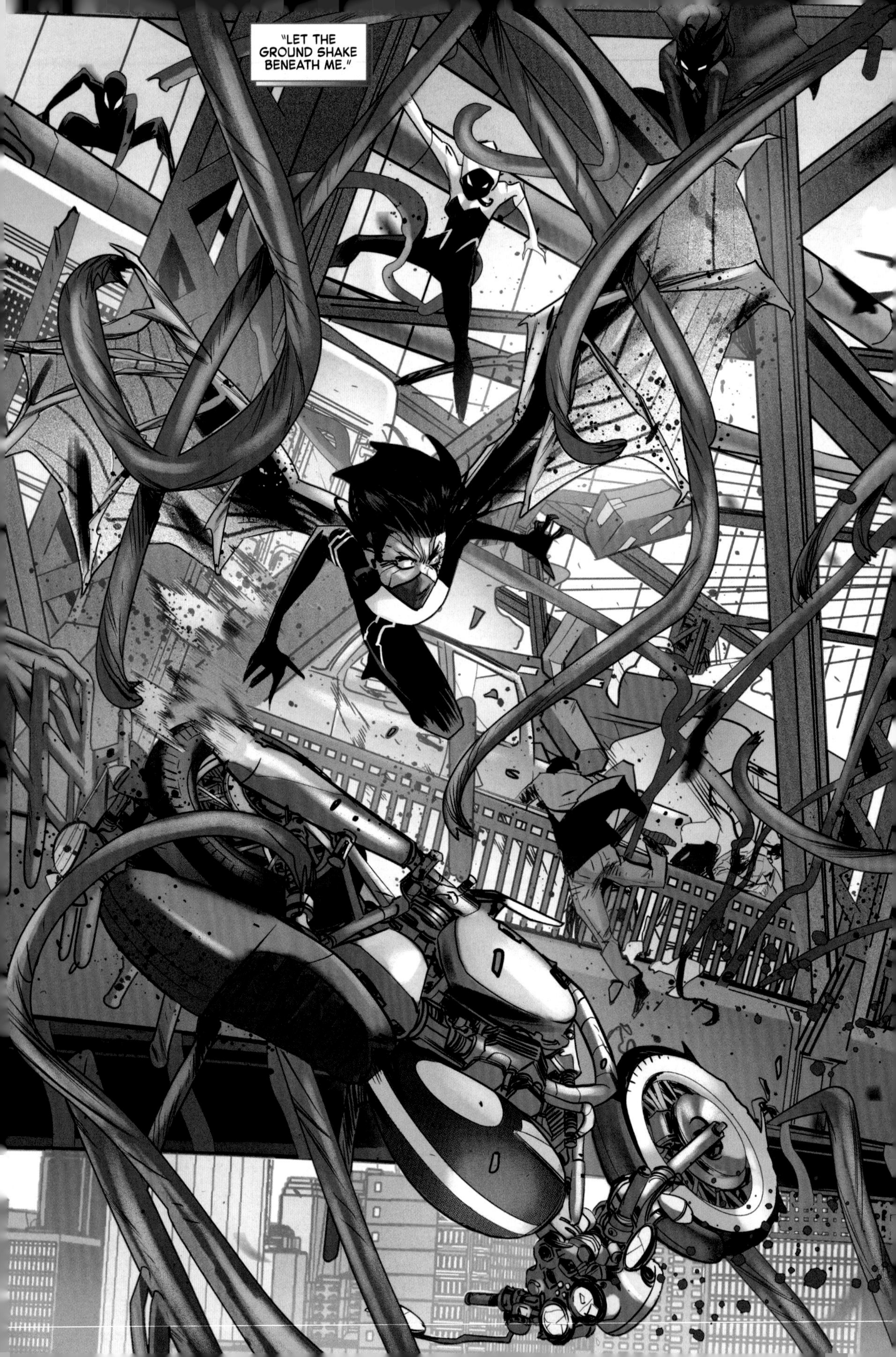
"LET THE GROUND SHAKE BENEATH ME."

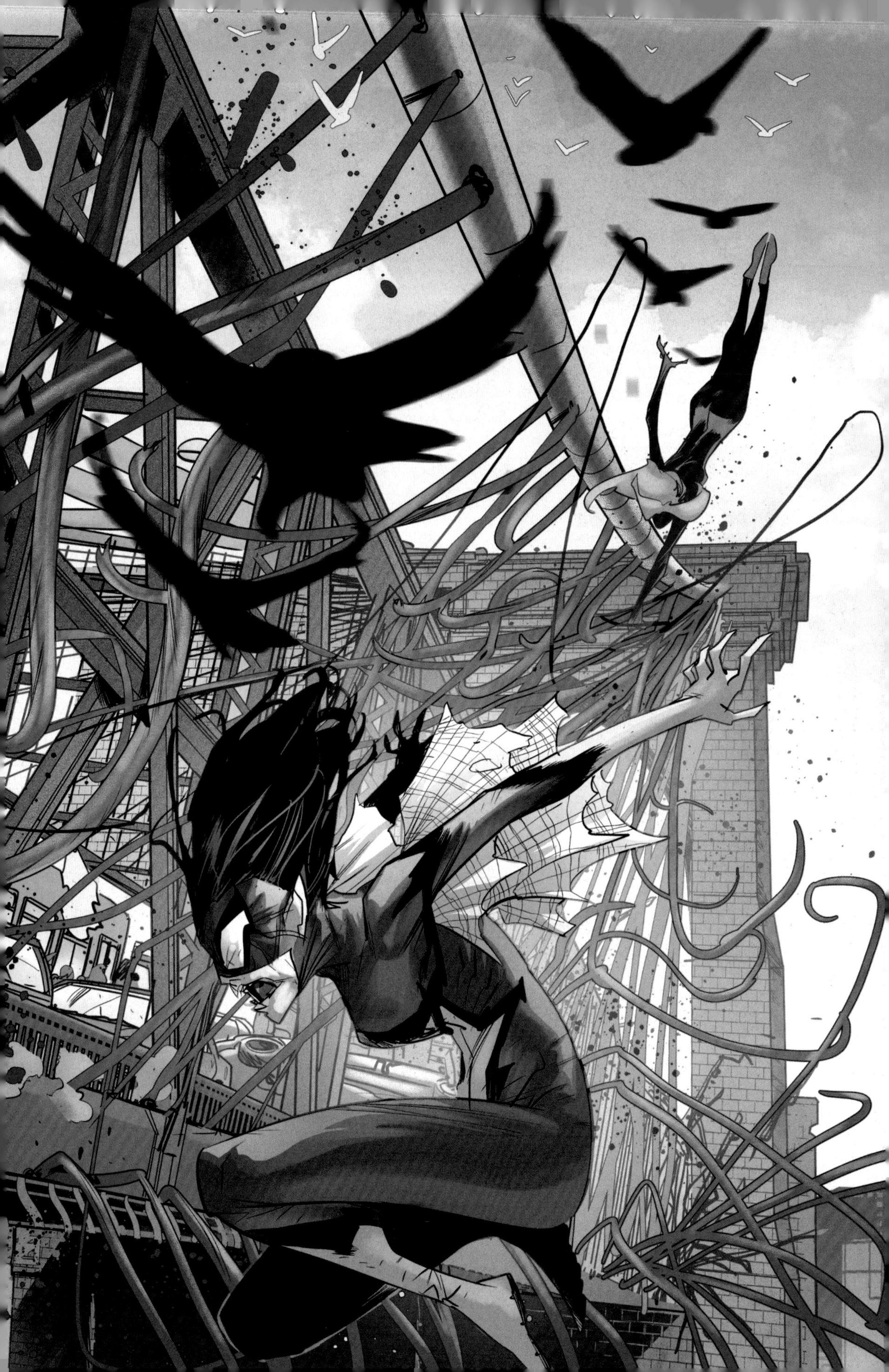

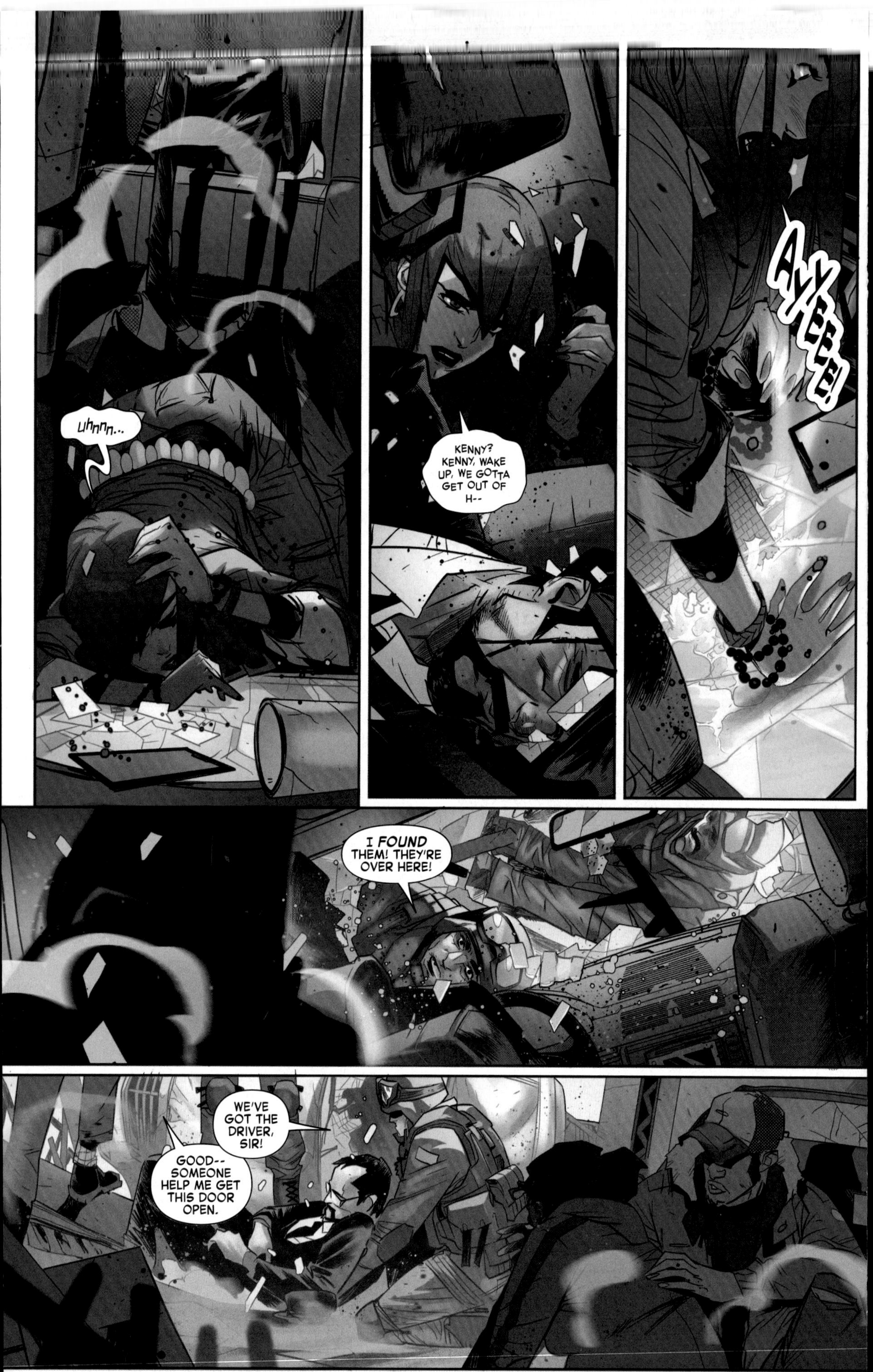
UHNNN...
KENNY? KENNY, WAKE UP, WE GOTTA GET OUT OF H--
AYYEEE!
I FOUND THEM! THEY'RE OVER HERE!
WE'VE GOT THE DRIVER, SIR!
GOOD-- SOMEONE HELP ME GET THIS DOOR OPEN.

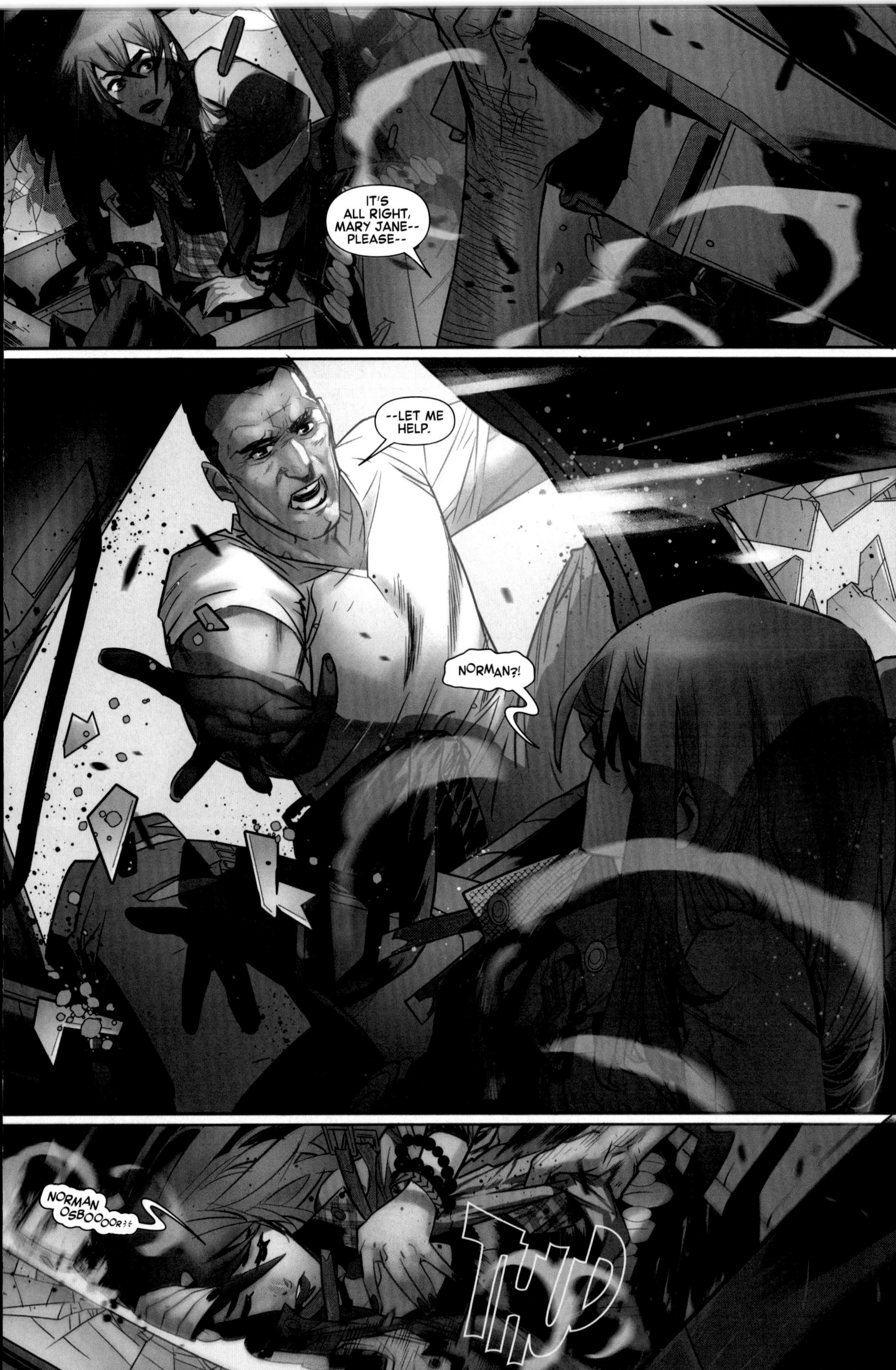

IT'S ALL RIGHT, MARY JANE-- PLEASE--
--LET ME HELP.
NORMAN?!
NORMAN OSBOOOOR?!
THUD

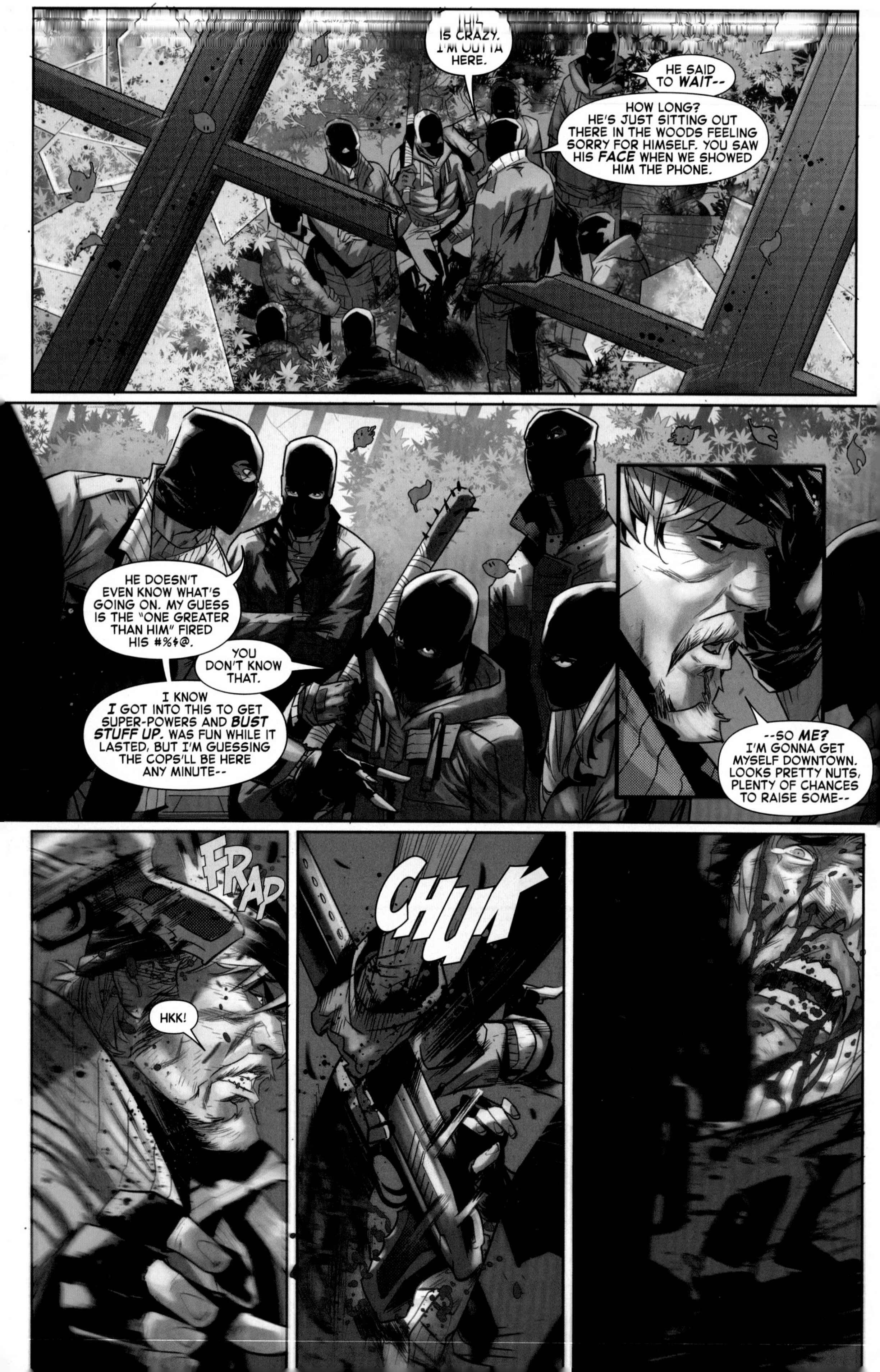
THIS IS CRAZY. I'M OUTTA HERE.
HE SAID TO WAIT--
HOW LONG? HE'S JUST SITTING OUT THERE IN THE WOODS FEELING SORRY FOR HIMSELF. YOU SAW HIS FACE WHEN WE SHOWED HIM THE PHONE.
HE DOESN'T EVEN KNOW WHAT'S GOING ON. MY GUESS IS THE "ONE GREATER THAN HIM" FIRED HIS #%$@.
YOU DON'T KNOW THAT.
I KNOW I GOT INTO THIS TO GET SUPER-POWERS AND BUST STUFF UP. WAS FUN WHILE IT LASTED, BUT I'M GUESSING THE COPS'LL BE HERE ANY MINUTE--
--SO ME? I'M GONNA GET MYSELF DOWNTOWN. LOOKS PRETTY NUTS, PLENTY OF CHANCES TO RAISE SOME--
FRAP
HKK!
CHUK

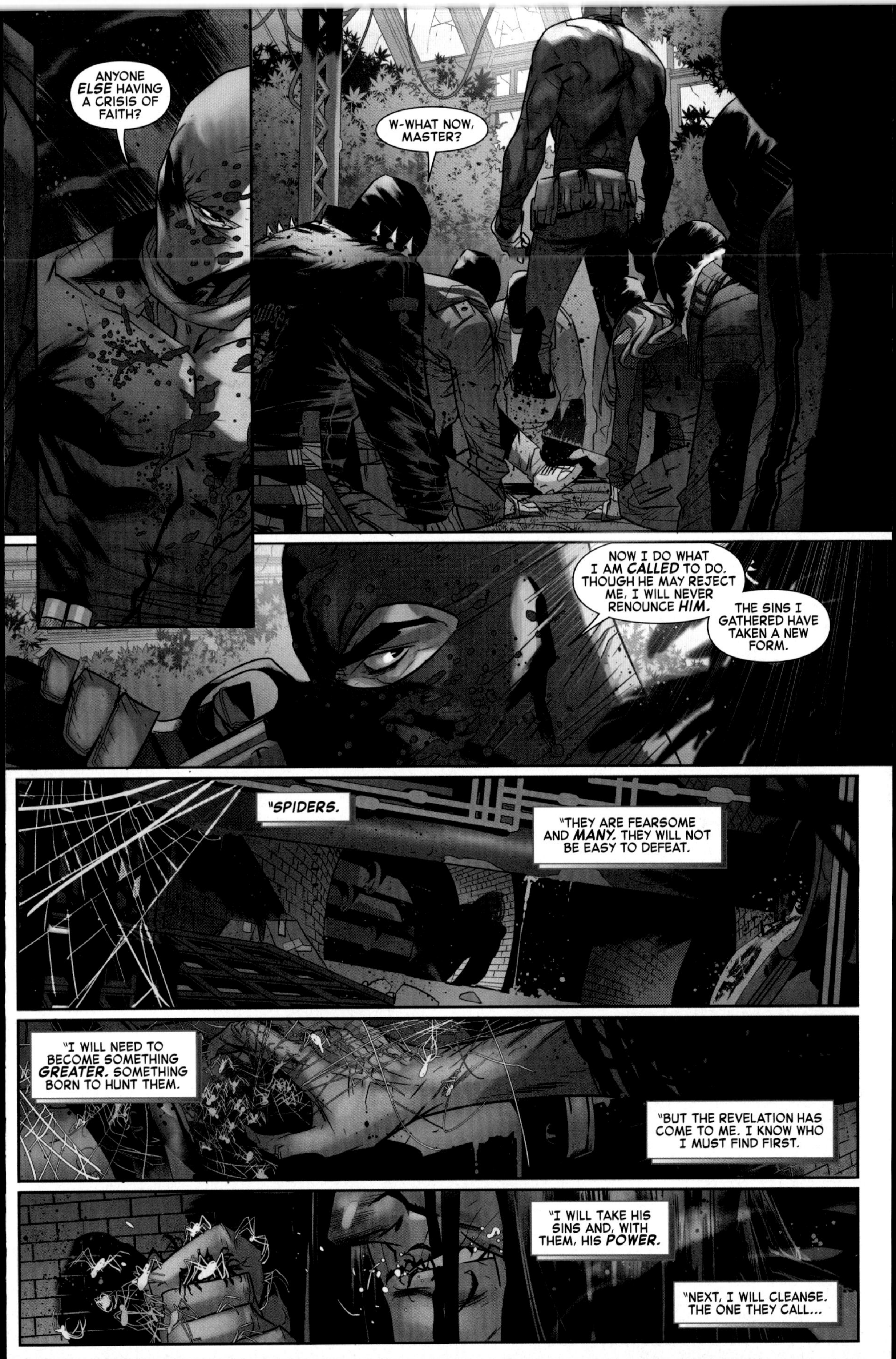
ANYONE ELSE HAVING A CRISIS OF FAITH?
W-WHAT NOW, MASTER?
NOW I DO WHAT I AM CALLED TO DO. THOUGH HE MAY REJECT ME, I WILL NEVER RENOUNCE HIM.
THE SINS I GATHERED HAVE TAKEN A NEW FORM.
"SPIDERS.
"THEY ARE FEARSOME AND MANY. THEY WILL NOT BE EASY TO DEFEAT.
"I WILL NEED TO BECOME SOMETHING GREATER. SOMETHING BORN TO HUNT THEM.
"BUT THE REVELATION HAS COME TO ME. I KNOW WHO I MUST FIND FIRST.
"I WILL TAKE HIS SINS AND, WITH THEM, HIS POWER.
"NEXT, I WILL CLEANSE. THE ONE THEY CALL...

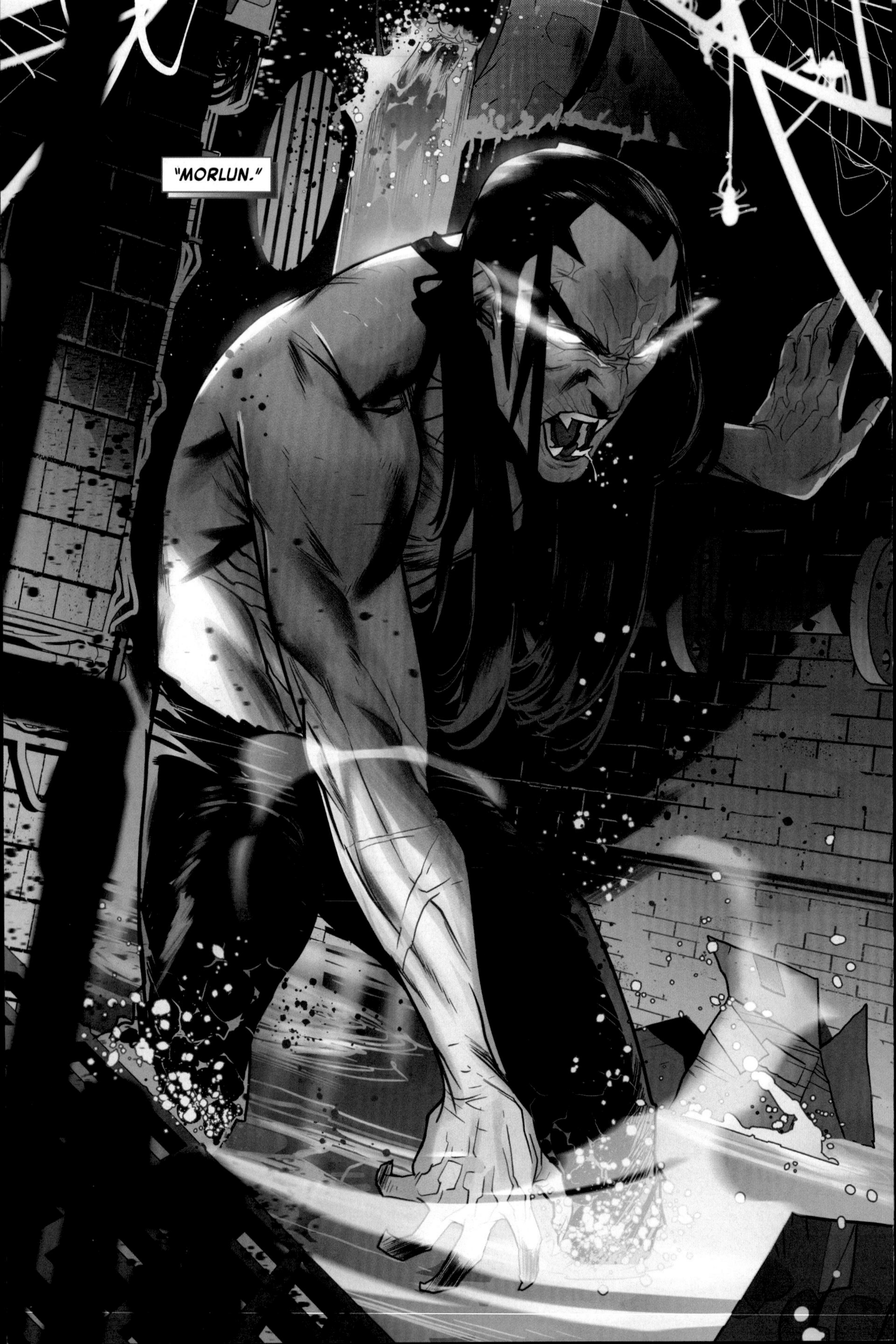
"MORLUN."

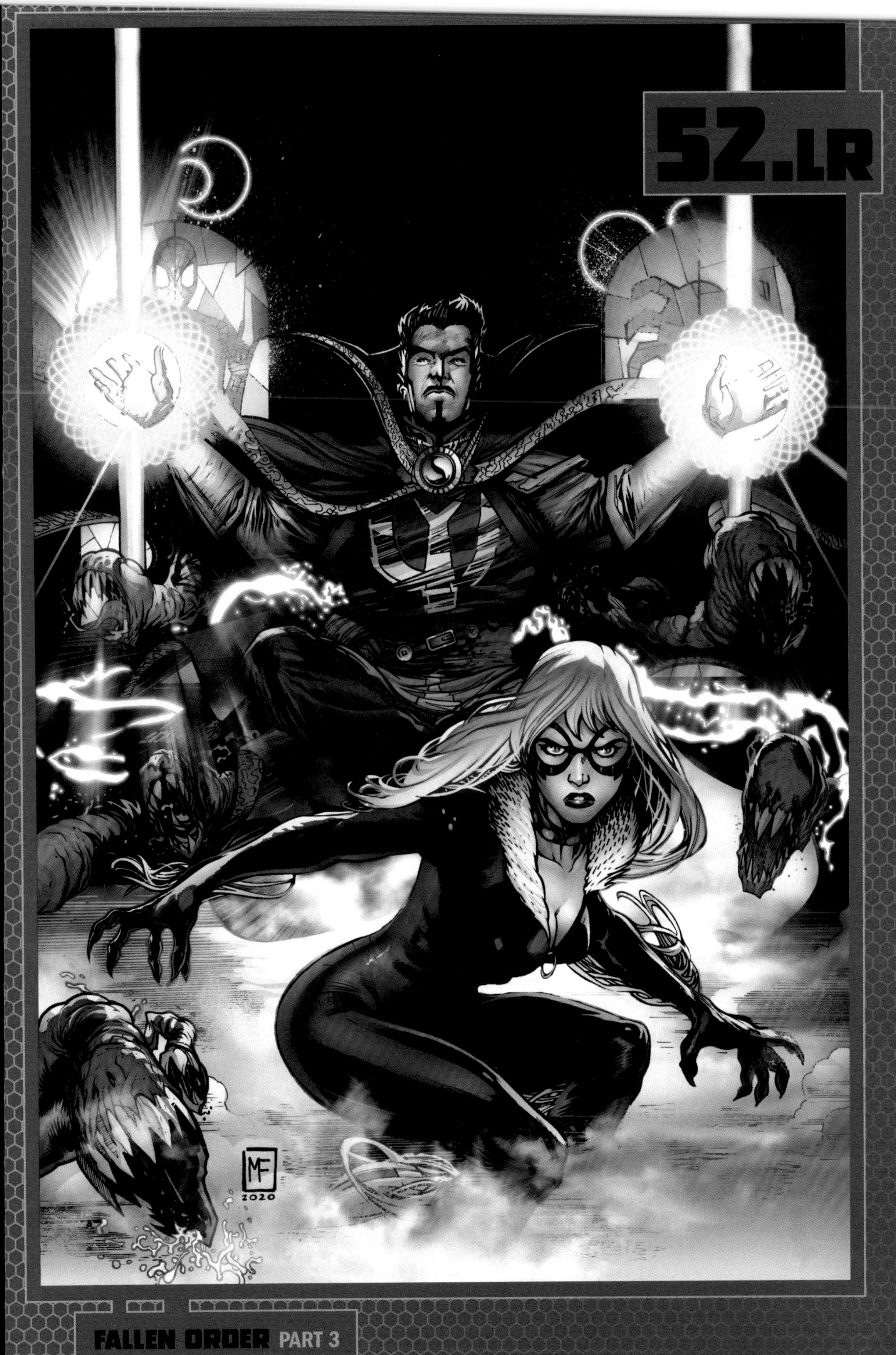
52.LR
MF 2020

FALLEN ORDER PART 3

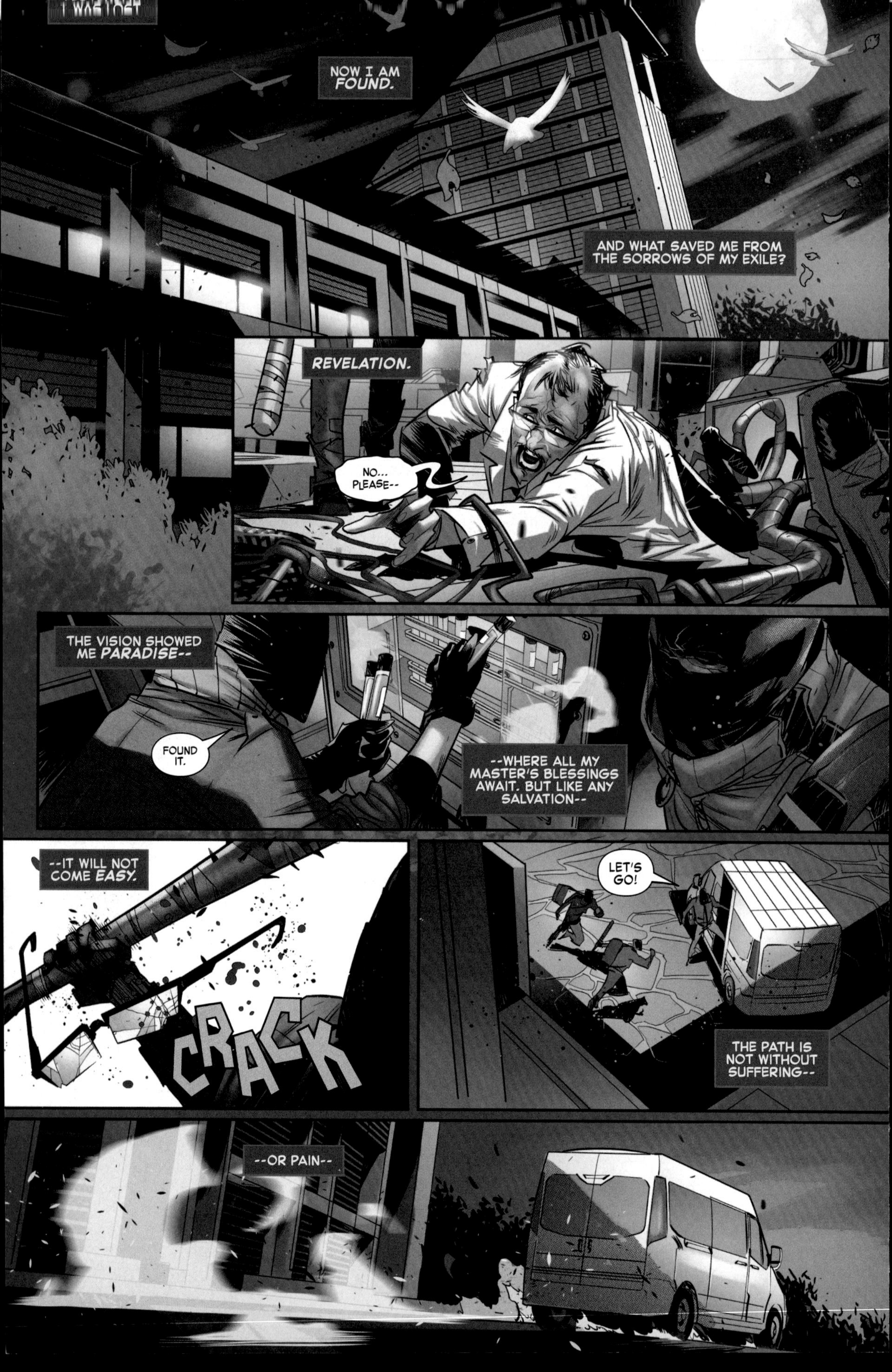
NOW I AM FOUND.
AND WHAT SAVED ME FROM THE SORROWS OF MY EXILE?
REVELATION.
NO... PLEASE--
THE VISION SHOWED ME PARADISE--
FOUND IT.
--WHERE ALL MY MASTER'S BLESSINGS AWAIT. BUT LIKE ANY SALVATION--
--IT WILL NOT COME EASY.
CRACK
LET'S GO!
THE PATH IS NOT WITHOUT SUFFERING--
--OR PAIN--

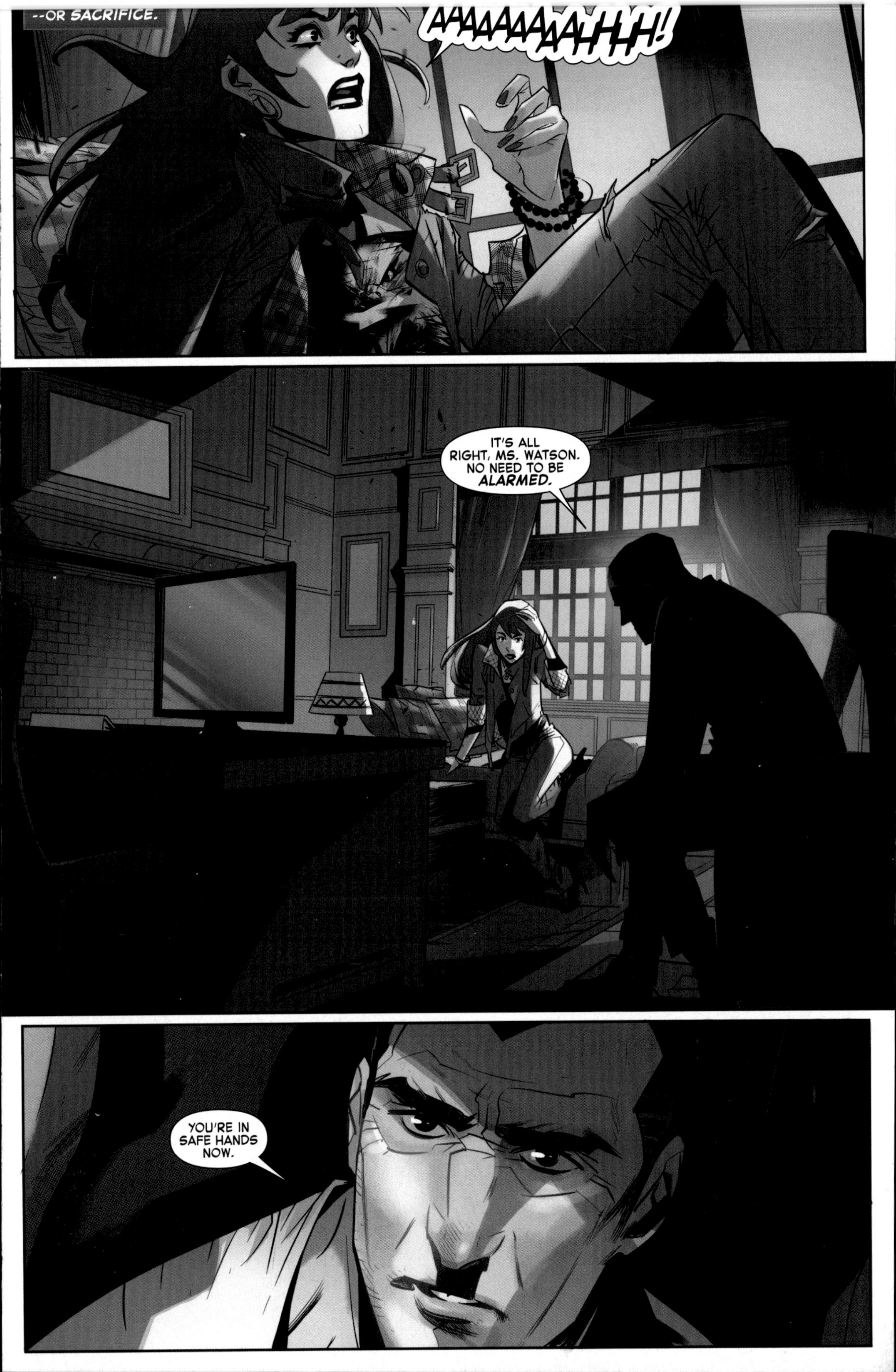
--OR SACRIFICE.
AAAAAAAAAHHHH!
IT'S ALL RIGHT, MS. WATSON. NO NEED TO BE ALARMED.
YOU'RE IN SAFE HANDS NOW.

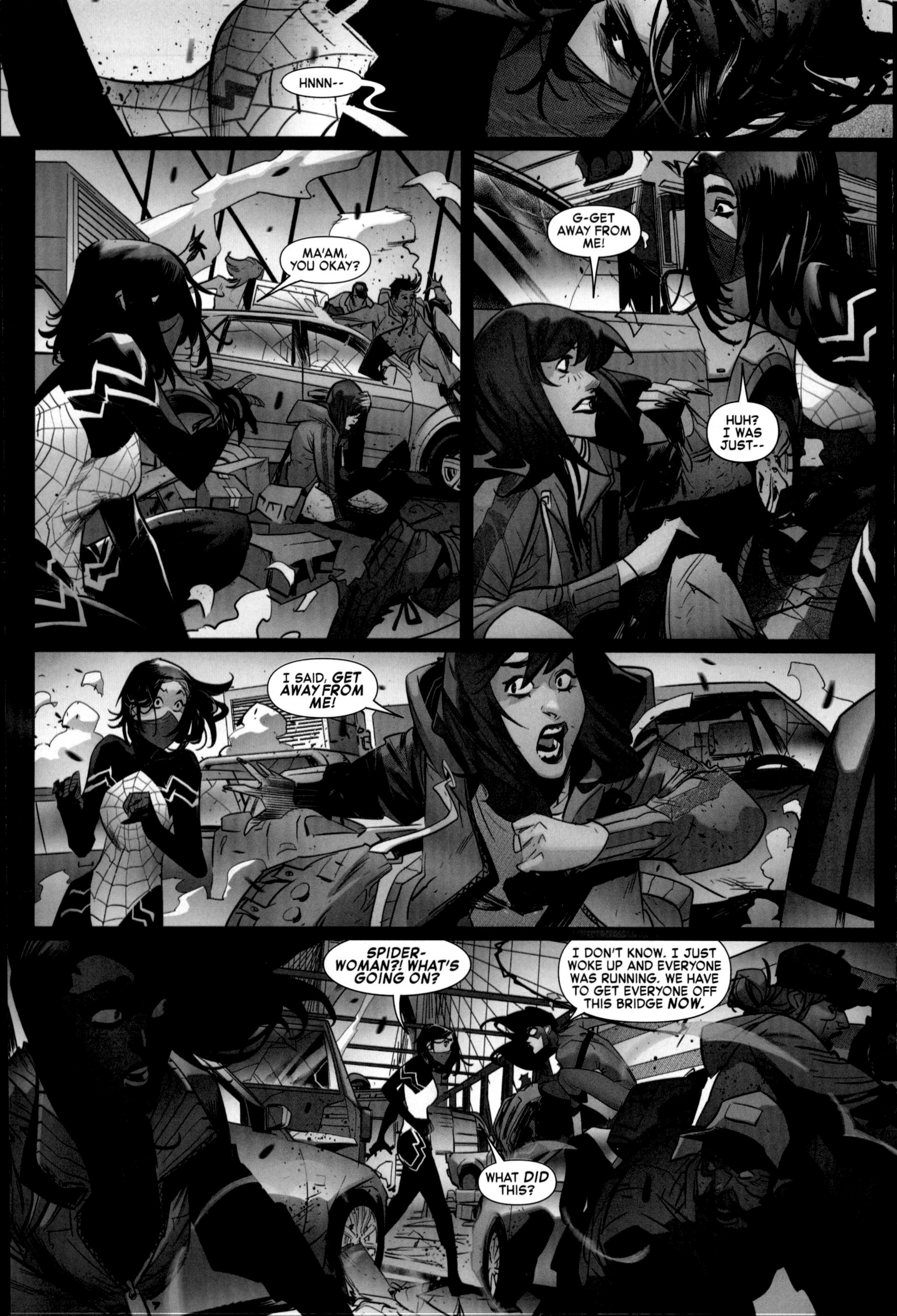
HNNN--
MA'AM, YOU OKAY?
G-GET AWAY FROM ME!
HUH? I WAS JUST--
I SAID, **GET AWAY FROM ME!**
SPIDER-WOMAN?! WHAT'S GOING ON?
I DON'T KNOW. I JUST WOKE UP AND EVERYONE WAS RUNNING. WE HAVE TO GET EVERYONE OFF THIS BRIDGE ***NOW.***
WHAT ***DID*** THIS?

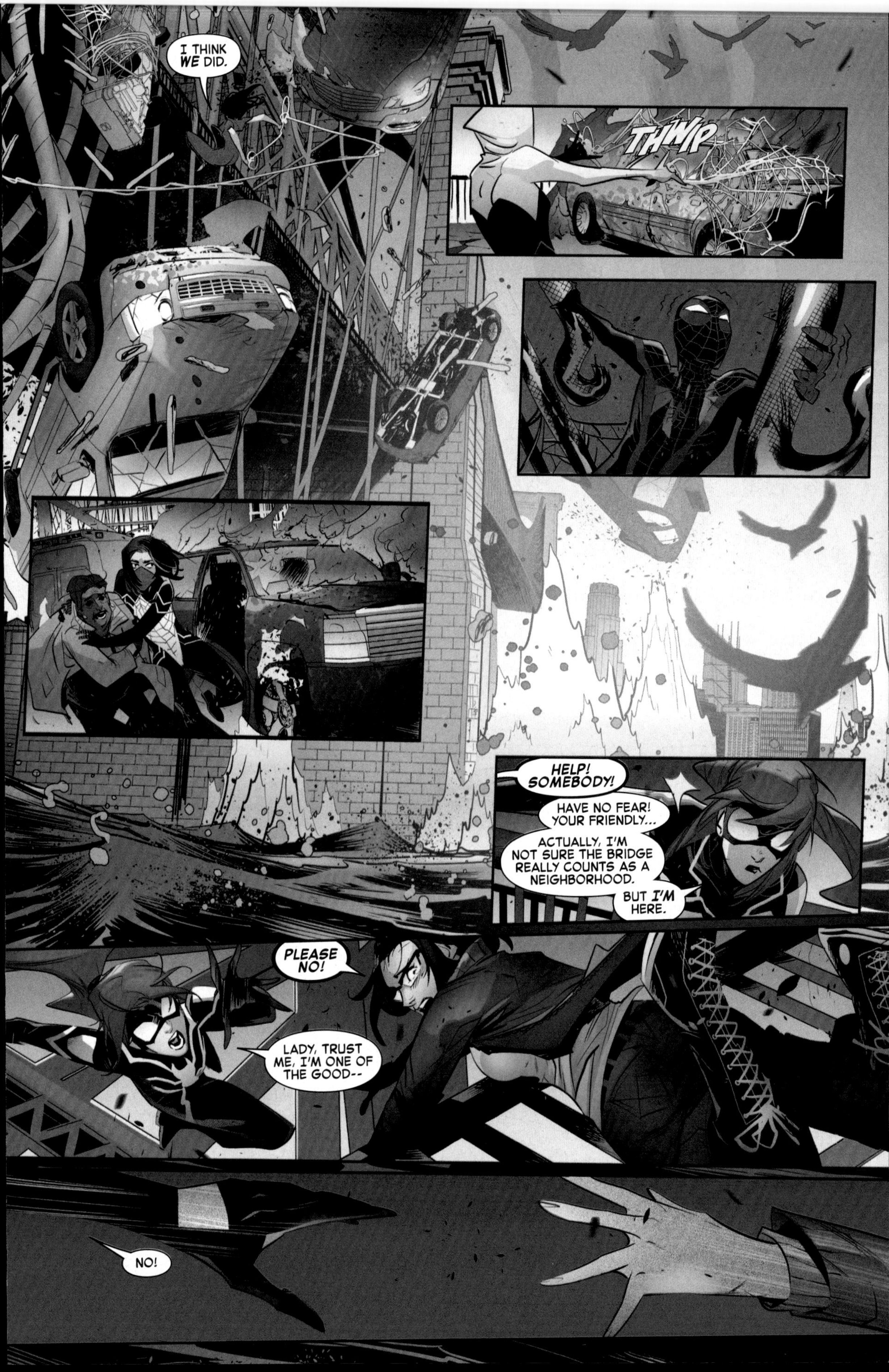
I THINK WE DID.
THWIP
HELP! SOMEBODY!
HAVE NO FEAR! YOUR FRIENDLY...
ACTUALLY, I'M NOT SURE THE BRIDGE REALLY COUNTS AS A NEIGHBORHOOD.
BUT I'M HERE.
PLEASE NO!
LADY, TRUST ME, I'M ONE OF THE GOOD--
NO!

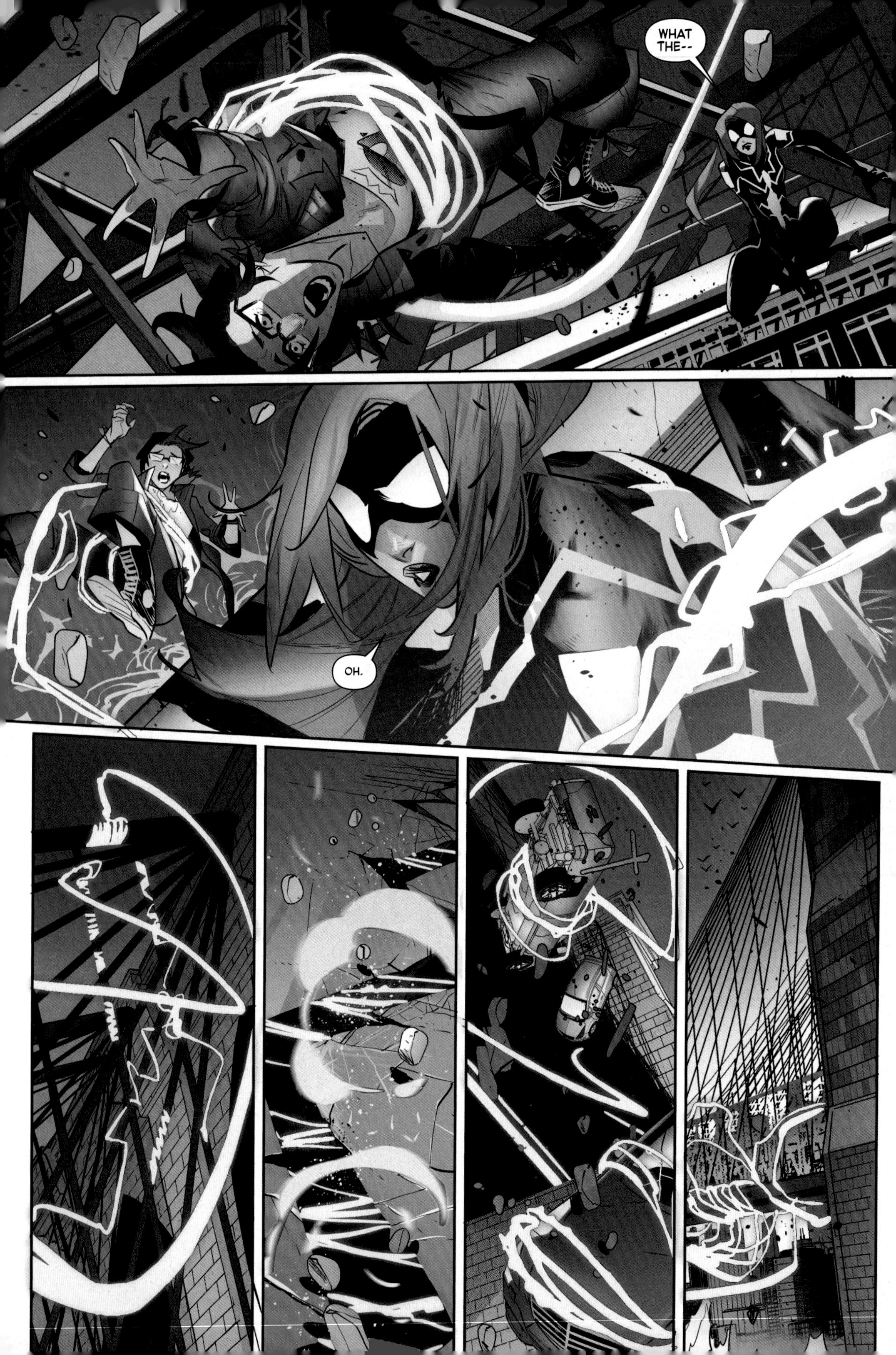
WHAT THE--
OH.

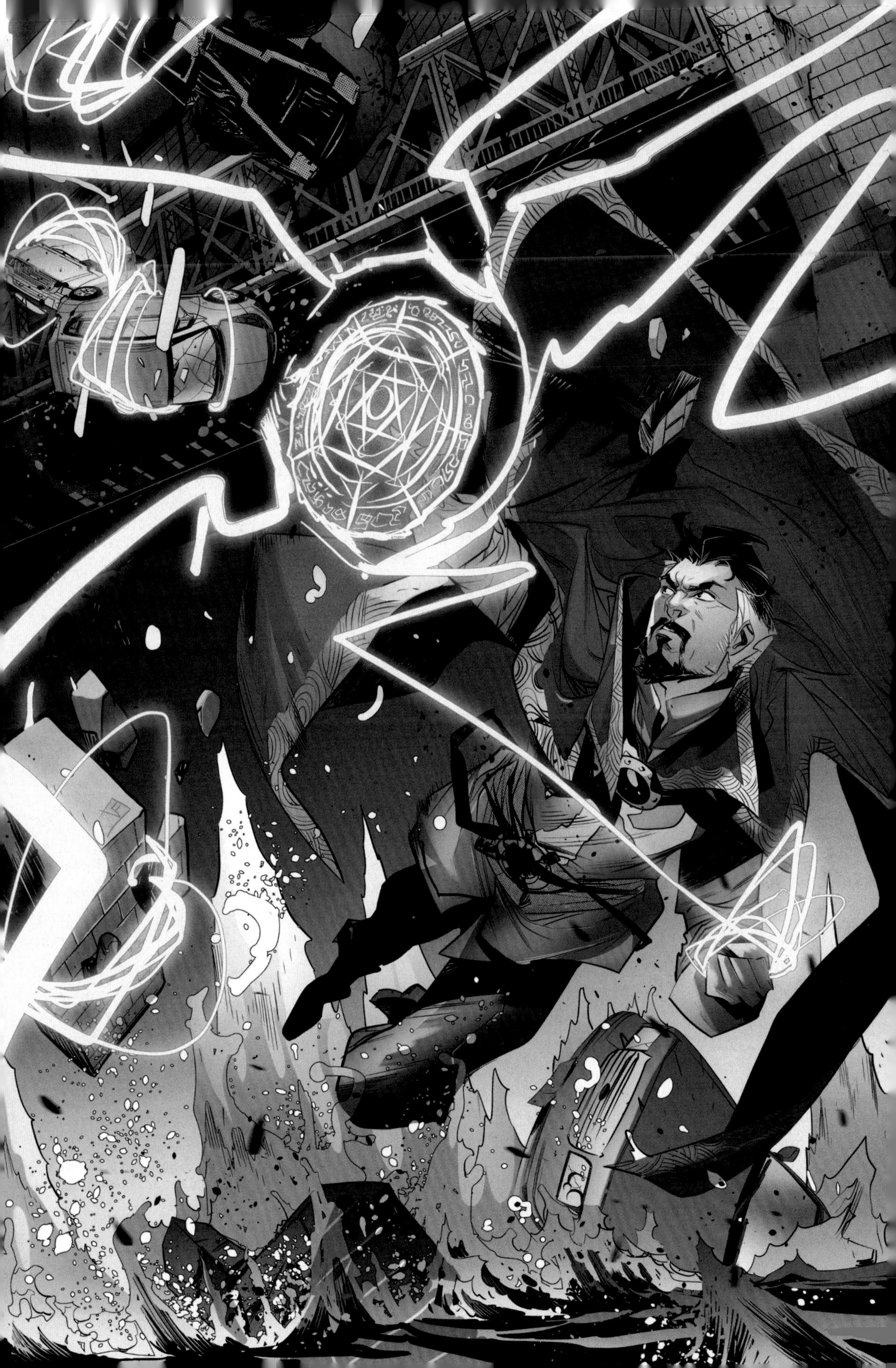

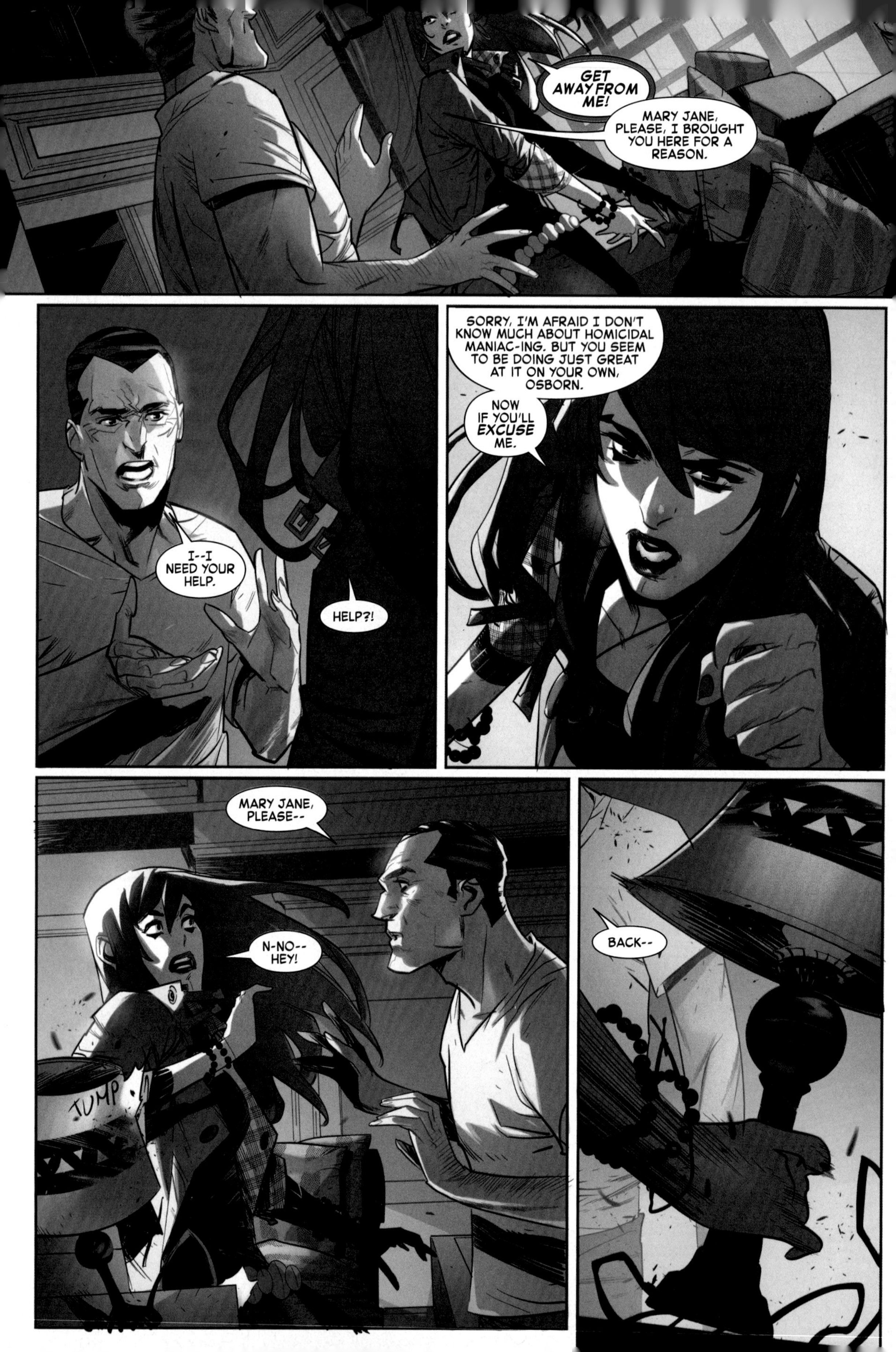
GET AWAY FROM ME!
MARY JANE, PLEASE, I BROUGHT YOU HERE FOR A REASON.
I--I NEED YOUR HELP.
HELP?!
SORRY, I'M AFRAID I DON'T KNOW MUCH ABOUT HOMICIDAL MANIAC-ING. BUT YOU SEEM TO BE DOING JUST GREAT AT IT ON YOUR OWN, OSBORN.
NOW IF YOU'LL EXCUSE ME.
MARY JANE, PLEASE--
N-NO-- HEY!
JUMP
BACK--

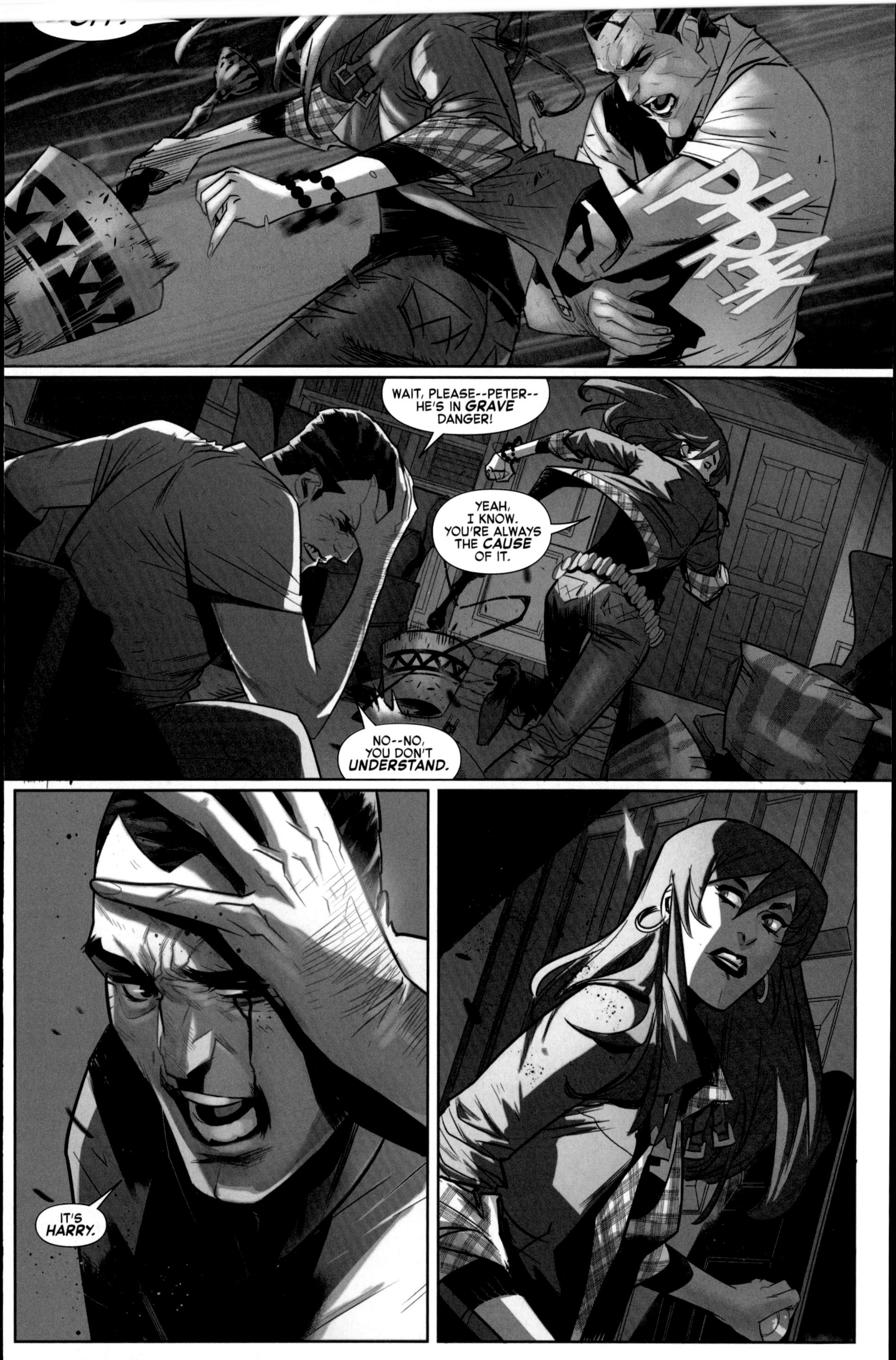
WAIT, PLEASE--PETER--HE'S IN GRAVE DANGER!
YEAH, I KNOW. YOU'RE ALWAYS THE CAUSE OF IT.
NO--NO, YOU DON'T UNDERSTAND.
IT'S HARRY.

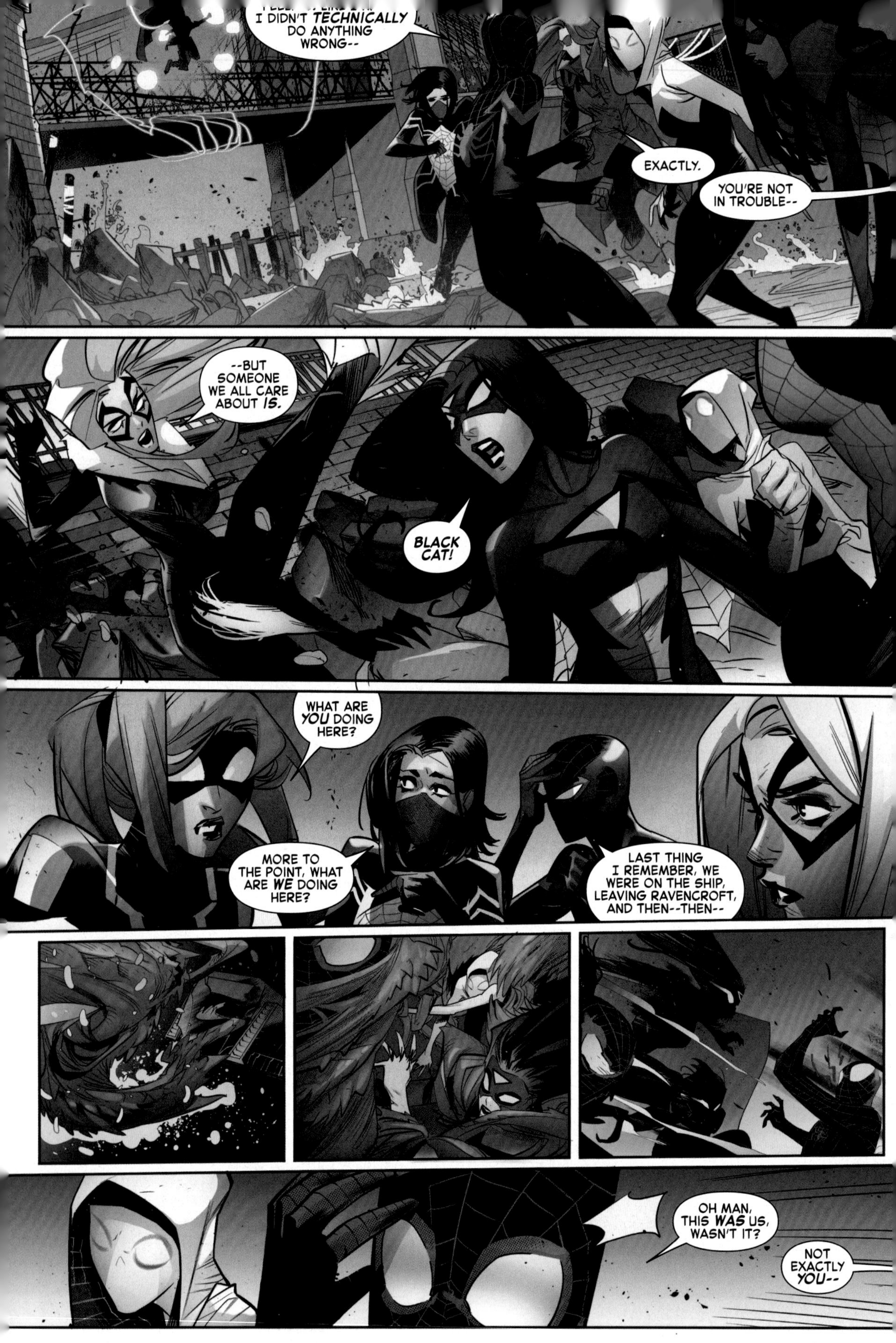
I DIDN'T TECHNICALLY DO ANYTHING WRONG--
EXACTLY.
YOU'RE NOT IN TROUBLE--
--BUT SOMEONE WE ALL CARE ABOUT IS.
BLACK CAT!
WHAT ARE YOU DOING HERE?
MORE TO THE POINT, WHAT ARE WE DOING HERE?
LAST THING I REMEMBER, WE WERE ON THE SHIP, LEAVING RAVENCROFT, AND THEN--THEN--
OH MAN, THIS WAS US, WASN'T IT?
NOT EXACTLY YOU--

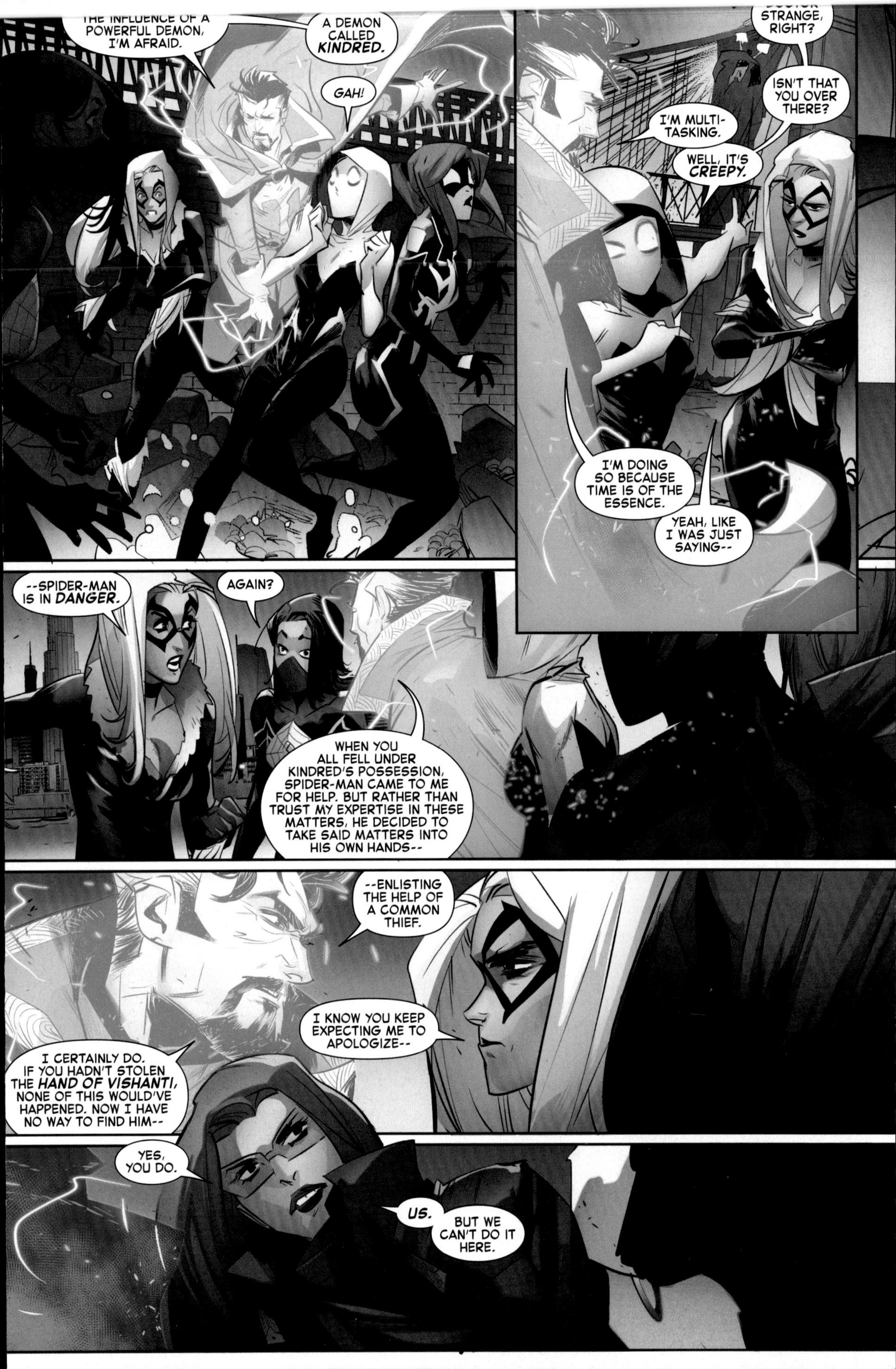

THE INFLUENCE OF A POWERFUL DEMON, I'M AFRAID.
A DEMON CALLED KINDRED.
GAH!
STRANGE, RIGHT?
ISN'T THAT YOU OVER THERE?
I'M MULTI-TASKING.
WELL, IT'S CREEPY.
I'M DOING SO BECAUSE TIME IS OF THE ESSENCE.
YEAH, LIKE I WAS JUST SAYING--
--SPIDER-MAN IS IN DANGER.
AGAIN?
WHEN YOU ALL FELL UNDER KINDRED'S POSSESSION, SPIDER-MAN CAME TO ME FOR HELP. BUT RATHER THAN TRUST MY EXPERTISE IN THESE MATTERS, HE DECIDED TO TAKE SAID MATTERS INTO HIS OWN HANDS--
--ENLISTING THE HELP OF A COMMON THIEF.
I KNOW YOU KEEP EXPECTING ME TO APOLOGIZE--
I CERTAINLY DO. IF YOU HADN'T STOLEN THE HAND OF VISHANTI, NONE OF THIS WOULD'VE HAPPENED. NOW I HAVE NO WAY TO FIND HIM--
YES, YOU DO.
US.
BUT WE CAN'T DO IT HERE.

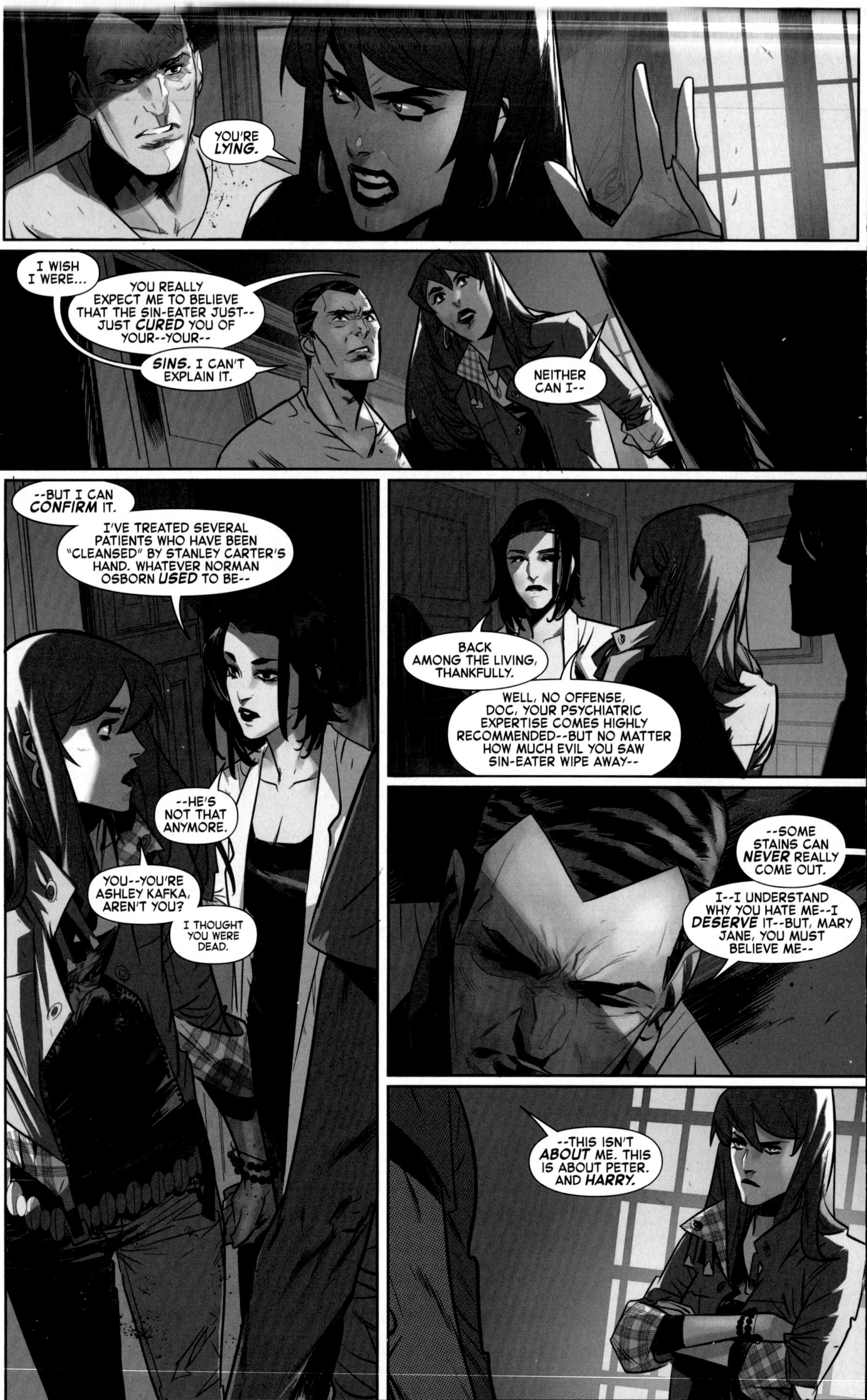
YOU'RE LYING.
I WISH I WERE...
YOU REALLY EXPECT ME TO BELIEVE THAT THE SIN-EATER JUST-- JUST CURED YOU OF YOUR--YOUR--
SINS. I CAN'T EXPLAIN IT.
NEITHER CAN I--
--BUT I CAN CONFIRM IT.
I'VE TREATED SEVERAL PATIENTS WHO HAVE BEEN "CLEANSED" BY STANLEY CARTER'S HAND. WHATEVER NORMAN OSBORN USED TO BE--
--HE'S NOT THAT ANYMORE.
YOU--YOU'RE ASHLEY KAFKA, AREN'T YOU?
I THOUGHT YOU WERE DEAD.
BACK AMONG THE LIVING, THANKFULLY.
WELL, NO OFFENSE, DOC, YOUR PSYCHIATRIC EXPERTISE COMES HIGHLY RECOMMENDED--BUT NO MATTER HOW MUCH EVIL YOU SAW SIN-EATER WIPE AWAY--
--SOME STAINS CAN NEVER REALLY COME OUT.
I--I UNDERSTAND WHY YOU HATE ME--I DESERVE IT--BUT, MARY JANE, YOU MUST BELIEVE ME--
--THIS ISN'T ABOUT ME. THIS IS ABOUT PETER. AND HARRY.

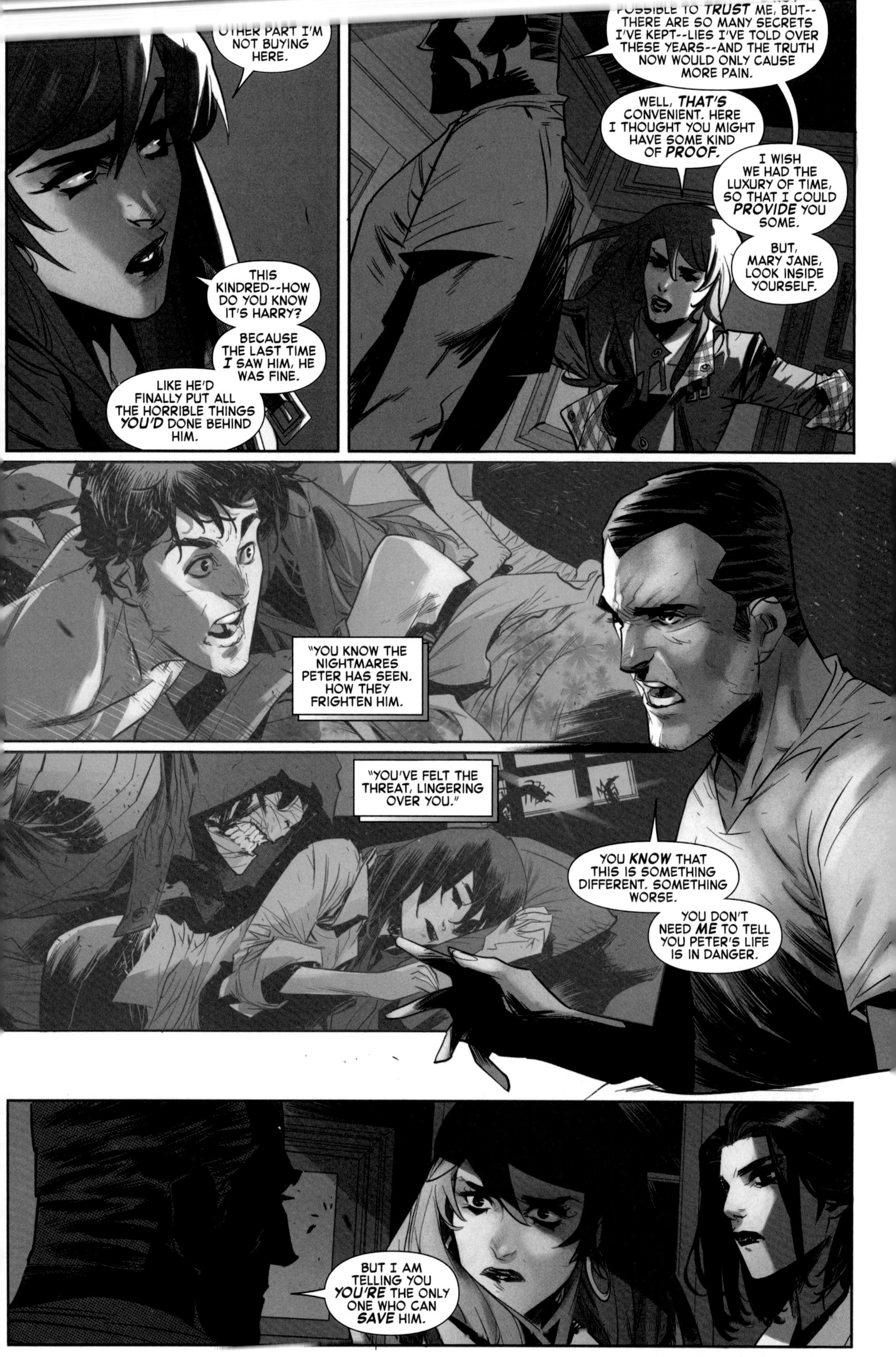

OTHER PART I'M NOT BUYING HERE.
THIS KINDRED--HOW DO YOU KNOW IT'S HARRY?
BECAUSE THE LAST TIME *I* SAW HIM, HE WAS FINE.
LIKE HE'D FINALLY PUT ALL THE HORRIBLE THINGS *YOU'D* DONE BEHIND HIM.
POSSIBLE TO *TRUST* ME, BUT-- THERE ARE SO MANY SECRETS I'VE KEPT--LIES I'VE TOLD OVER THESE YEARS--AND THE TRUTH NOW WOULD ONLY CAUSE MORE PAIN.
WELL, *THAT'S* CONVENIENT. HERE I THOUGHT YOU MIGHT HAVE SOME KIND OF *PROOF.*
I WISH WE HAD THE LUXURY OF TIME, SO THAT I COULD *PROVIDE* YOU SOME.
BUT, MARY JANE, LOOK INSIDE YOURSELF.
"YOU KNOW THE NIGHTMARES PETER HAS SEEN. HOW THEY FRIGHTEN HIM.
"YOU'VE FELT THE THREAT, LINGERING OVER YOU."
YOU *KNOW* THAT THIS IS SOMETHING DIFFERENT. SOMETHING WORSE.
YOU DON'T NEED *ME* TO TELL YOU PETER'S LIFE IS IN DANGER.
BUT I AM TELLING YOU *YOU'RE* THE ONLY ONE WHO CAN *SAVE* HIM.

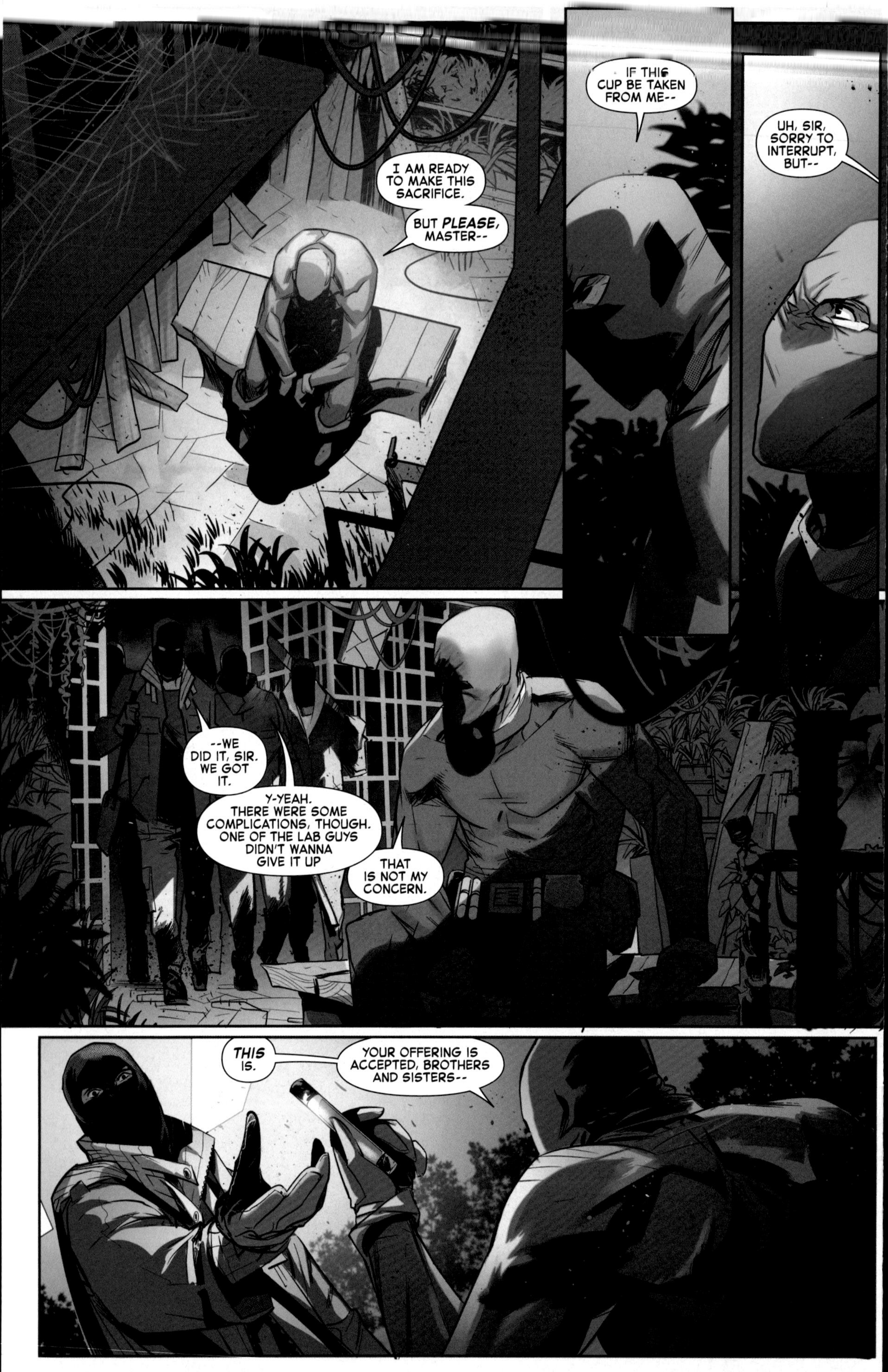
I AM READY TO MAKE THIS SACRIFICE.
BUT *PLEASE,* MASTER--
IF THIS CUP BE TAKEN FROM ME--
UH, SIR, SORRY TO INTERRUPT, BUT--
--WE DID IT, SIR. WE GOT IT.
Y-YEAH. THERE WERE SOME COMPLICATIONS, THOUGH. ONE OF THE LAB GUYS DIDN'T WANNA GIVE IT UP
THAT IS NOT MY CONCERN.
THIS IS.
YOUR OFFERING IS ACCEPTED, BROTHERS AND SISTERS--

--AND IT PLEASES ME.

WHAT *IS* IT, SIR?

A BIOLOGICAL WEAPON. SOME TIME AGO, A MADWOMAN ATTEMPTED TO INFECT ALL OF MANHATTAN WITH IT--

--USING IT TO TURN THE INFECTED INTO SOMETHING TRULY TERRIFYING.

THE THREAT WAS ERADICATED, BUT A FEW VIALS OF THE AGENT WERE PRESERVED-- FOR RESEARCH PURPOSES.

SO... WHAT ARE *YOU* GONNA DO WITH IT?

USE IT FOR *BAIT.*

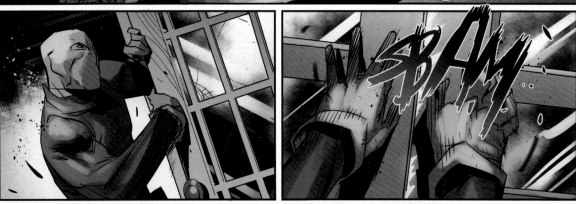

SBAM

I'M SO SORRY, ALL OF YOU. SUFFERING IS THE WAY OF THIS WORLD.

BUT KNOW THAT YOUR FAITH WILL BE *REWARDED.*

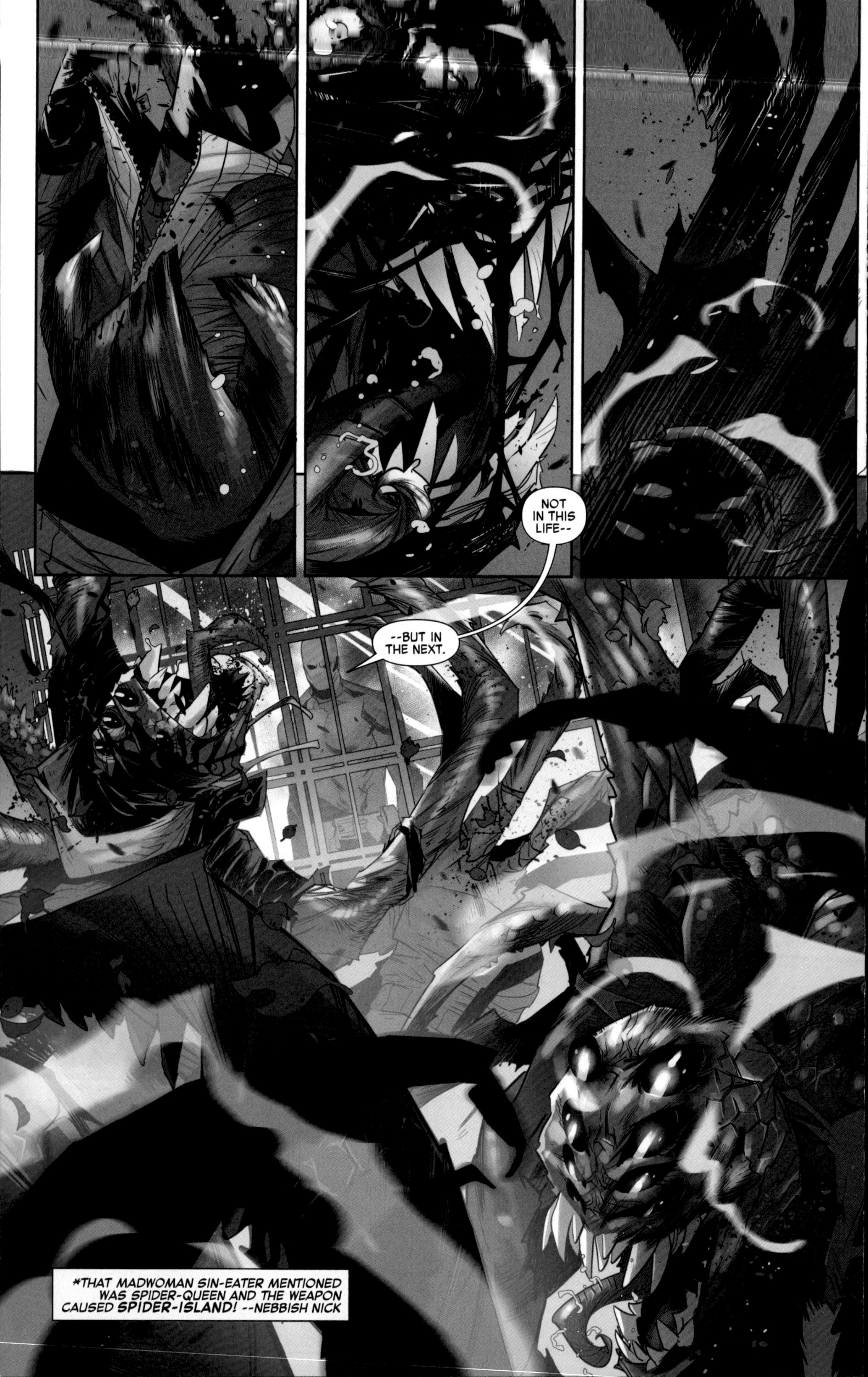
NOT IN THIS LIFE--
--BUT IN THE NEXT.
*THAT MADWOMAN SIN-EATER MENTIONED WAS SPIDER-QUEEN AND THE WEAPON CAUSED SPIDER-ISLAND! --NEBBISH NICK

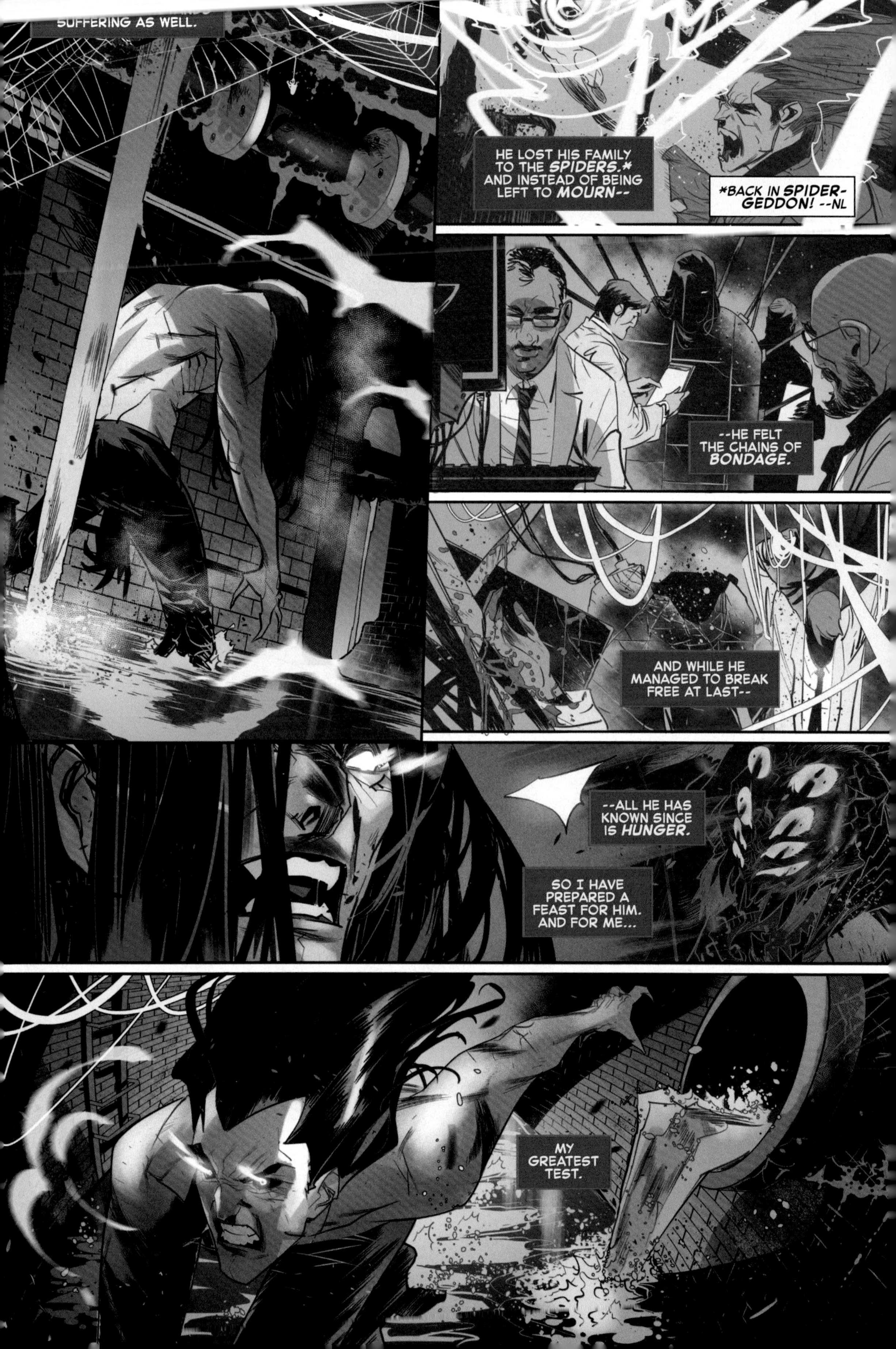
SUFFERING AS WELL.
HE LOST HIS FAMILY TO THE SPIDERS.* AND INSTEAD OF BEING LEFT TO MOURN--
*BACK IN SPIDER-GEDDON! --NL
--HE FELT THE CHAINS OF BONDAGE.
AND WHILE HE MANAGED TO BREAK FREE AT LAST--
--ALL HE HAS KNOWN SINCE IS HUNGER.
SO I HAVE PREPARED A FEAST FOR HIM. AND FOR ME...
MY GREATEST TEST.

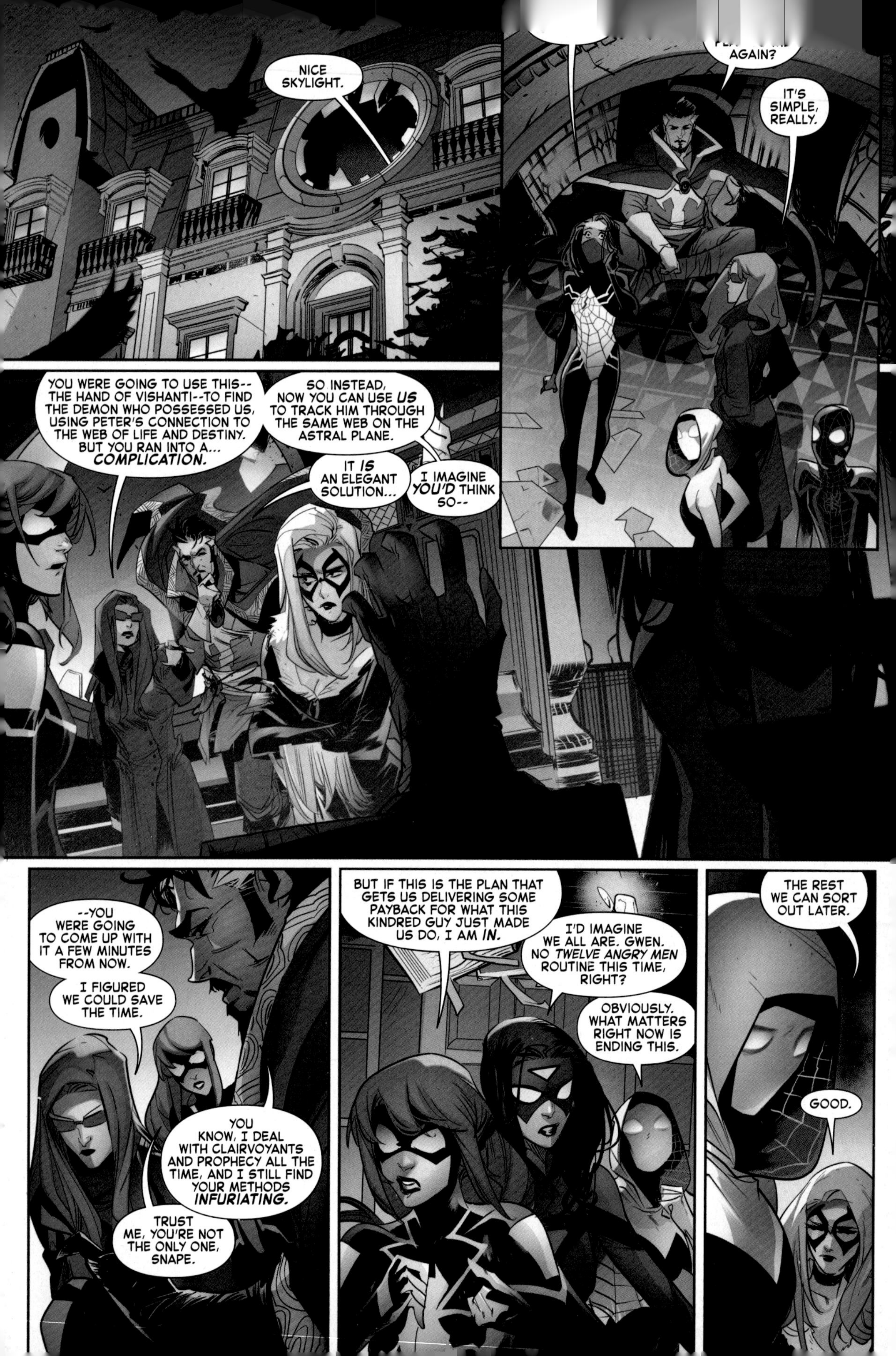
NICE SKYLIGHT.
AGAIN?
IT'S SIMPLE, REALLY.
YOU WERE GOING TO USE THIS-- THE HAND OF VISHANTI--TO FIND THE DEMON WHO POSSESSED US, USING PETER'S CONNECTION TO THE WEB OF LIFE AND DESTINY. BUT YOU RAN INTO A... COMPLICATION.
SO INSTEAD, NOW YOU CAN USE US TO TRACK HIM THROUGH THE SAME WEB ON THE ASTRAL PLANE.
IT IS AN ELEGANT SOLUTION...
I IMAGINE YOU'D THINK SO--
--YOU WERE GOING TO COME UP WITH IT A FEW MINUTES FROM NOW.
I FIGURED WE COULD SAVE THE TIME.
YOU KNOW, I DEAL WITH CLAIRVOYANTS AND PROPHECY ALL THE TIME, AND I STILL FIND YOUR METHODS INFURIATING.
TRUST ME, YOU'RE NOT THE ONLY ONE, SNAPE.
BUT IF THIS IS THE PLAN THAT GETS US DELIVERING SOME PAYBACK FOR WHAT THIS KINDRED GUY JUST MADE US DO, I AM IN.
I'D IMAGINE WE ALL ARE. GWEN. NO TWELVE ANGRY MEN ROUTINE THIS TIME, RIGHT?
OBVIOUSLY. WHAT MATTERS RIGHT NOW IS ENDING THIS.
THE REST WE CAN SORT OUT LATER.
GOOD.

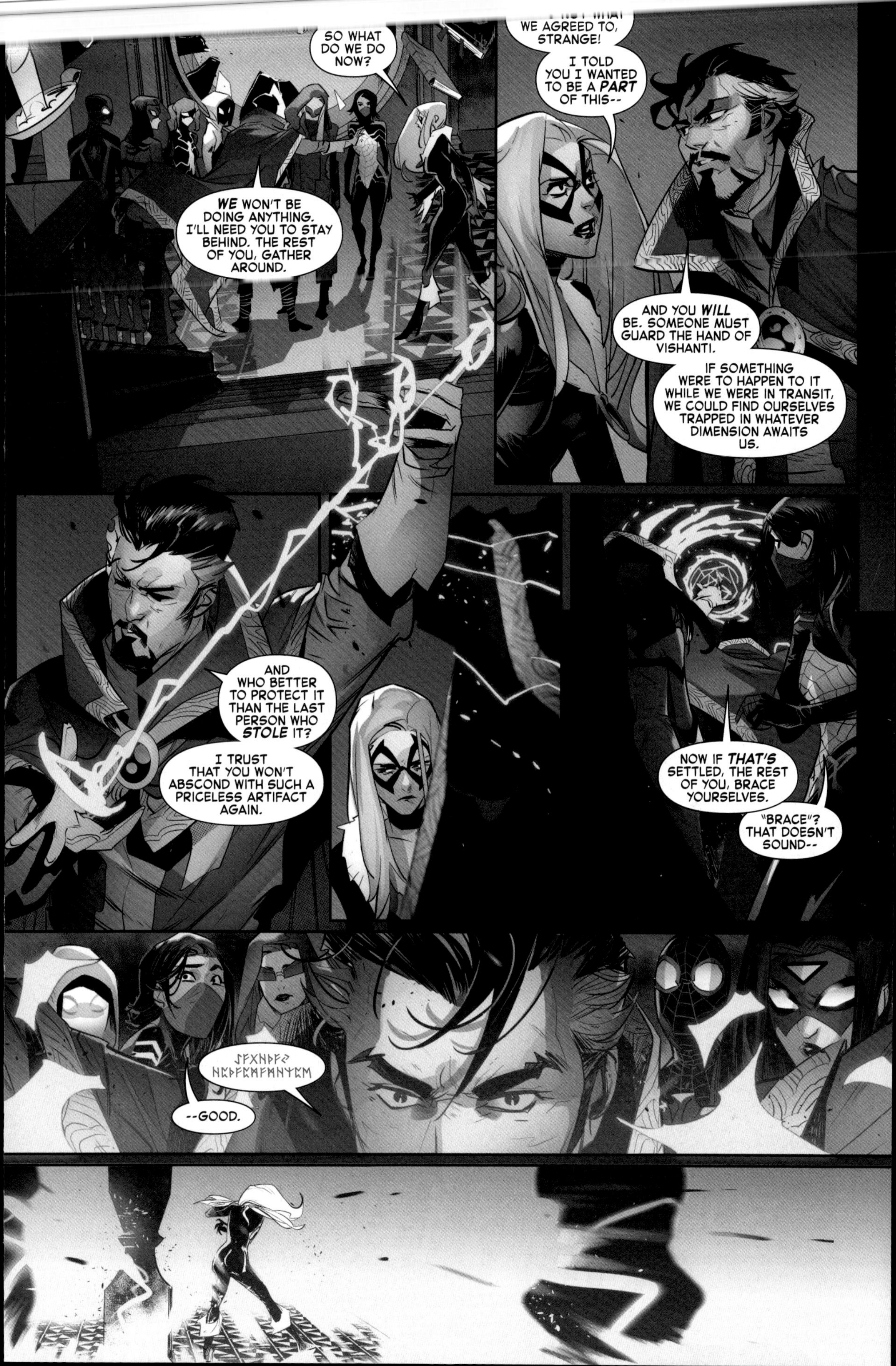
SO WHAT DO WE DO NOW?
WE AGREED TO, STRANGE!
I TOLD YOU I WANTED TO BE A PART OF THIS--
WE WON'T BE DOING ANYTHING. I'LL NEED YOU TO STAY BEHIND. THE REST OF YOU, GATHER AROUND.
AND YOU WILL BE. SOMEONE MUST GUARD THE HAND OF VISHANTI.
IF SOMETHING WERE TO HAPPEN TO IT WHILE WE WERE IN TRANSIT, WE COULD FIND OURSELVES TRAPPED IN WHATEVER DIMENSION AWAITS US.
AND WHO BETTER TO PROTECT IT THAN THE LAST PERSON WHO STOLE IT?
I TRUST THAT YOU WON'T ABSCOND WITH SUCH A PRICELESS ARTIFACT AGAIN.
NOW IF THAT'S SETTLED, THE REST OF YOU, BRACE YOURSELVES.
"BRACE"? THAT DOESN'T SOUND--
--GOOD.

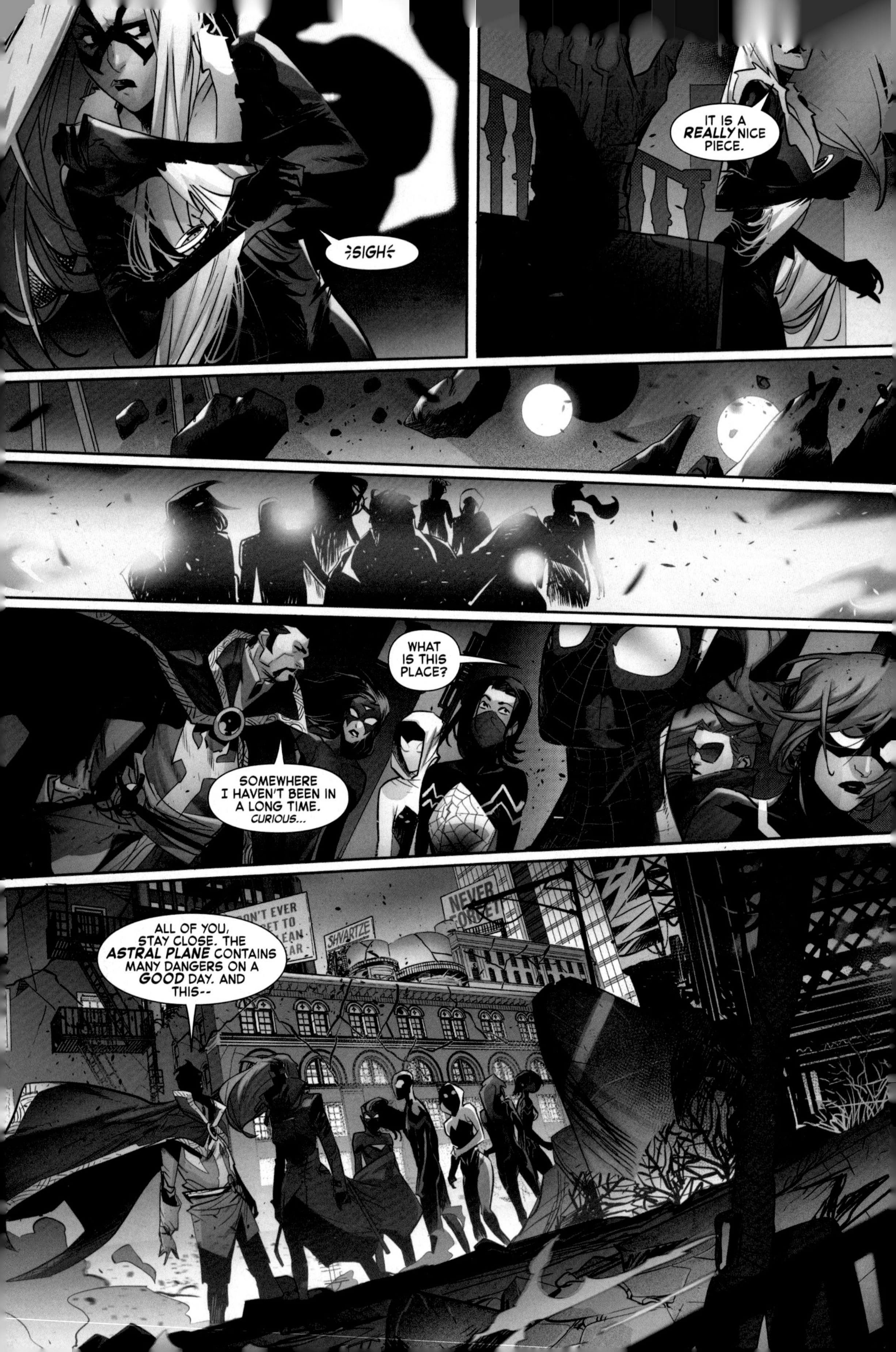

⚡SIGH⚡
IT IS A REALLY NICE PIECE.
WHAT IS THIS PLACE?
SOMEWHERE I HAVEN'T BEEN IN A LONG TIME. CURIOUS...
NEVER FORGET
SHVARTZE
ALL OF YOU, STAY CLOSE. THE ASTRAL PLANE CONTAINS MANY DANGERS ON A GOOD DAY. AND THIS--

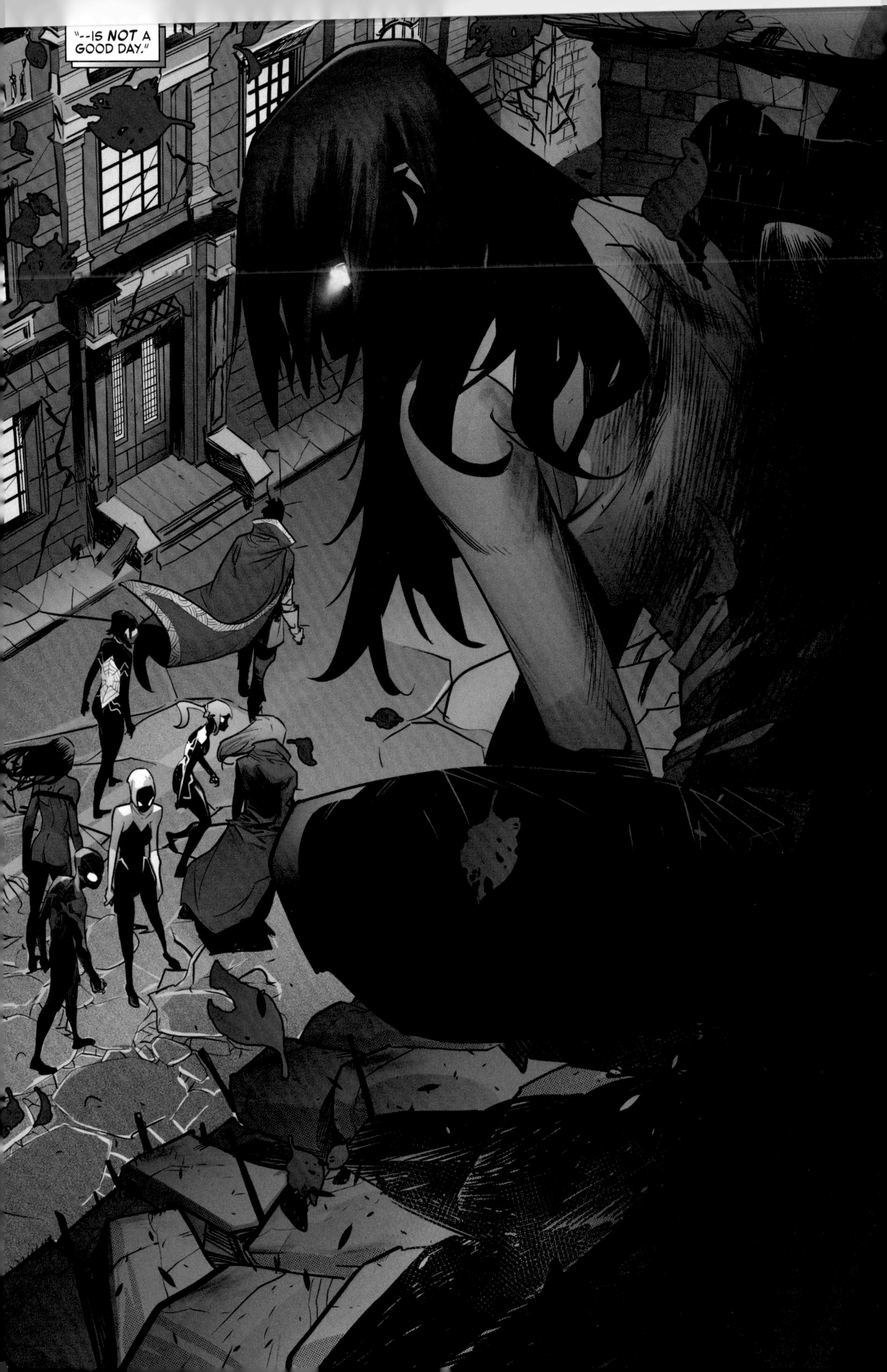
"--IS NOT A GOOD DAY."

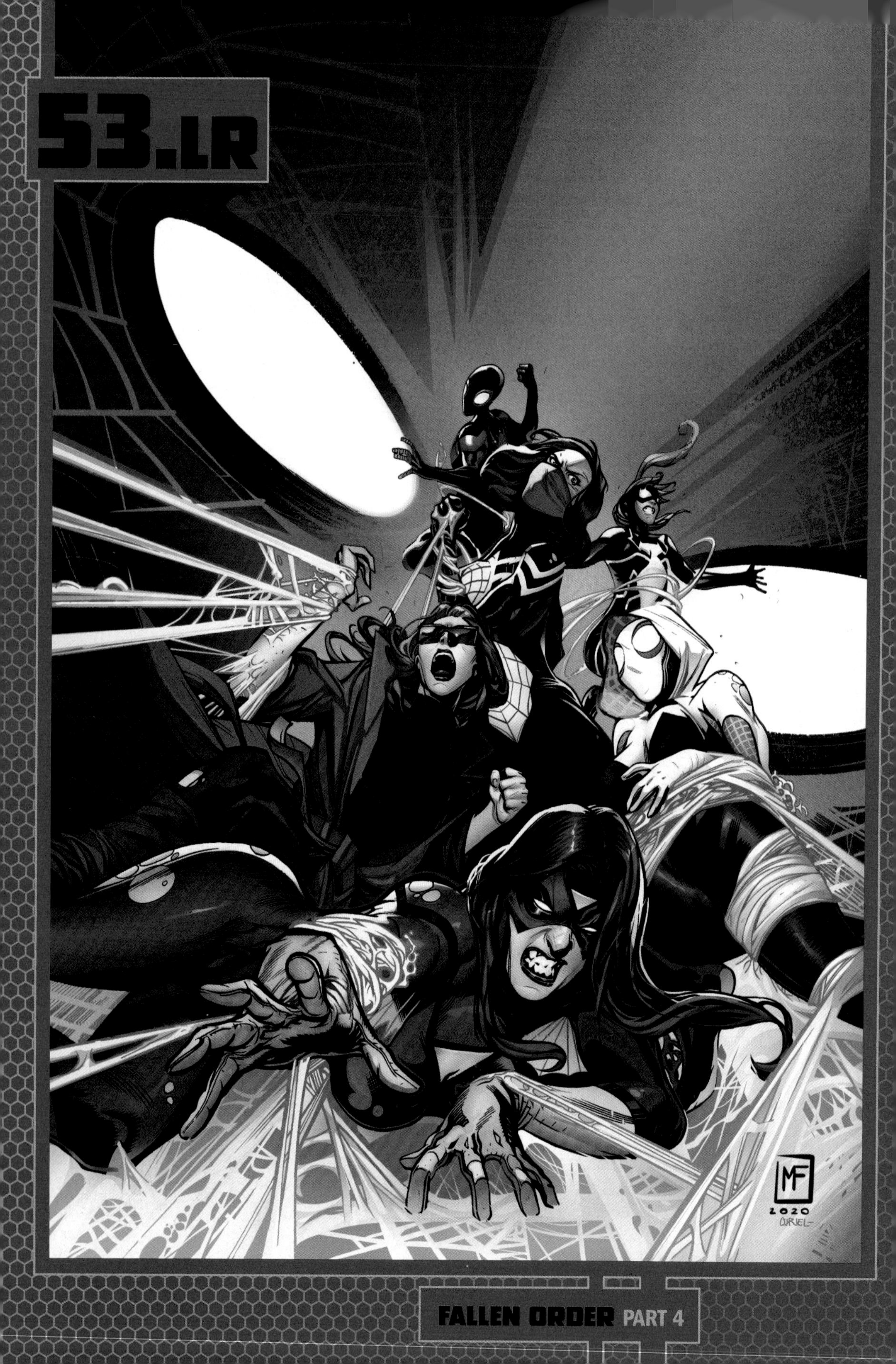
53.LR
FALLEN ORDER PART 4

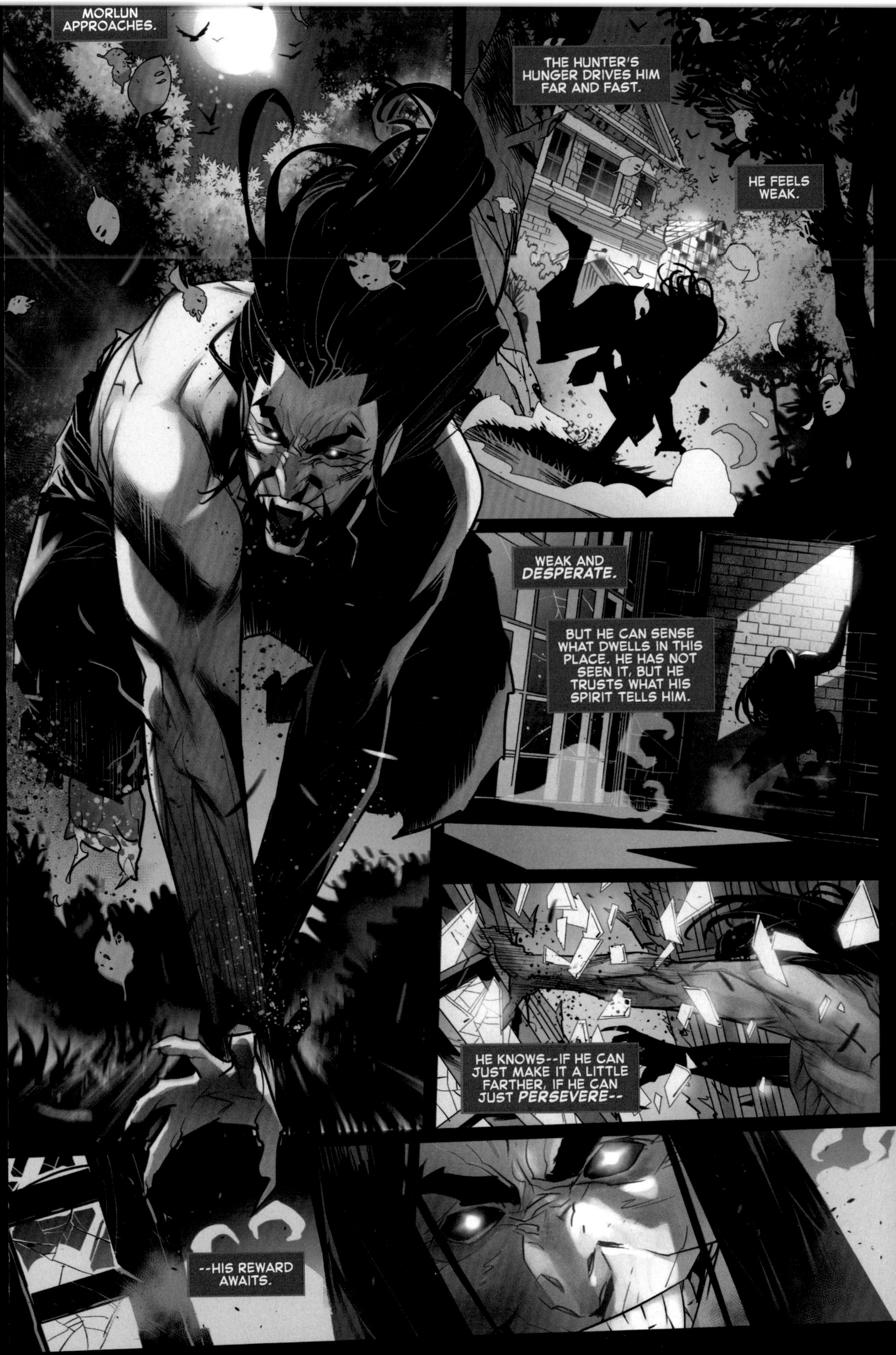

MORLUN APPROACHES.
THE HUNTER'S HUNGER DRIVES HIM FAR AND FAST.
HE FEELS WEAK.
WEAK AND *DESPERATE.*
BUT HE CAN SENSE WHAT DWELLS IN THIS PLACE. HE HAS NOT SEEN IT, BUT HE TRUSTS WHAT HIS SPIRIT TELLS HIM.
HE KNOWS--IF HE CAN JUST MAKE IT A LITTLE FARTHER, IF HE CAN JUST *PERSEVERE*--
--HIS REWARD AWAITS.

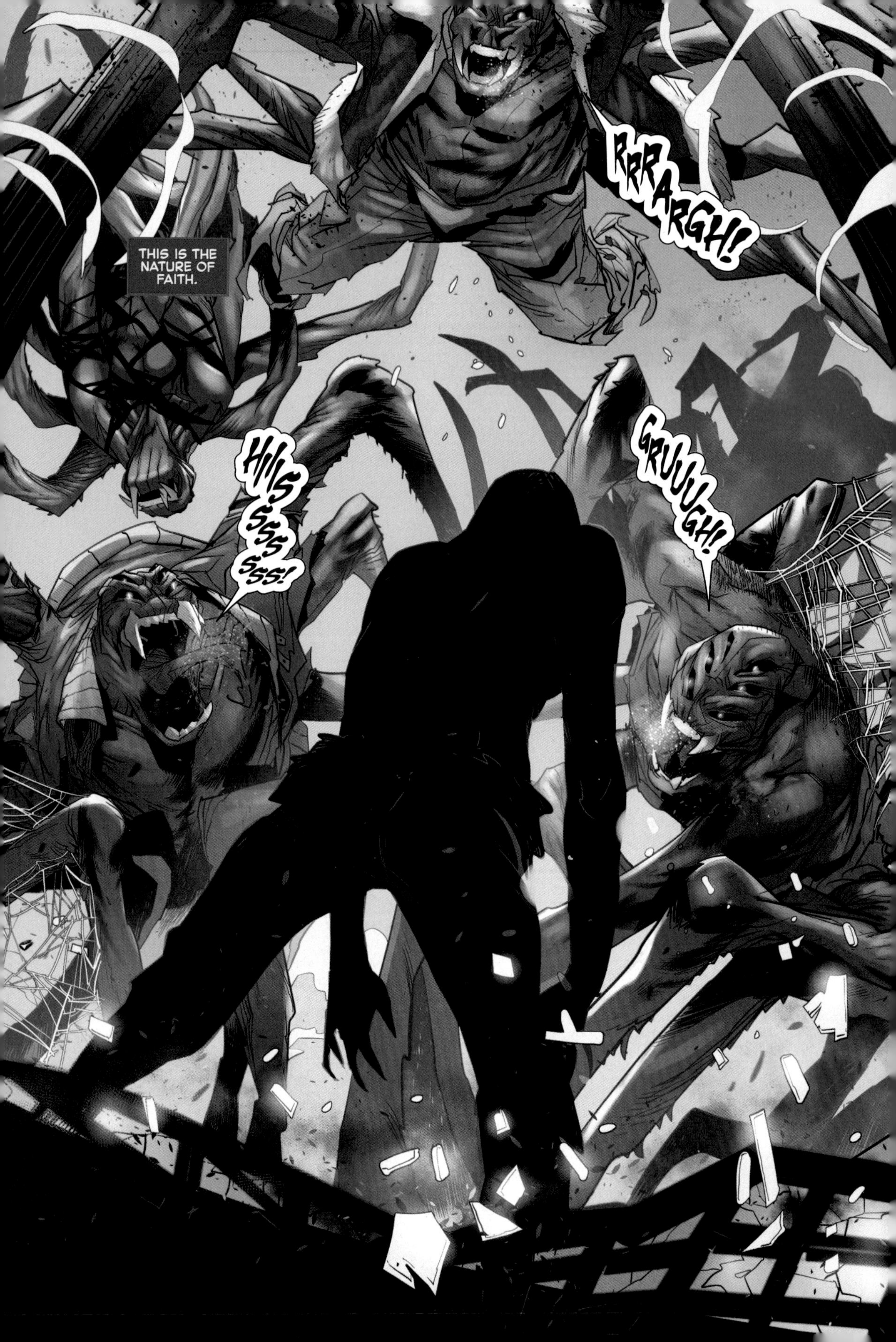
THIS IS THE NATURE OF FAITH.
RRRARGH!
HHSSSSSSS!
GRUUUGH!

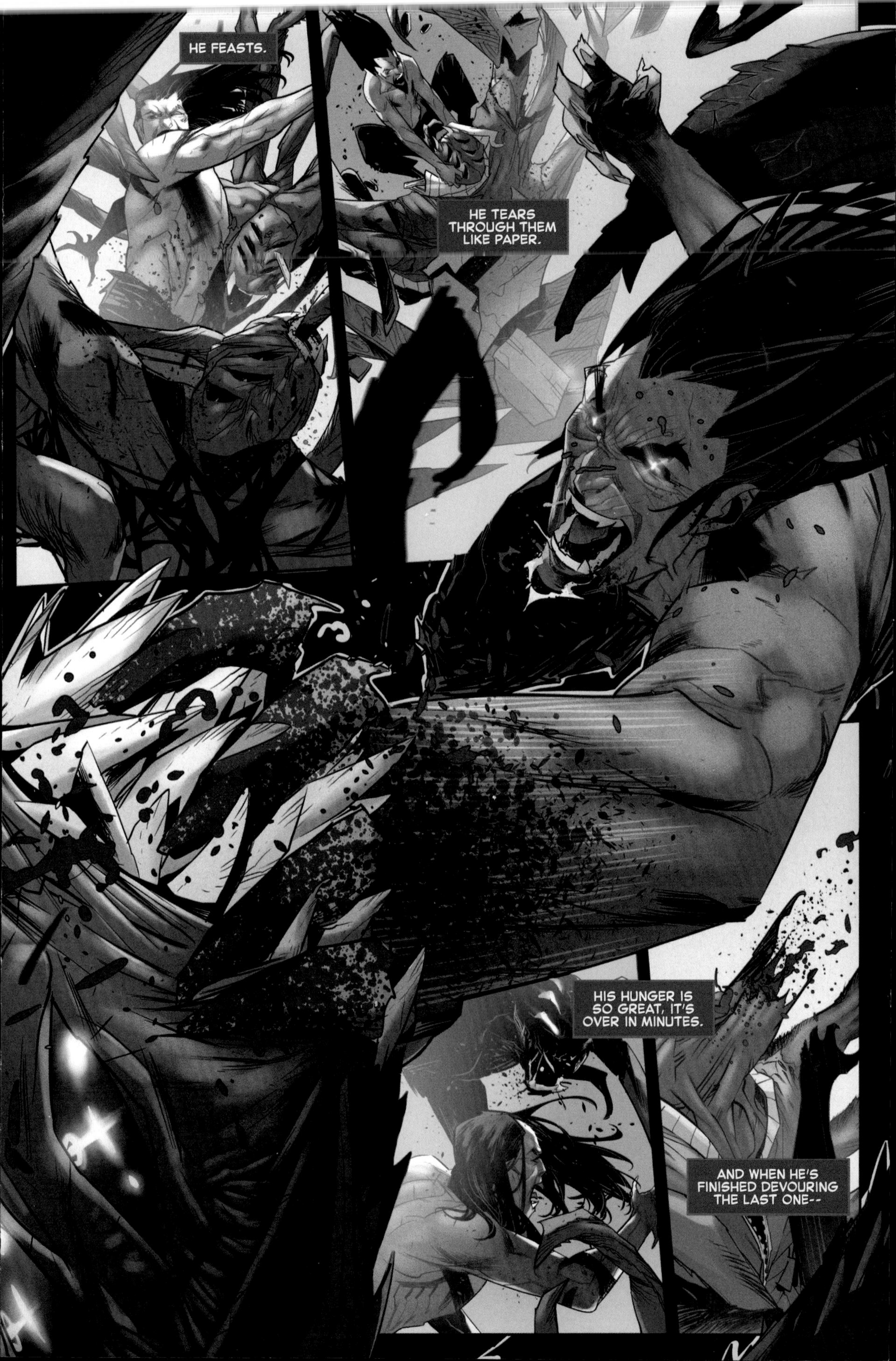
HE FEASTS.
HE TEARS THROUGH THEM LIKE PAPER.
HIS HUNGER IS SO GREAT, IT'S OVER IN MINUTES.
AND WHEN HE'S FINISHED DEVOURING THE LAST ONE--

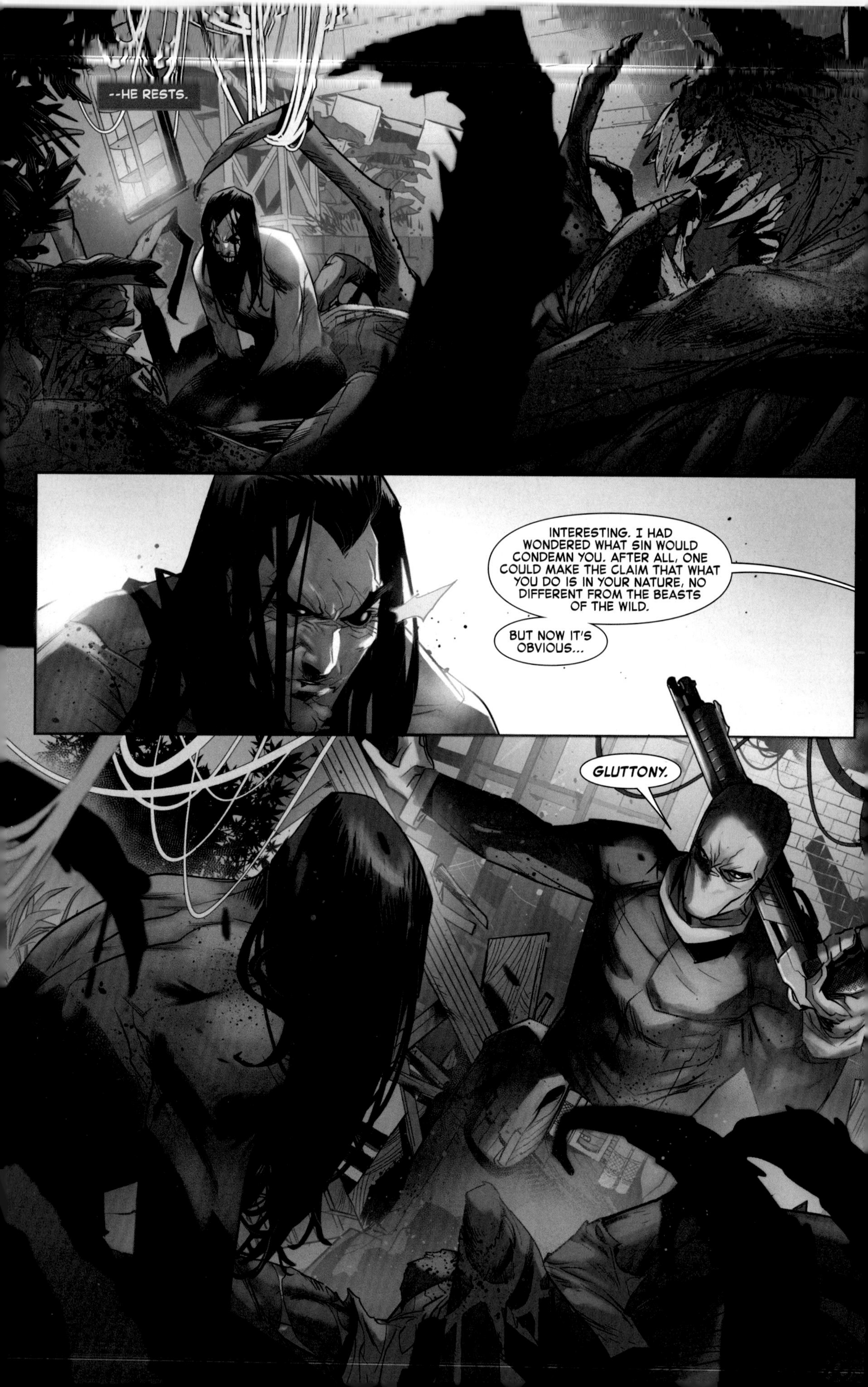
--HE RESTS.
INTERESTING. I HAD WONDERED WHAT SIN WOULD CONDEMN YOU. AFTER ALL, ONE COULD MAKE THE CLAIM THAT WHAT YOU DO IS IN YOUR NATURE, NO DIFFERENT FROM THE BEASTS OF THE WILD.
BUT NOW IT'S OBVIOUS...
GLUTTONY.

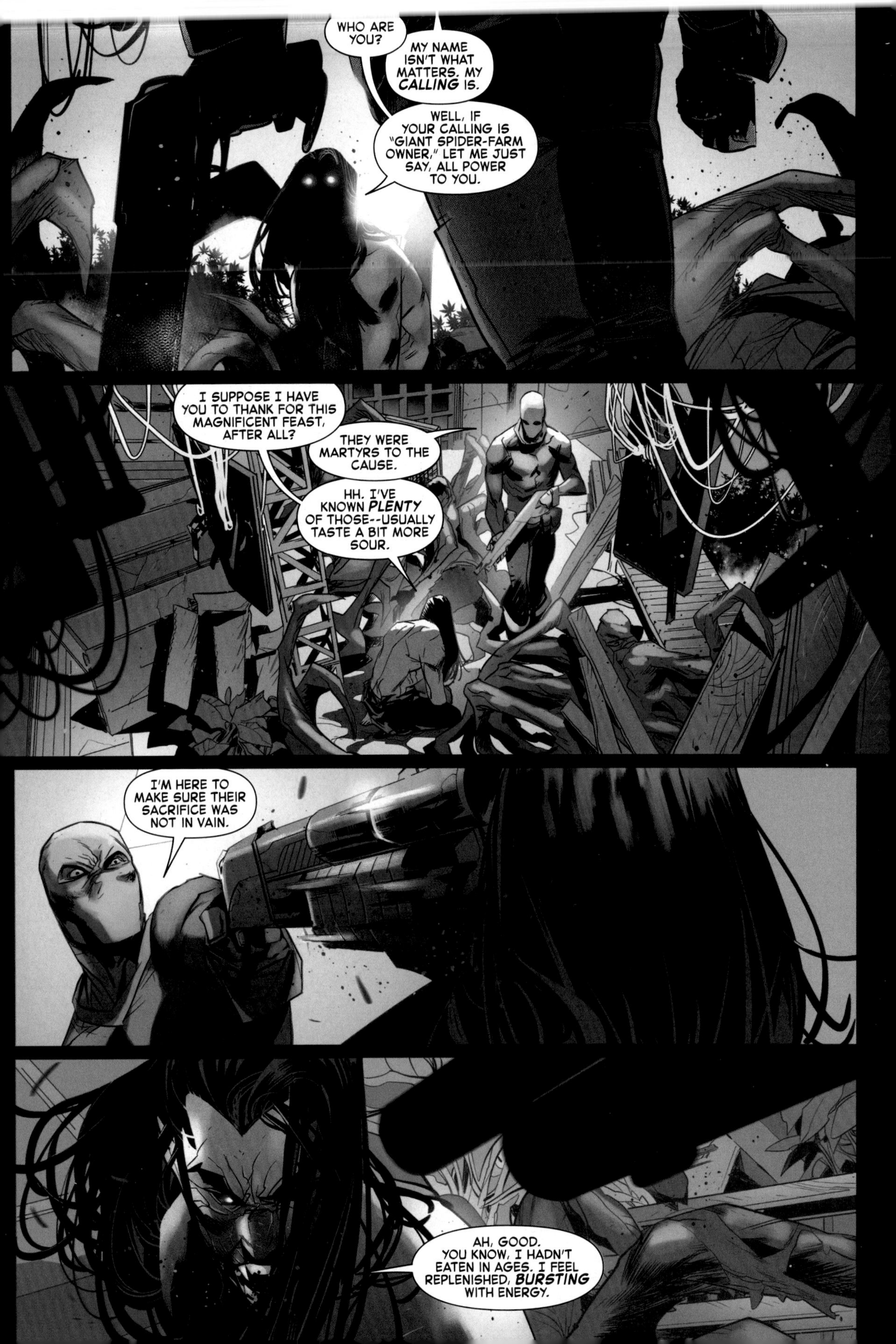
WHO ARE YOU?
MY NAME ISN'T WHAT MATTERS. MY CALLING IS.
WELL, IF YOUR CALLING IS "GIANT SPIDER-FARM OWNER," LET ME JUST SAY, ALL POWER TO YOU.
I SUPPOSE I HAVE YOU TO THANK FOR THIS MAGNIFICENT FEAST, AFTER ALL?
THEY WERE MARTYRS TO THE CAUSE.
HH. I'VE KNOWN PLENTY OF THOSE--USUALLY TASTE A BIT MORE SOUR.
I'M HERE TO MAKE SURE THEIR SACRIFICE WAS NOT IN VAIN.
AH, GOOD. YOU KNOW, I HADN'T EATEN IN AGES. I FEEL REPLENISHED, BURSTING WITH ENERGY.

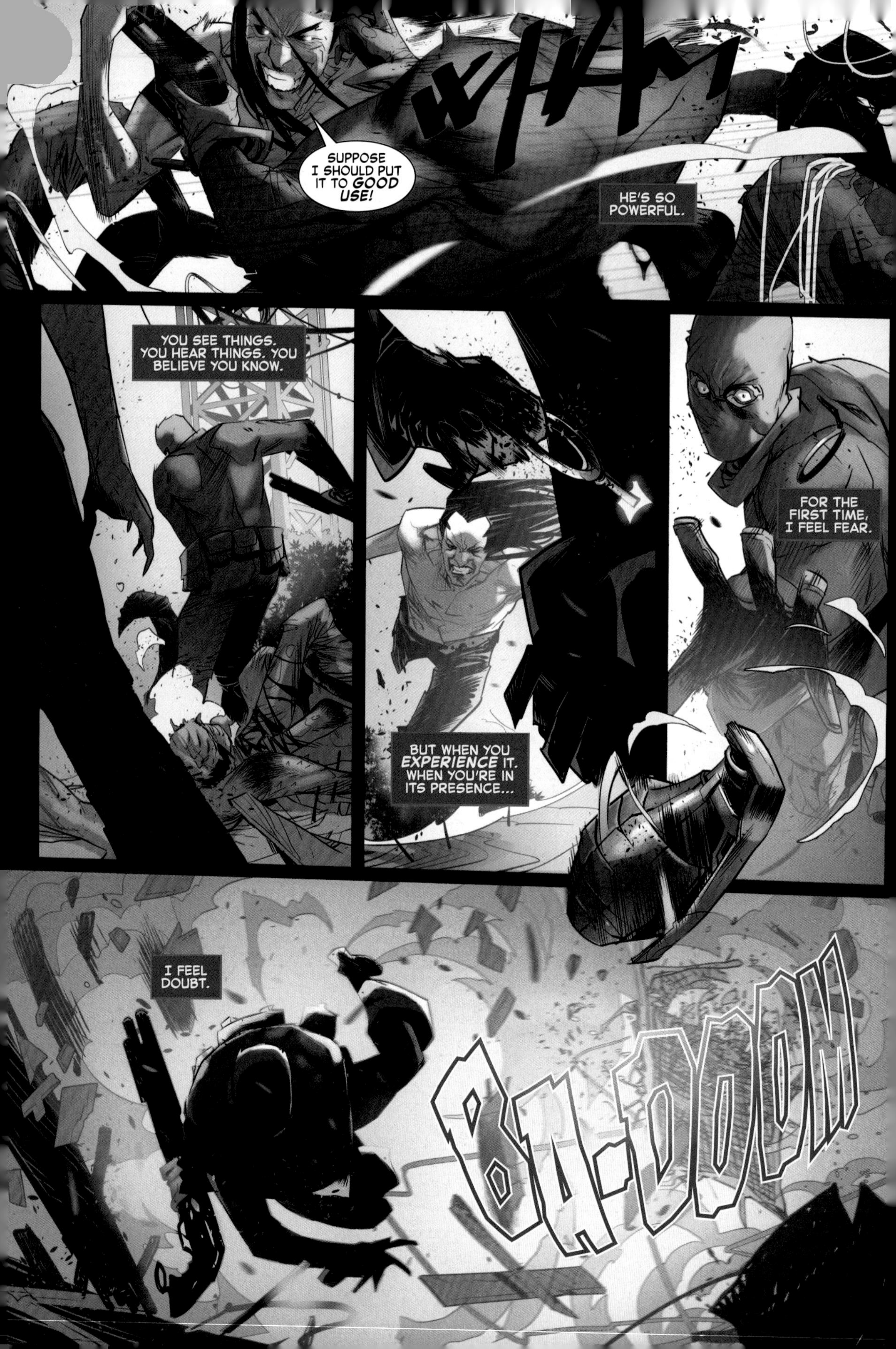

WHHM
SUPPOSE I SHOULD PUT IT TO GOOD USE!
HE'S SO POWERFUL.
YOU SEE THINGS. YOU HEAR THINGS. YOU BELIEVE YOU KNOW.
BUT WHEN YOU EXPERIENCE IT. WHEN YOU'RE IN ITS PRESENCE...
FOR THE FIRST TIME, I FEEL FEAR.
I FEEL DOUBT.
BA-DOOOM

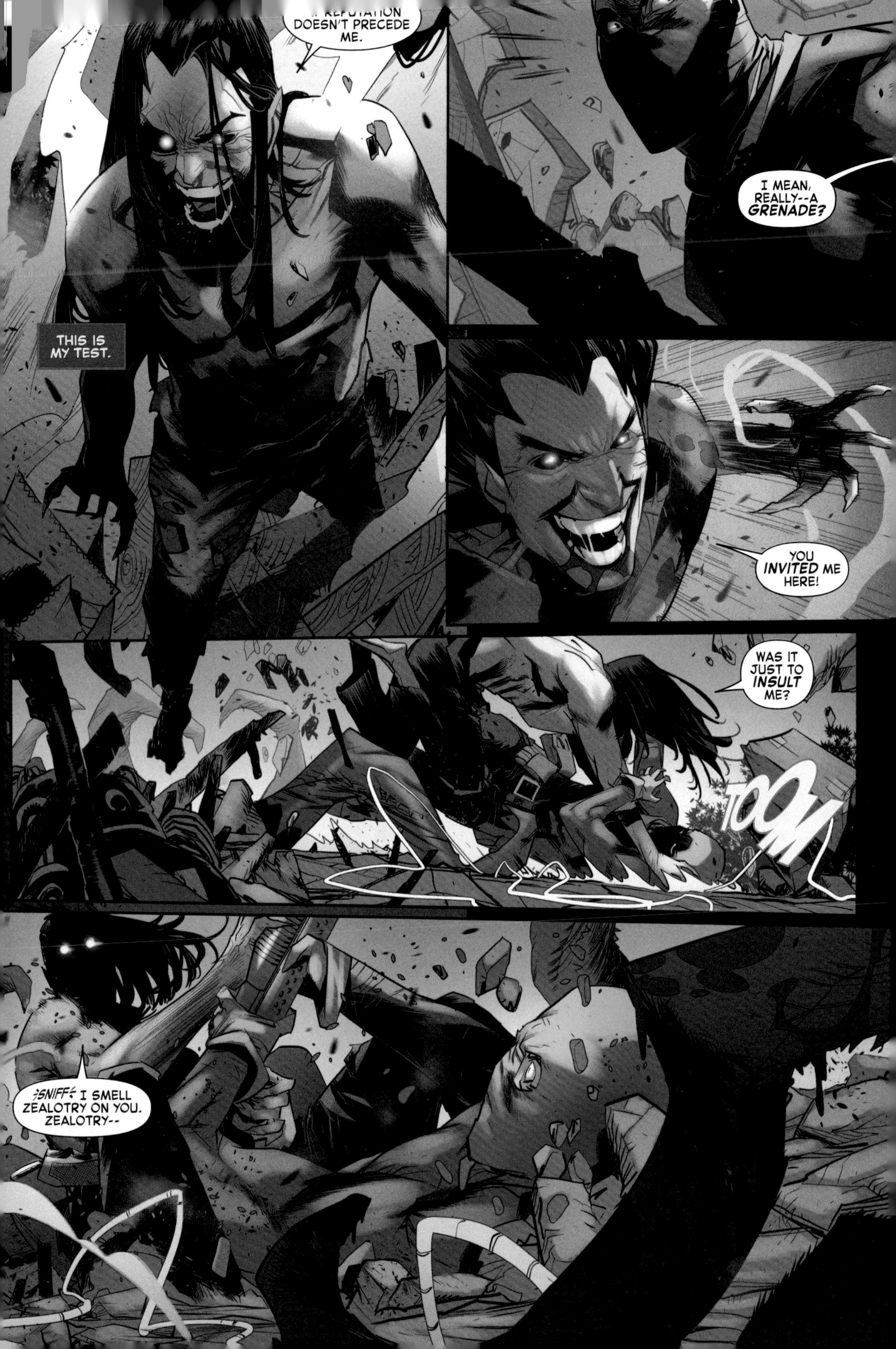
DOESN'T PRECEDE ME.
THIS IS MY TEST.
I MEAN, REALLY--A GRENADE?
YOU INVITED ME HERE!
WAS IT JUST TO INSULT ME?
TOOM
SNIFF I SMELL ZEALOTRY ON YOU. ZEALOTRY--

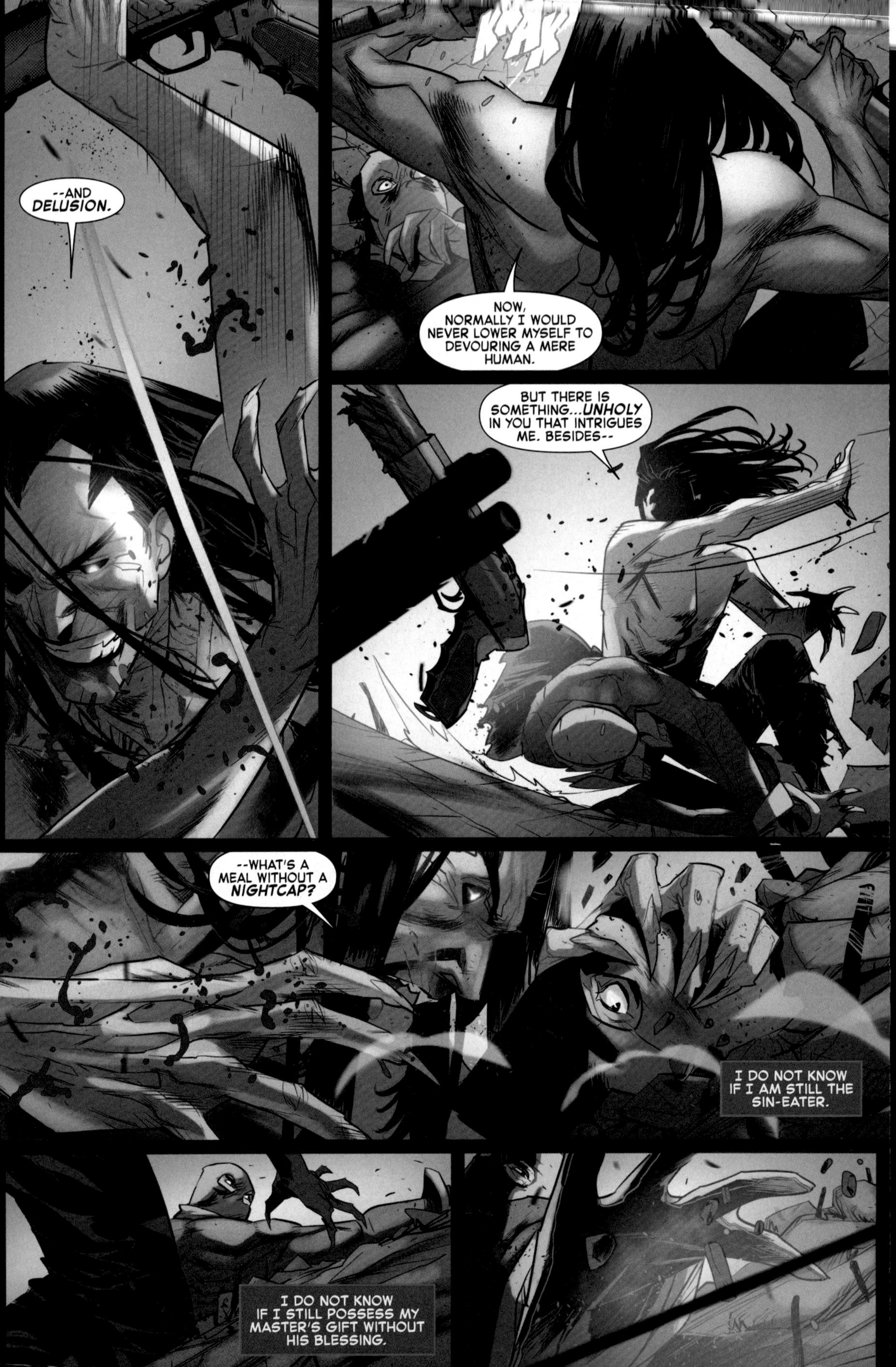
KRAK
--AND DELUSION.
NOW, NORMALLY I WOULD NEVER LOWER MYSELF TO DEVOURING A MERE HUMAN.
BUT THERE IS SOMETHING...UNHOLY IN YOU THAT INTRIGUES ME. BESIDES--
--WHAT'S A MEAL WITHOUT A NIGHTCAP?
I DO NOT KNOW IF I AM STILL THE SIN-EATER.
I DO NOT KNOW IF I STILL POSSESS MY MASTER'S GIFT WITHOUT HIS BLESSING.

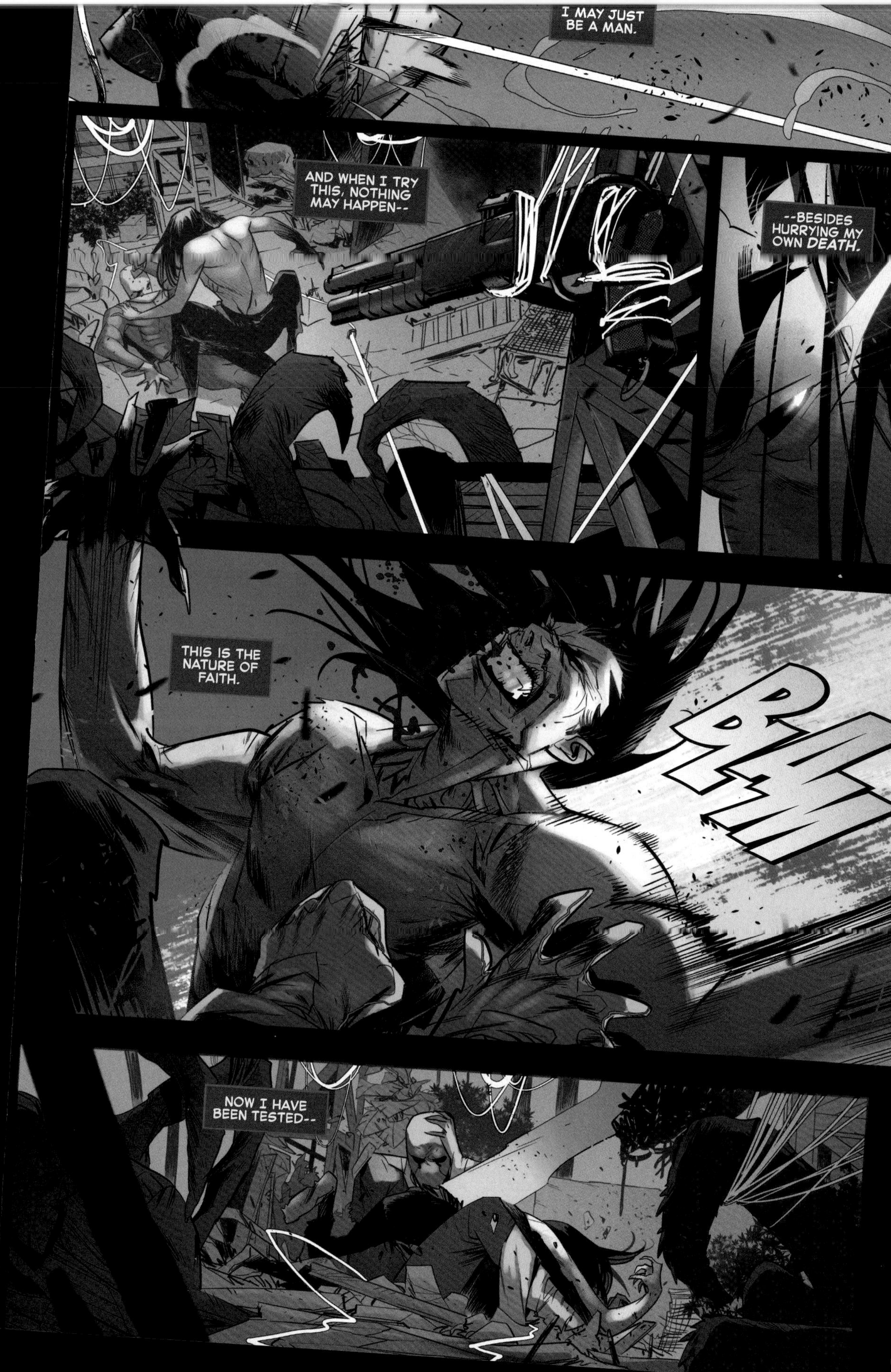
I MAY JUST BE A MAN.
AND WHEN I TRY THIS, NOTHING MAY HAPPEN--
--BESIDES HURRYING MY OWN DEATH.
THIS IS THE NATURE OF FAITH.
NOW I HAVE BEEN TESTED--

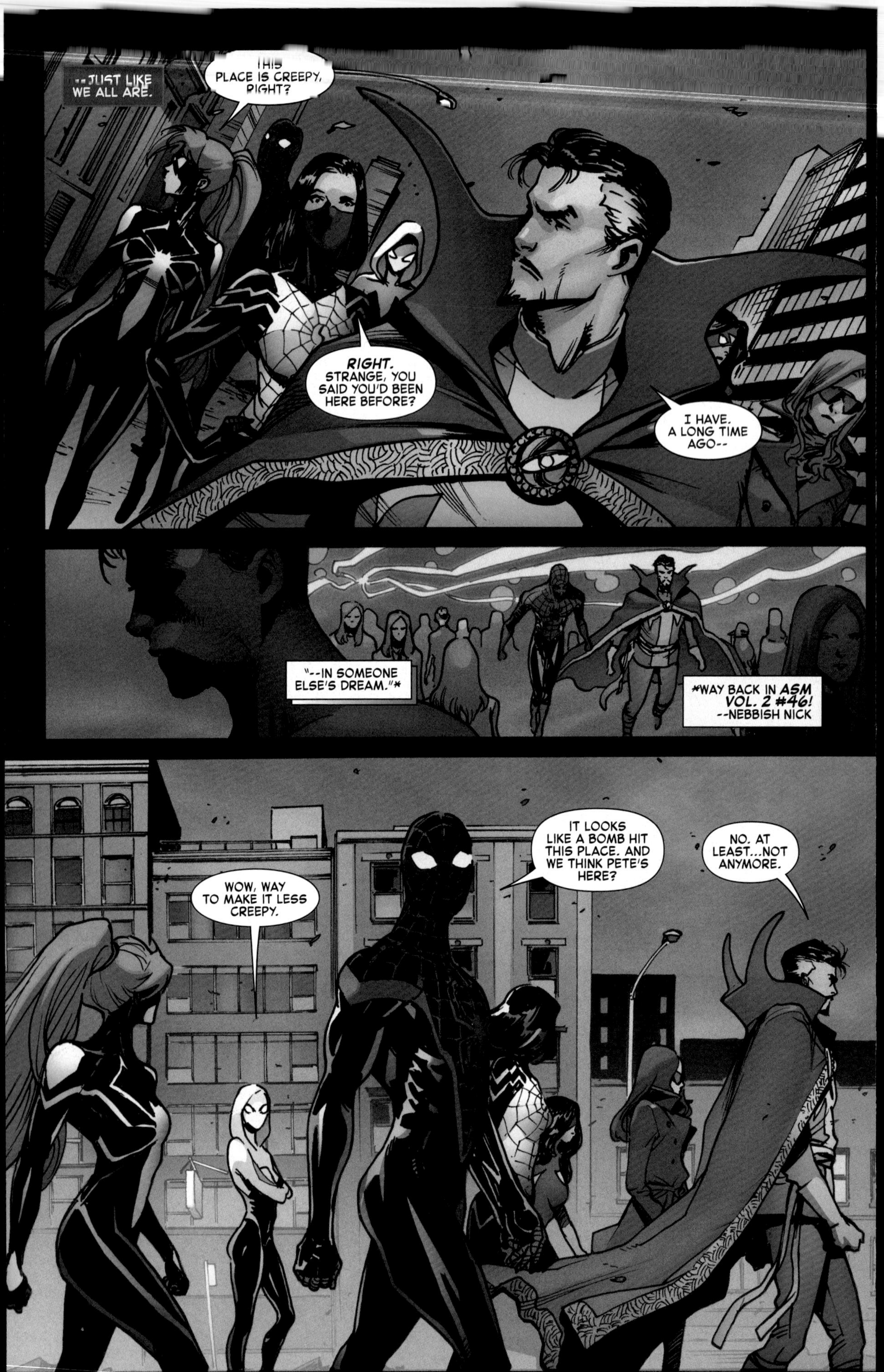
--JUST LIKE WE ALL ARE.
THIS PLACE IS CREEPY, RIGHT?
RIGHT. STRANGE, YOU SAID YOU'D BEEN HERE BEFORE?
I HAVE. A LONG TIME AGO--
"--IN SOMEONE ELSE'S DREAM."*
*WAY BACK IN ***ASM VOL. 2 #46!*** --NEBBISH NICK
WOW, WAY TO MAKE IT LESS CREEPY.
IT LOOKS LIKE A BOMB HIT THIS PLACE. AND WE THINK PETE'S HERE?
NO. AT LEAST...NOT ANYMORE.

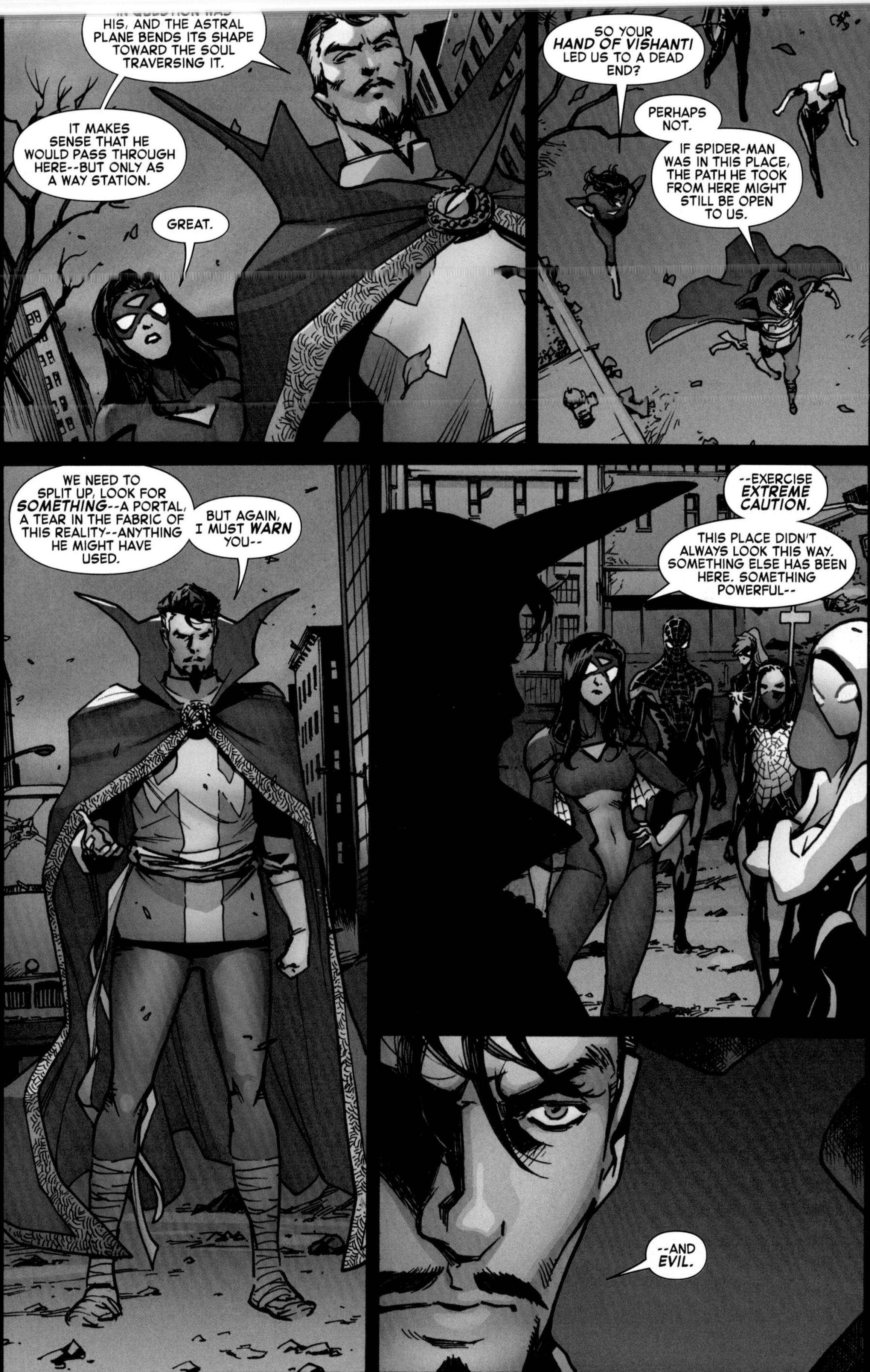

HIS, AND THE ASTRAL PLANE BENDS ITS SHAPE TOWARD THE SOUL TRAVERSING IT.
IT MAKES SENSE THAT HE WOULD PASS THROUGH HERE--BUT ONLY AS A WAY STATION.
GREAT.
SO YOUR HAND OF VISHANTI LED US TO A DEAD END?
PERHAPS NOT.
IF SPIDER-MAN WAS IN THIS PLACE, THE PATH HE TOOK FROM HERE MIGHT STILL BE OPEN TO US.
WE NEED TO SPLIT UP, LOOK FOR SOMETHING--A PORTAL, A TEAR IN THE FABRIC OF THIS REALITY--ANYTHING HE MIGHT HAVE USED.
BUT AGAIN, I MUST WARN YOU--
--EXERCISE EXTREME CAUTION.
THIS PLACE DIDN'T ALWAYS LOOK THIS WAY. SOMETHING ELSE HAS BEEN HERE. SOMETHING POWERFUL--
--AND EVIL.

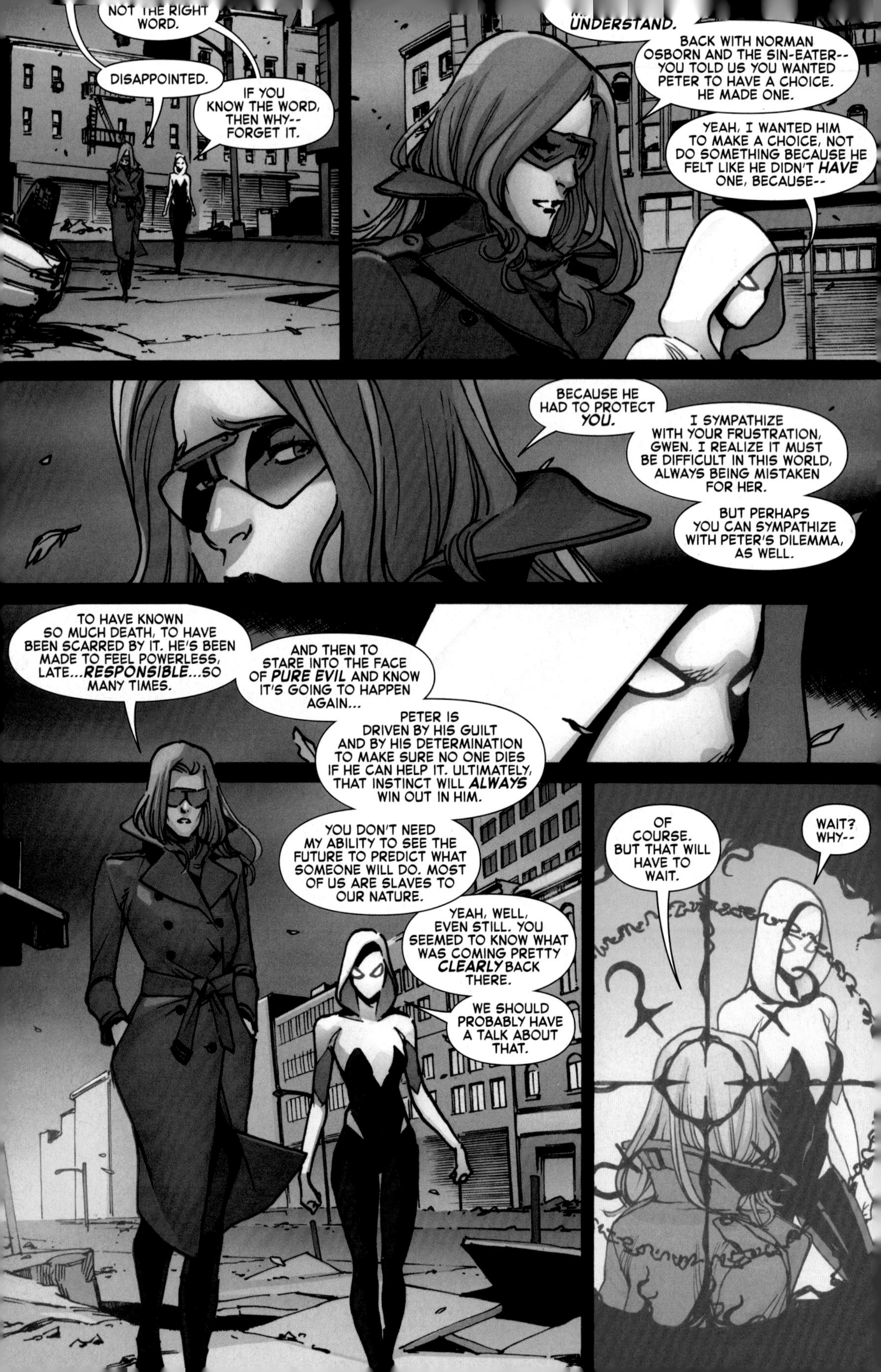
NOT THE RIGHT WORD.
DISAPPOINTED.
IF YOU KNOW THE WORD, THEN WHY-- FORGET IT.
UNDERSTAND.
BACK WITH NORMAN OSBORN AND THE SIN-EATER-- YOU TOLD US YOU WANTED PETER TO HAVE A CHOICE. HE MADE ONE.
YEAH, I WANTED HIM TO MAKE A CHOICE, NOT DO SOMETHING BECAUSE HE FELT LIKE HE DIDN'T HAVE ONE, BECAUSE--
BECAUSE HE HAD TO PROTECT YOU.
I SYMPATHIZE WITH YOUR FRUSTRATION, GWEN. I REALIZE IT MUST BE DIFFICULT IN THIS WORLD, ALWAYS BEING MISTAKEN FOR HER.
BUT PERHAPS YOU CAN SYMPATHIZE WITH PETER'S DILEMMA, AS WELL.
TO HAVE KNOWN SO MUCH DEATH, TO HAVE BEEN SCARRED BY IT. HE'S BEEN MADE TO FEEL POWERLESS, LATE...RESPONSIBLE...SO MANY TIMES.
AND THEN TO STARE INTO THE FACE OF PURE EVIL AND KNOW IT'S GOING TO HAPPEN AGAIN...
PETER IS DRIVEN BY HIS GUILT AND BY HIS DETERMINATION TO MAKE SURE NO ONE DIES IF HE CAN HELP IT. ULTIMATELY, THAT INSTINCT WILL ALWAYS WIN OUT IN HIM.
YOU DON'T NEED MY ABILITY TO SEE THE FUTURE TO PREDICT WHAT SOMEONE WILL DO. MOST OF US ARE SLAVES TO OUR NATURE.
YEAH, WELL, EVEN STILL. YOU SEEMED TO KNOW WHAT WAS COMING PRETTY CLEARLY BACK THERE.
WE SHOULD PROBABLY HAVE A TALK ABOUT THAT.
OF COURSE. BUT THAT WILL HAVE TO WAIT.
WAIT? WHY--

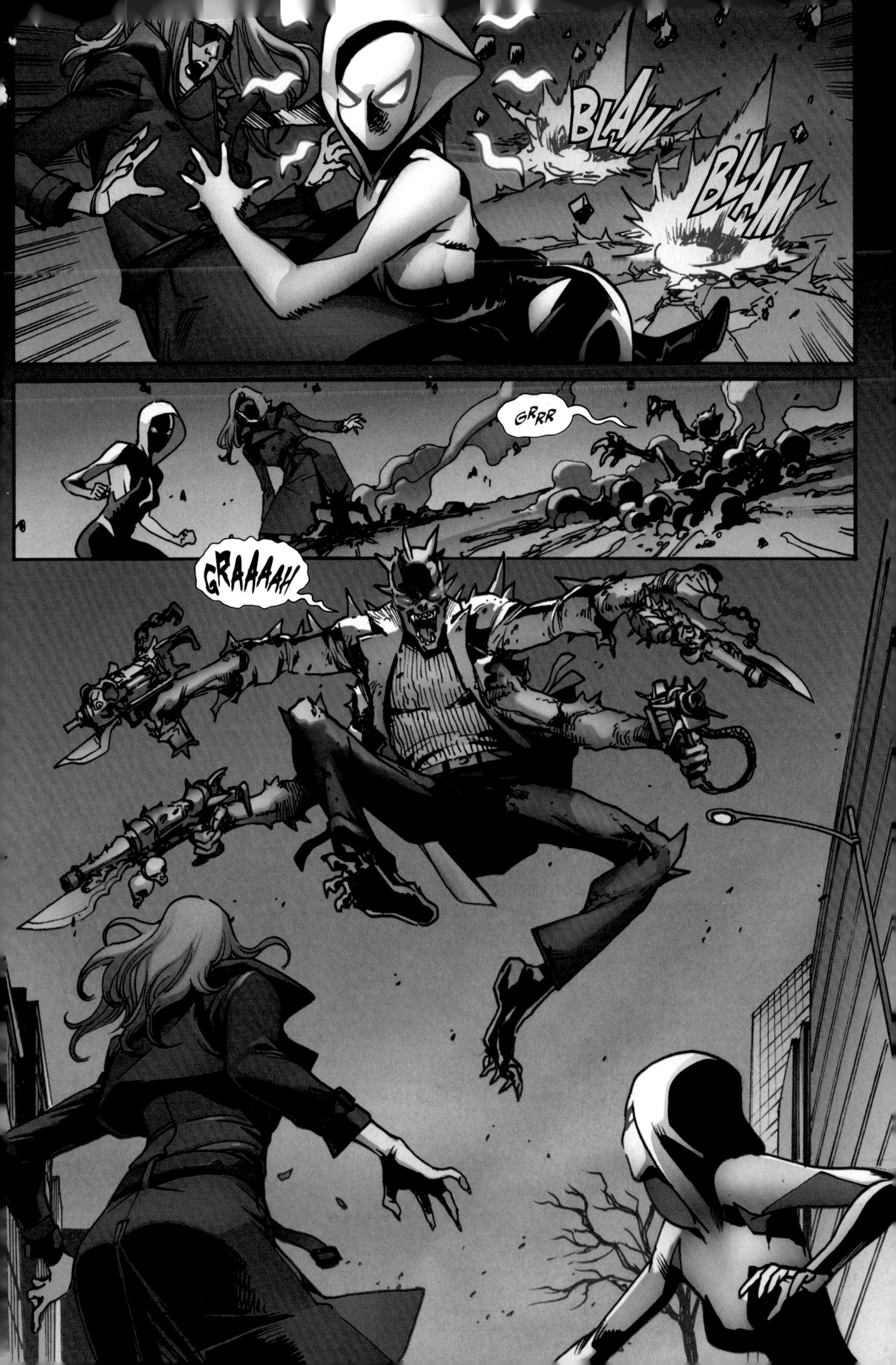
BLAM
BLAM
GRRR
GRAAAAH

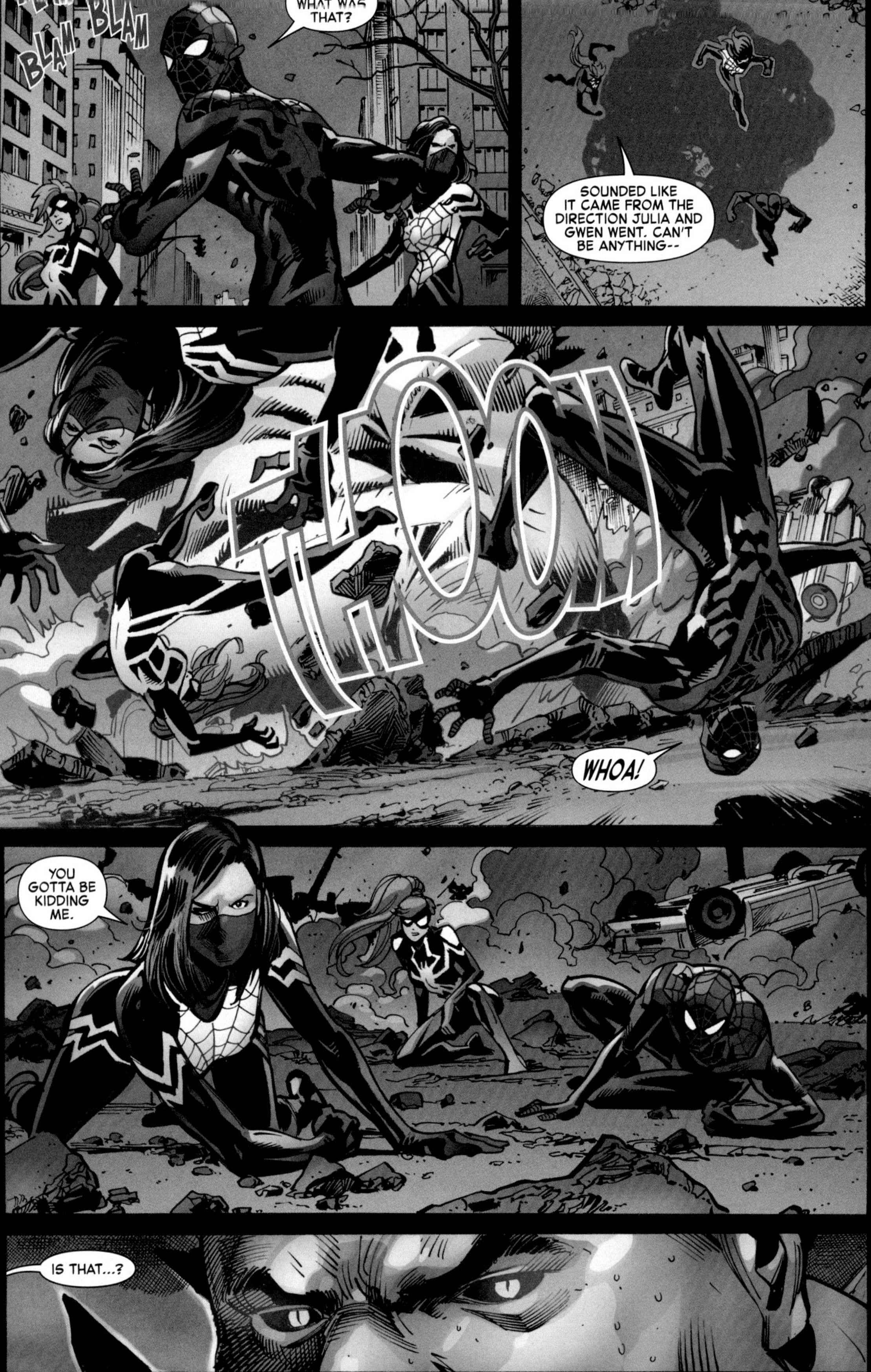
BLAM BLAM
WHAT WAS THAT?
SOUNDED LIKE IT CAME FROM THE DIRECTION JULIA AND GWEN WENT. CAN'T BE ANYTHING--
THOOM
WHOA!
YOU GOTTA BE KIDDING ME.
IS THAT...?

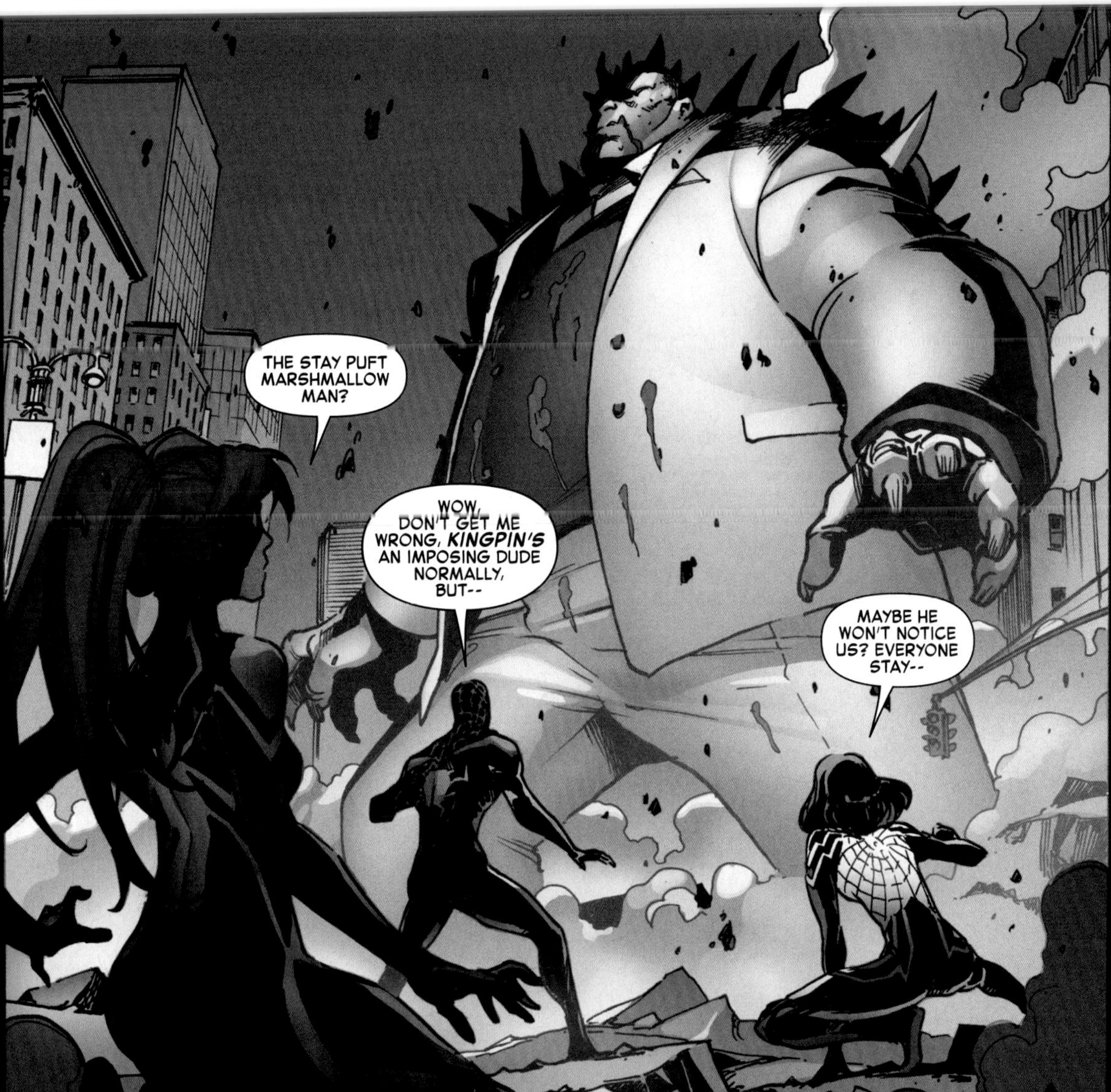
THE STAY PUFT MARSHMALLOW MAN?
WOW, DON'T GET ME WRONG, KINGPIN'S AN IMPOSING DUDE NORMALLY, BUT--
MAYBE HE WON'T NOTICE US? EVERYONE STAY--

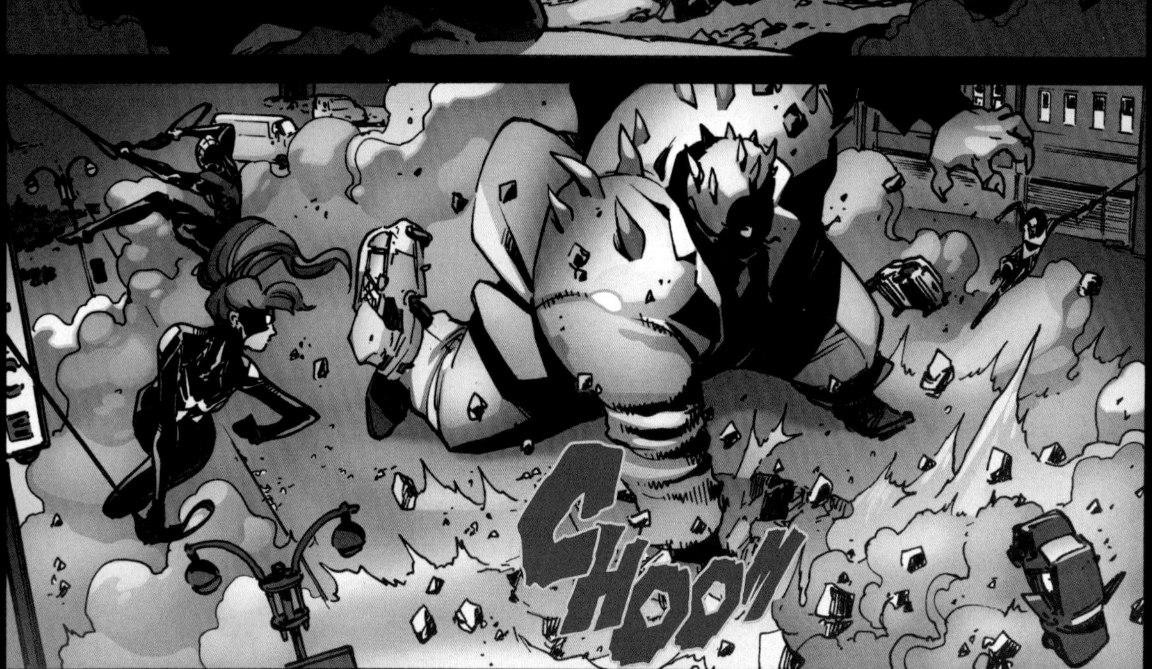
CHOOM

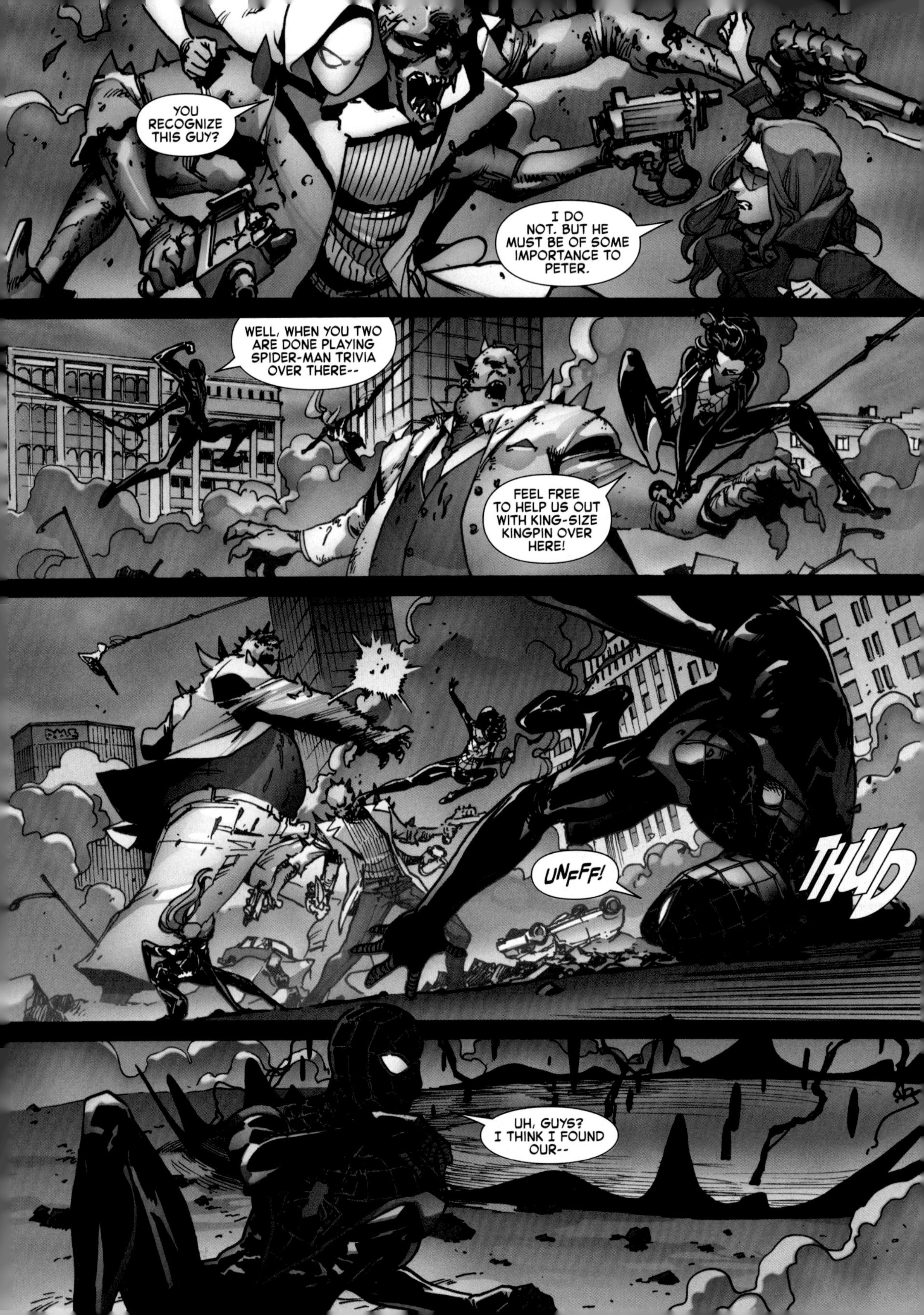
YOU RECOGNIZE THIS GUY?
I DO NOT. BUT HE MUST BE OF SOME IMPORTANCE TO PETER.
WELL, WHEN YOU TWO ARE DONE PLAYING SPIDER-MAN TRIVIA OVER THERE--
FEEL FREE TO HELP US OUT WITH KING-SIZE KINGPIN OVER HERE!
UNFFF!
THUD
UH, GUYS? I THINK I FOUND OUR--

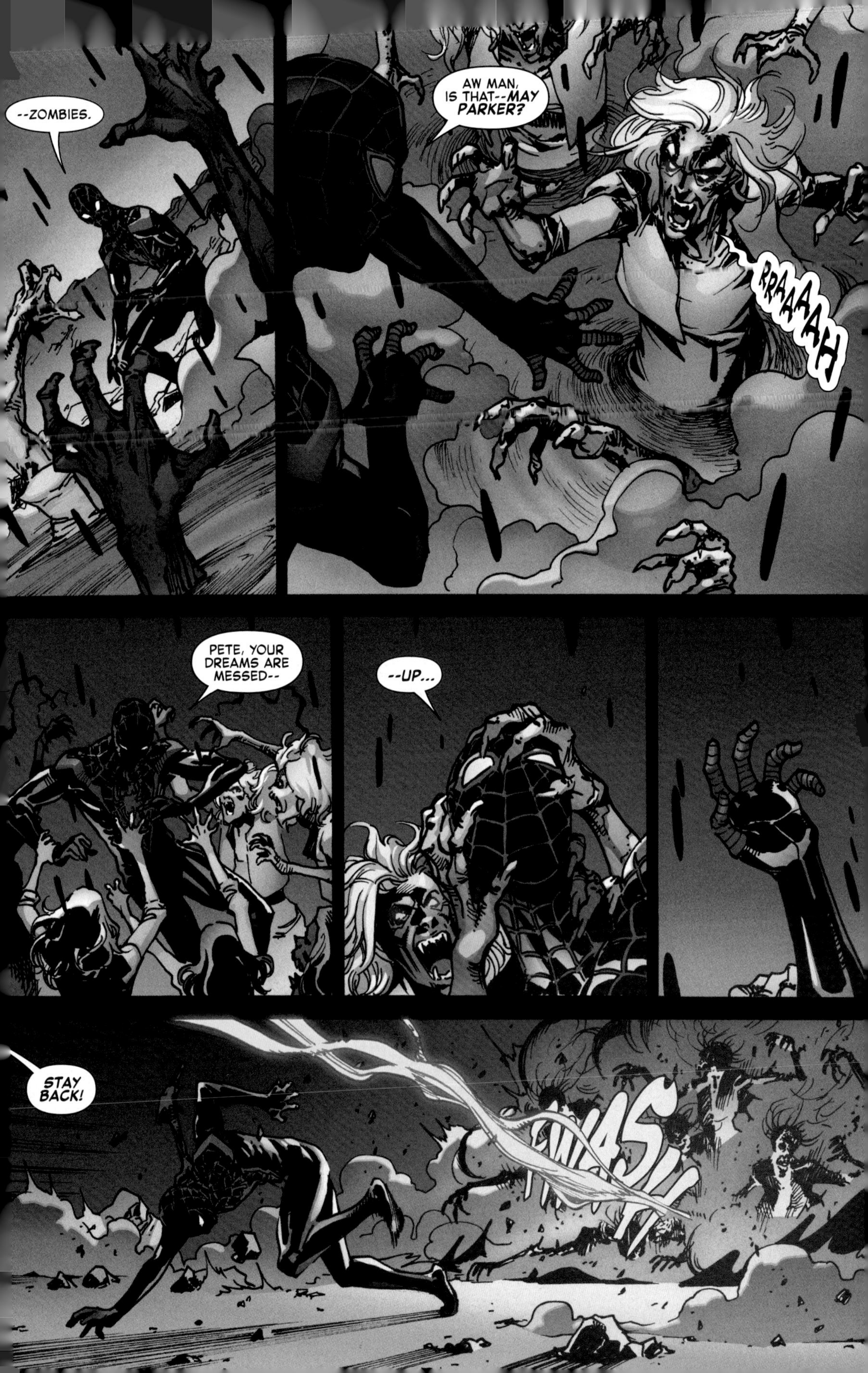
--ZOMBIES.
AW MAN, IS THAT--MAY PARKER?
RRAAAAAH
PETE, YOUR DREAMS ARE MESSED--
--UP...
STAY BACK!

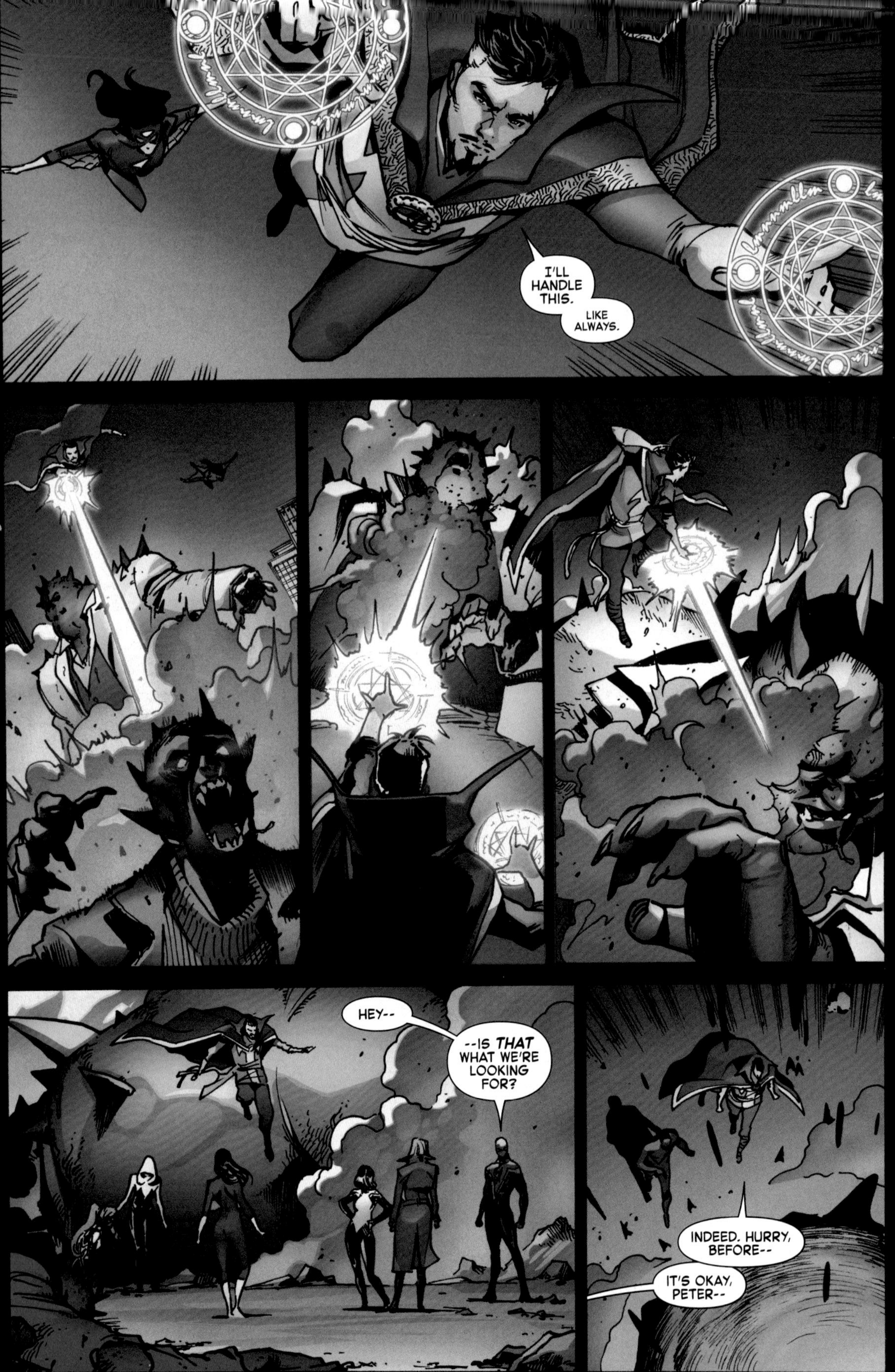
I'LL HANDLE THIS.
LIKE ALWAYS.
HEY--
--IS *THAT* WHAT WE'RE LOOKING FOR?
INDEED. HURRY, BEFORE--
IT'S OKAY, PETER--

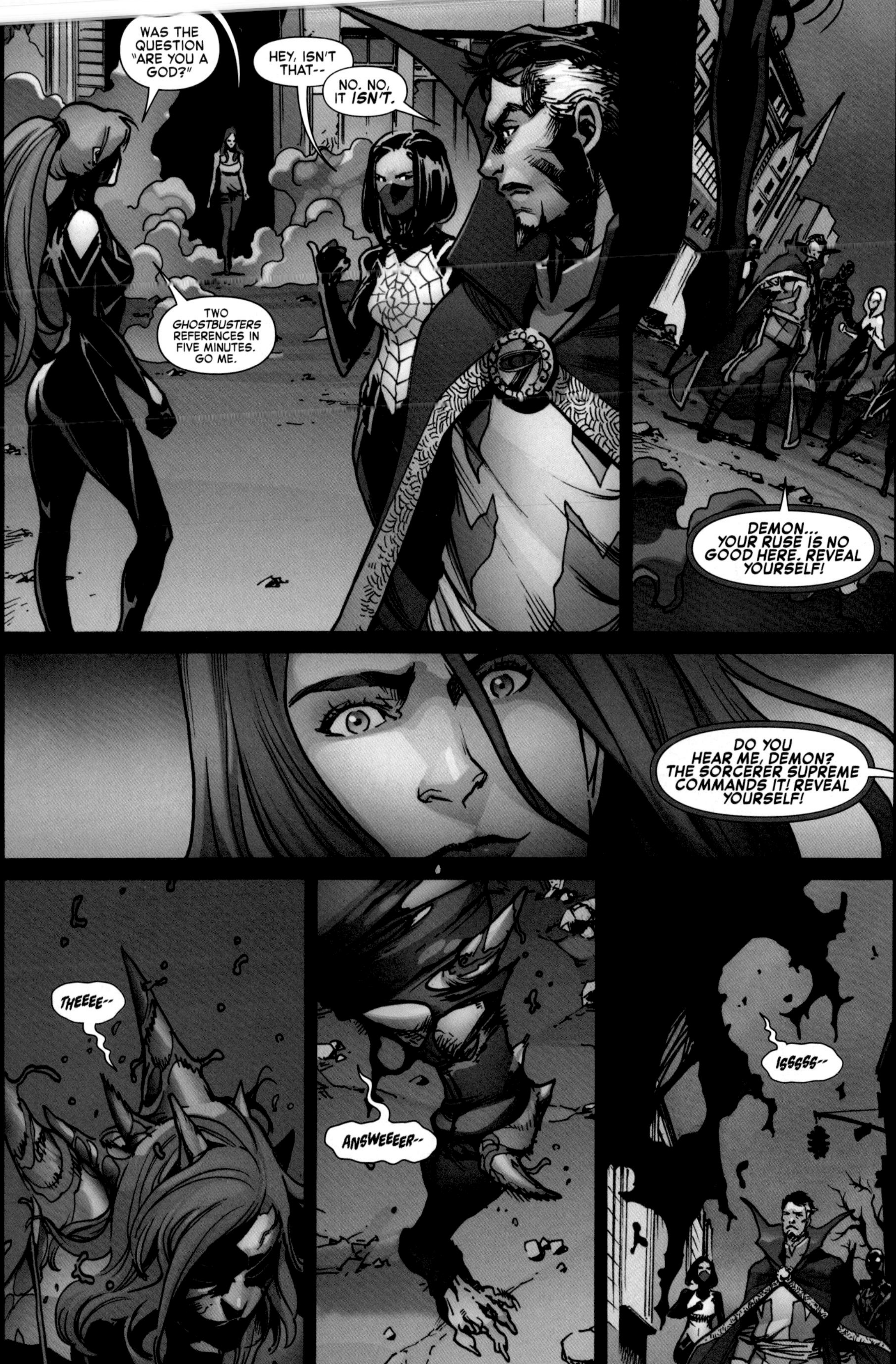
WAS THE QUESTION "ARE YOU A GOD?"
HEY, ISN'T THAT--
NO. NO, IT ISN'T.
TWO GHOSTBUSTERS REFERENCES IN FIVE MINUTES. GO ME.
DEMON... YOUR RUSE IS NO GOOD HERE. REVEAL YOURSELF!
DO YOU HEAR ME, DEMON? THE SORCERER SUPREME COMMANDS IT! REVEAL YOURSELF!
THEEEE--
ANSWEEEER--
ISSSSS--

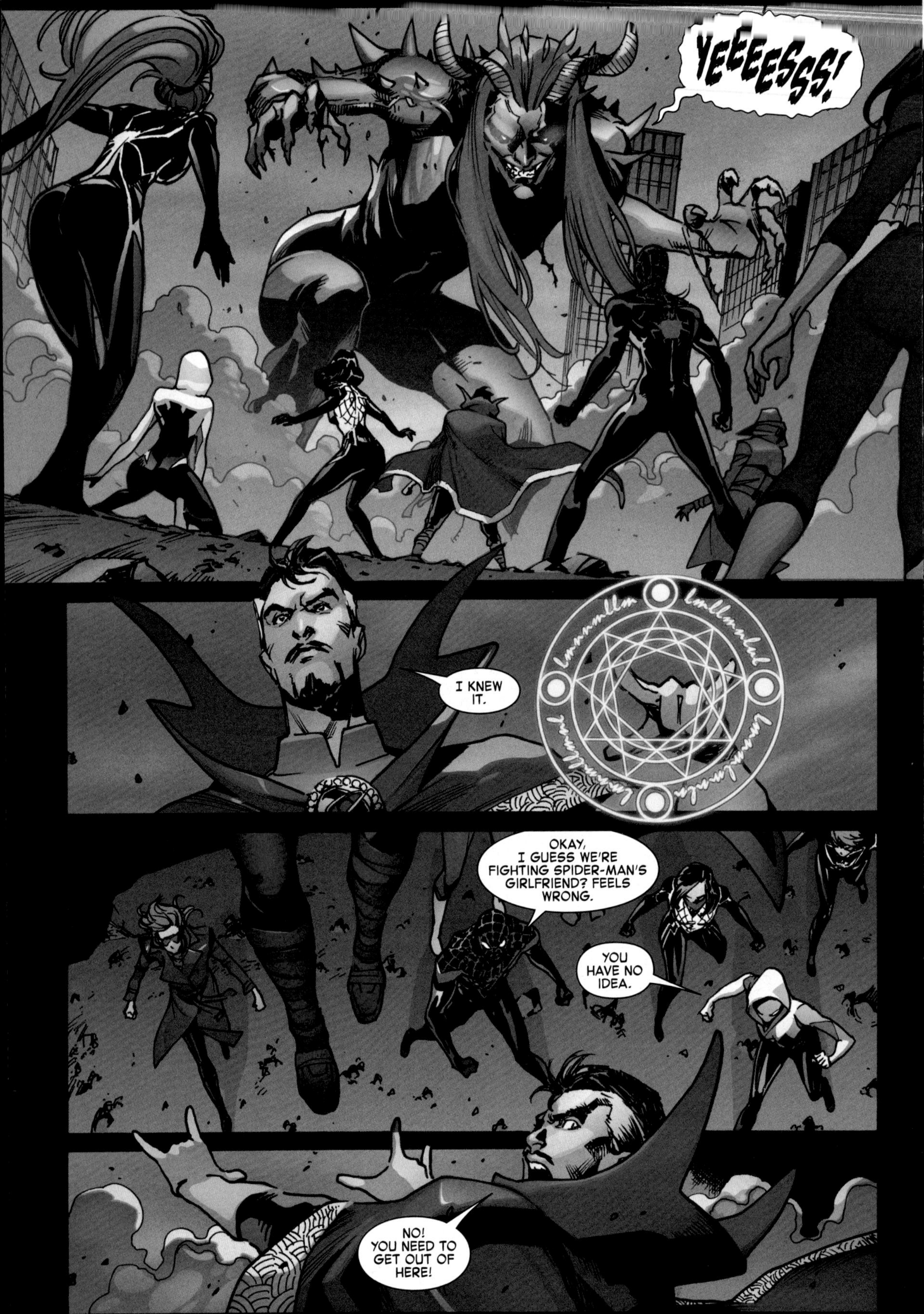
YEEEESSS!
I KNEW IT.
OKAY, I GUESS WE'RE FIGHTING SPIDER-MAN'S GIRLFRIEND? FEELS WRONG.
YOU HAVE NO IDEA.
NO! YOU NEED TO GET OUT OF HERE!

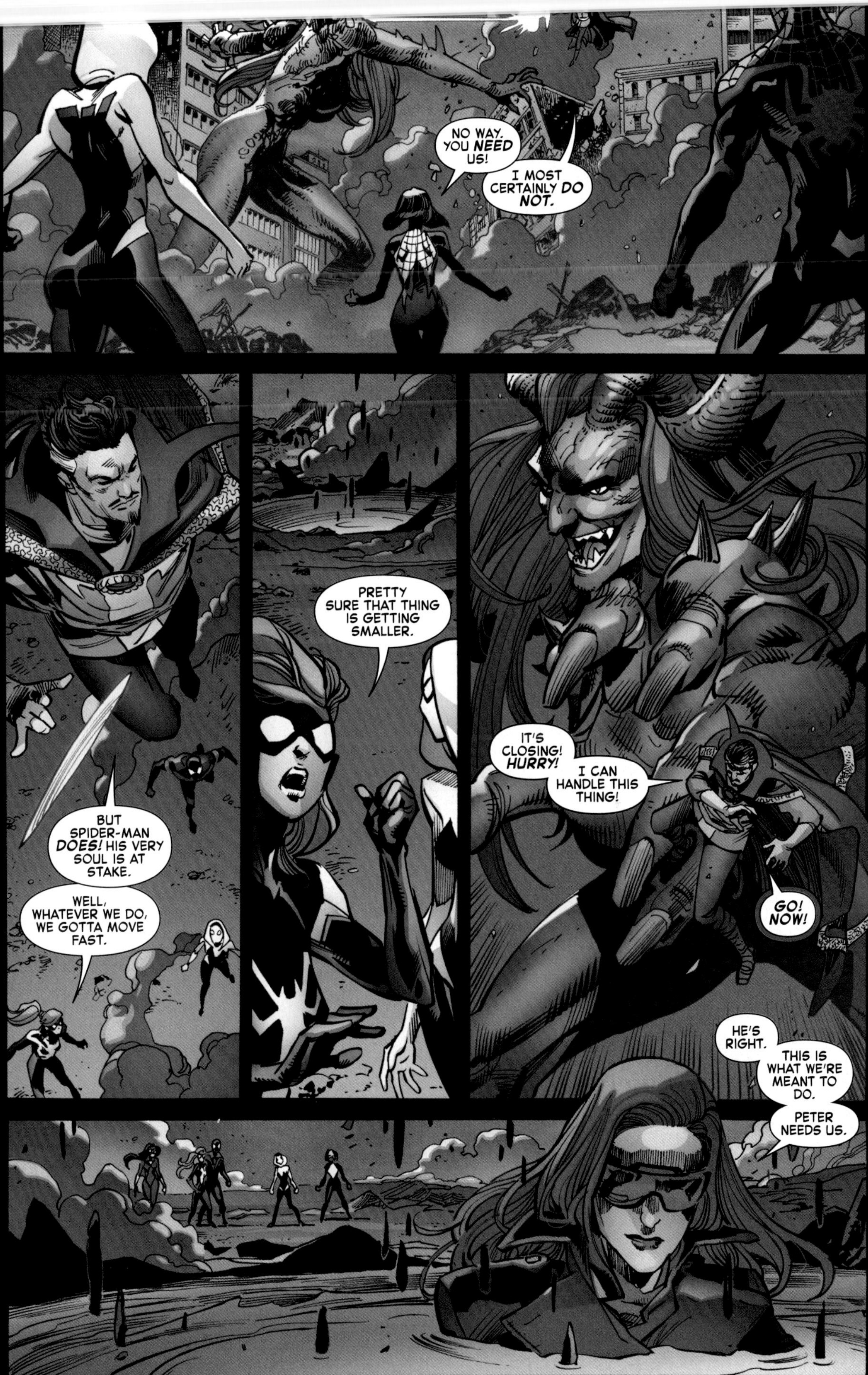

NO WAY. YOU NEED US!
I MOST CERTAINLY DO NOT.
BUT SPIDER-MAN DOES! HIS VERY SOUL IS AT STAKE.
WELL, WHATEVER WE DO, WE GOTTA MOVE FAST.
PRETTY SURE THAT THING IS GETTING SMALLER.
IT'S CLOSING! HURRY!
I CAN HANDLE THIS THING!
GO! NOW!
HE'S RIGHT.
THIS IS WHAT WE'RE MEANT TO DO.
PETER NEEDS US.

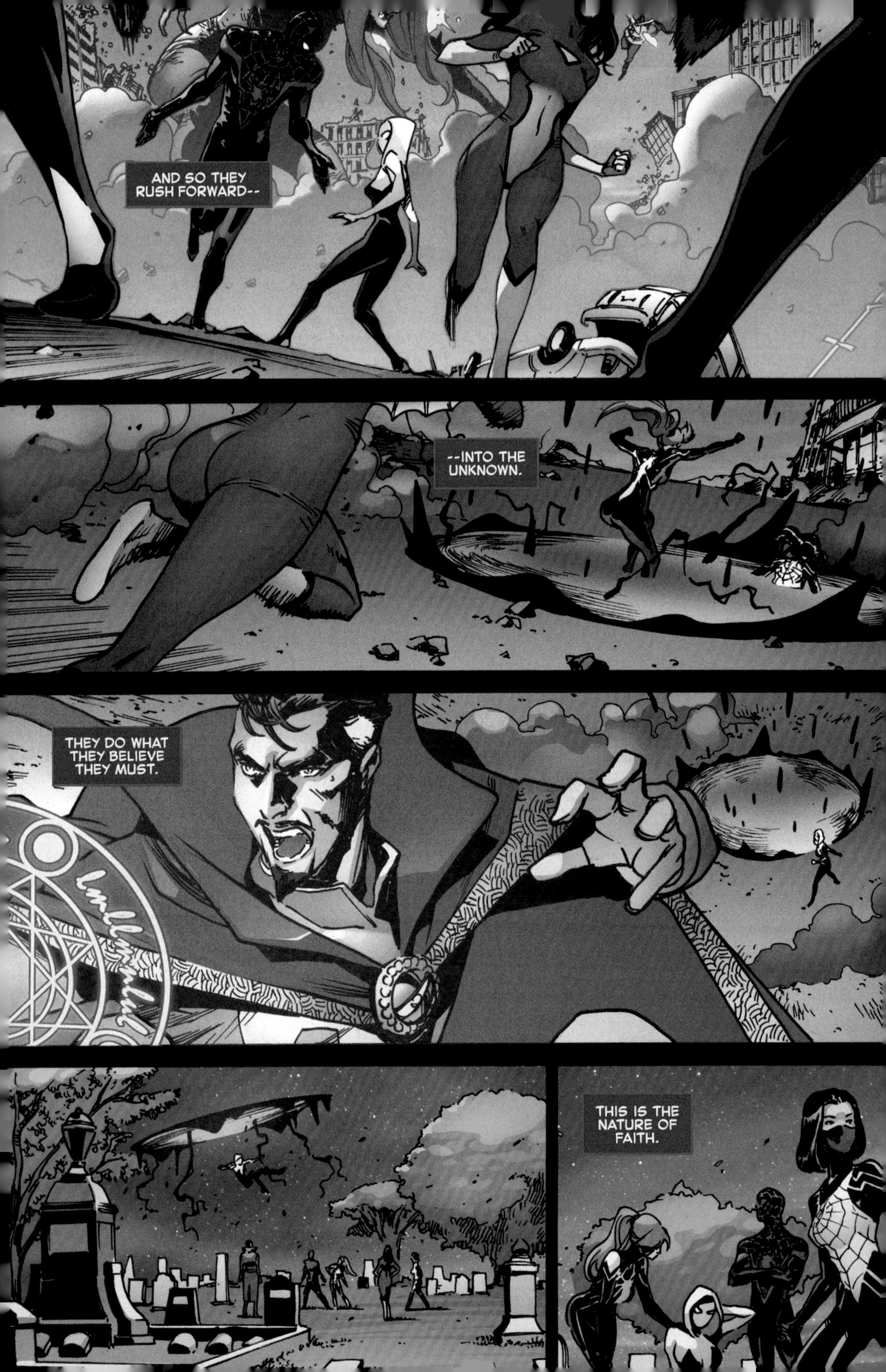
AND SO THEY RUSH FORWARD--
--INTO THE UNKNOWN.
THEY DO WHAT THEY BELIEVE THEY MUST.
THIS IS THE NATURE OF FAITH.

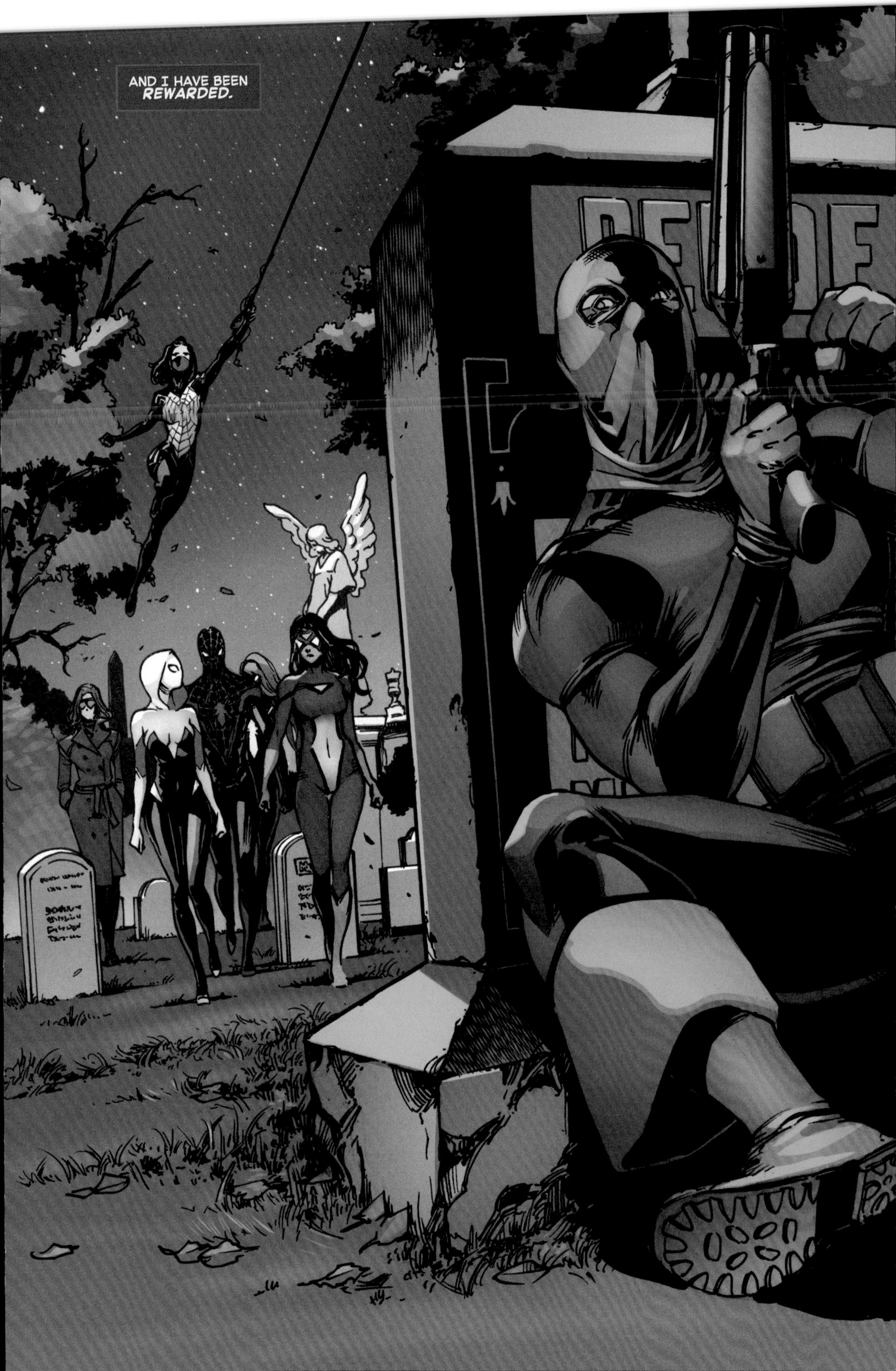
AND I HAVE BEEN
REWARDED.

54.LR

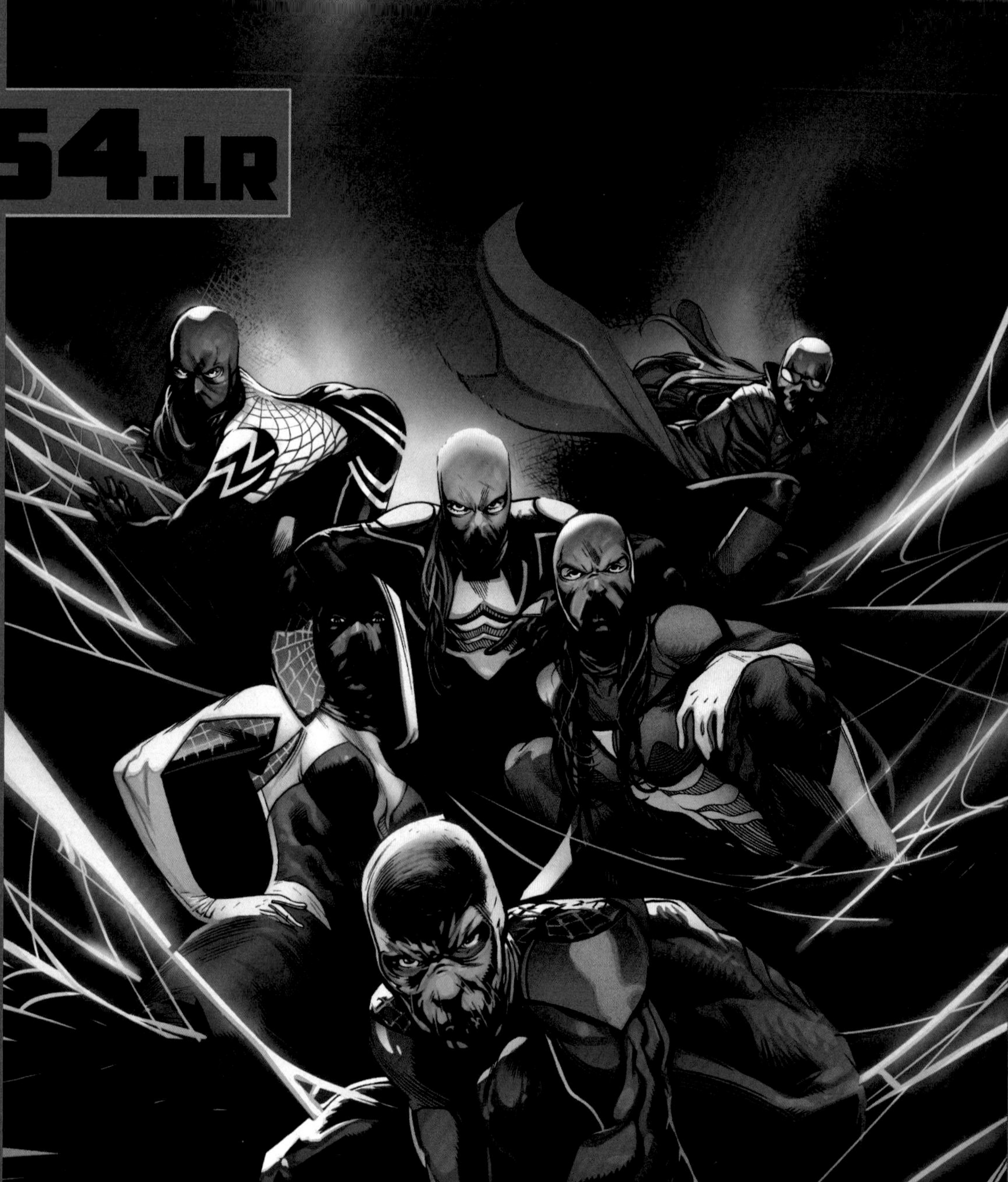
MF
2020

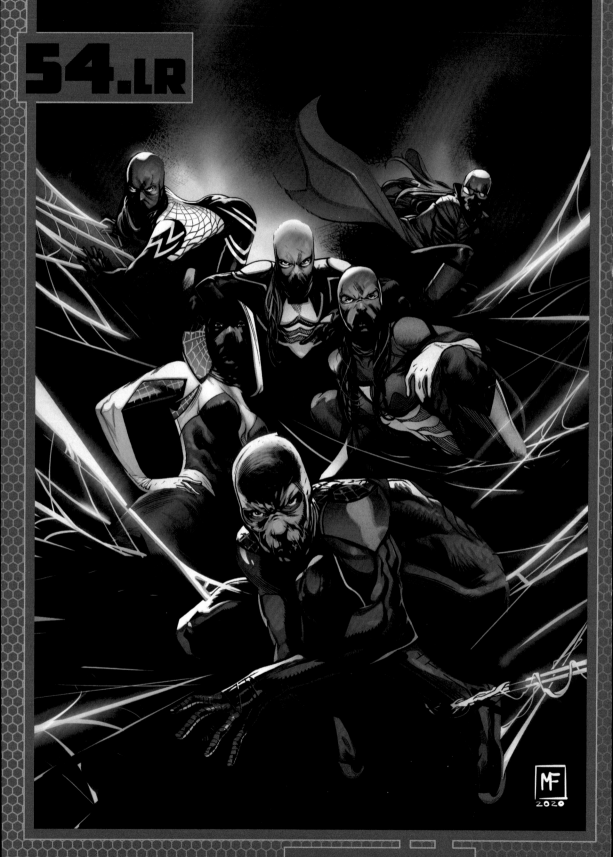

FALLEN ORDER PART 5

DON'T BE AN *IDIOT*, MARY JANE! STOP *STRUGGLING!*

YOU'LL *KILL US BOTH!*

THEN LET ME GO!

I WILL...I WILL...JUST AS SOON AS WE ARRIVE AT OUR *DESTINATION.*

WHERE, HARRY? WHERE ARE YOU *TAKING—*

OH NO!

YOU *REMEMBER,* DON'T YOU?

HOW COULD YOU...HOW COULD *ANY* OF US...EVER *FORGET?*

THE PLACE WHERE ALL OUR HEARTS WERE FOREVER BROKEN...ALL OUR LIVES FOREVER *SHATTERED.* THE PLACE—

—WHERE *GWEN STACY DIED!!*

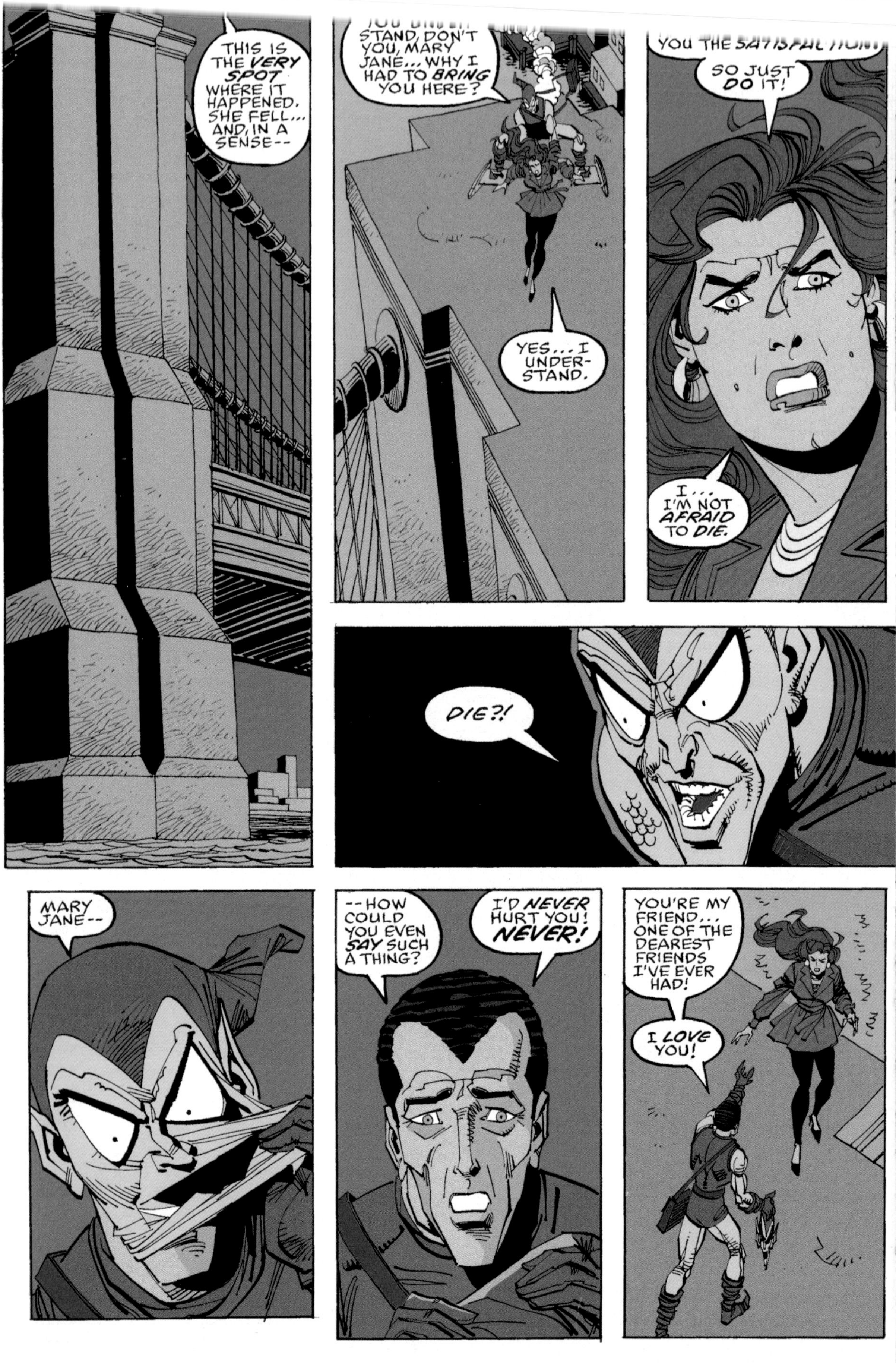
THIS IS THE VERY SPOT WHERE IT HAPPENED. SHE FELL... AND, IN A SENSE--
STAND, DON'T YOU, MARY JANE... WHY I HAD TO BRING YOU HERE?
YES... I UNDERSTAND.
SO JUST DO IT!
I... I'M NOT AFRAID TO DIE.
DIE?!
MARY JANE--
--HOW COULD YOU EVEN SAY SUCH A THING?
I'D NEVER HURT YOU! NEVER!
YOU'RE MY FRIEND... ONE OF THE DEAREST FRIENDS I'VE EVER HAD!
I LOVE YOU!

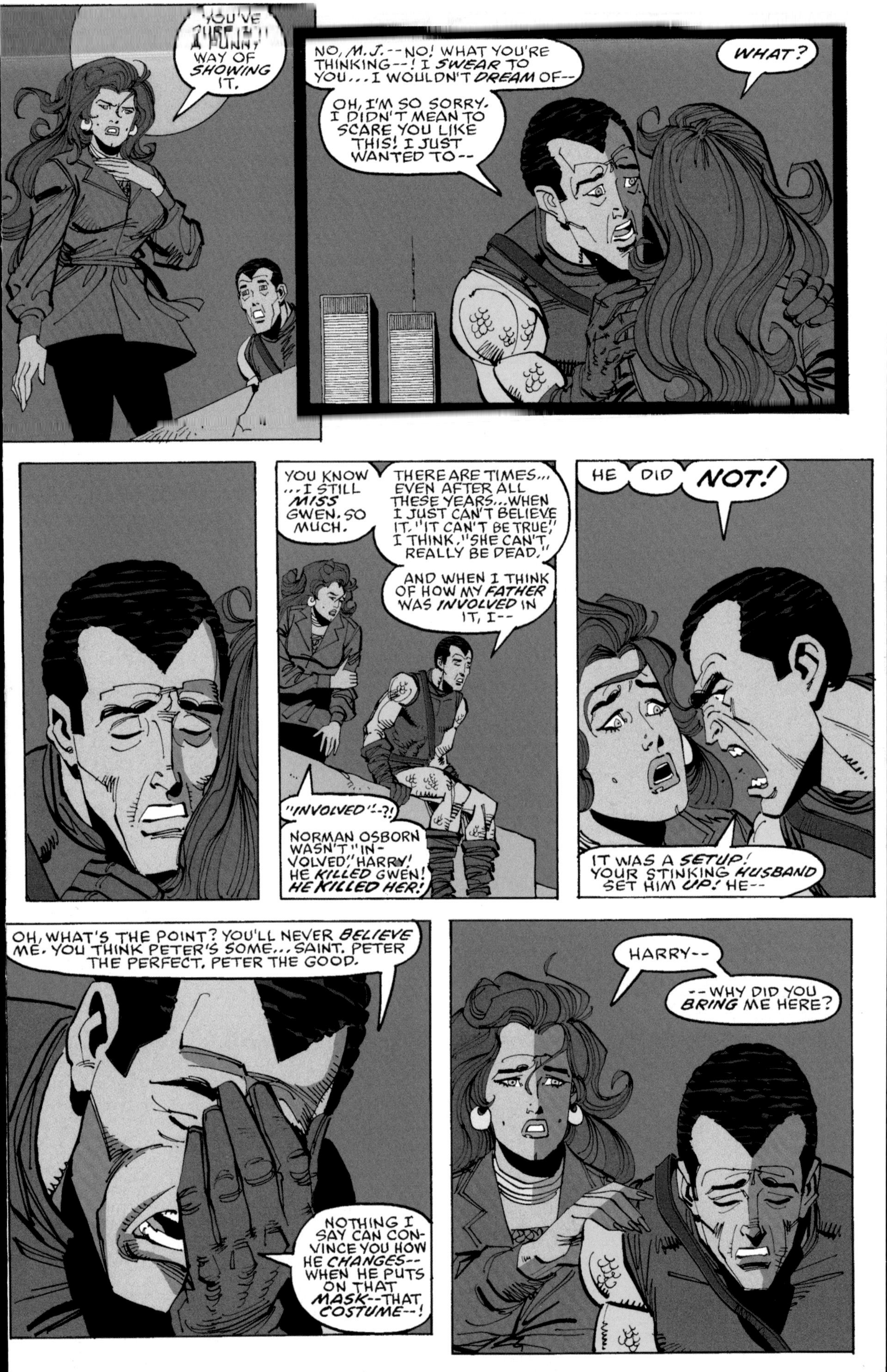

YOU'VE A FUNNY WAY OF SHOWING IT.
NO, M.J.--NO! WHAT YOU'RE THINKING--! I SWEAR TO YOU... I WOULDN'T DREAM OF--
OH, I'M SO SORRY. I DIDN'T MEAN TO SCARE YOU LIKE THIS! I JUST WANTED TO--
WHAT?
YOU KNOW ...I STILL MISS GWEN. SO MUCH.
THERE ARE TIMES... EVEN AFTER ALL THESE YEARS...WHEN I JUST CAN'T BELIEVE IT. "IT CAN'T BE TRUE," I THINK. "SHE CAN'T REALLY BE DEAD."
AND WHEN I THINK OF HOW MY FATHER WAS INVOLVED IN IT, I--
"INVOLVED"--?!
NORMAN OSBORN WASN'T "INVOLVED," HARRY! HE KILLED GWEN! HE KILLED HER!
HE DID NOT!
IT WAS A SETUP! YOUR STINKING HUSBAND SET HIM UP! HE--
OH, WHAT'S THE POINT? YOU'LL NEVER BELIEVE ME. YOU THINK PETER'S SOME... SAINT. PETER THE PERFECT. PETER THE GOOD.
NOTHING I SAY CAN CONVINCE YOU HOW HE CHANGES-- WHEN HE PUTS ON THAT MASK--THAT COSTUME--!
HARRY--
--WHY DID YOU BRING ME HERE?

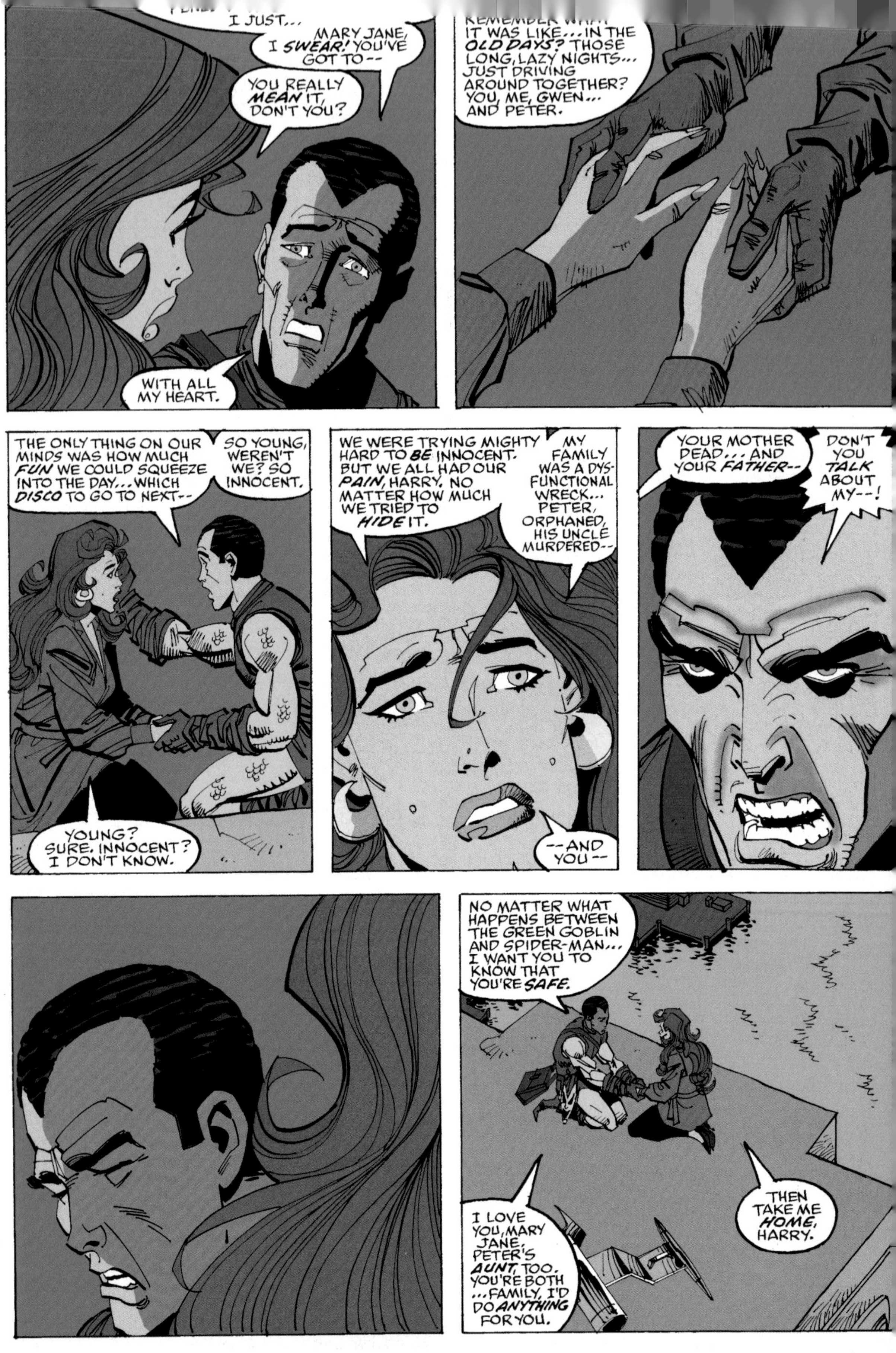

I JUST...
MARY JANE, I SWEAR! YOU'VE GOT TO--
YOU REALLY MEAN IT, DON'T YOU?
WITH ALL MY HEART.
REMEMBER WHAT IT WAS LIKE... IN THE OLD DAYS? THOSE LONG, LAZY NIGHTS... JUST DRIVING AROUND TOGETHER? YOU, ME, GWEN... AND PETER.
THE ONLY THING ON OUR MINDS WAS HOW MUCH FUN WE COULD SQUEEZE INTO THE DAY... WHICH DISCO TO GO TO NEXT--
SO YOUNG, WEREN'T WE? SO INNOCENT.
YOUNG? SURE. INNOCENT? I DON'T KNOW.
WE WERE TRYING MIGHTY HARD TO BE INNOCENT. BUT WE ALL HAD OUR PAIN, HARRY. NO MATTER HOW MUCH WE TRIED TO HIDE IT.
MY FAMILY WAS A DYS-FUNCTIONAL WRECK... PETER, ORPHANED, HIS UNCLE MURDERED--
--AND YOU--
YOUR MOTHER DEAD... AND YOUR FATHER--
DON'T YOU TALK ABOUT MY--!
NO MATTER WHAT HAPPENS BETWEEN THE GREEN GOBLIN AND SPIDER-MAN... I WANT YOU TO KNOW THAT YOU'RE SAFE.
I LOVE YOU, MARY JANE. PETER'S AUNT, TOO. YOU'RE BOTH ...FAMILY. I'D DO ANYTHING FOR YOU.
THEN TAKE ME HOME, HARRY.

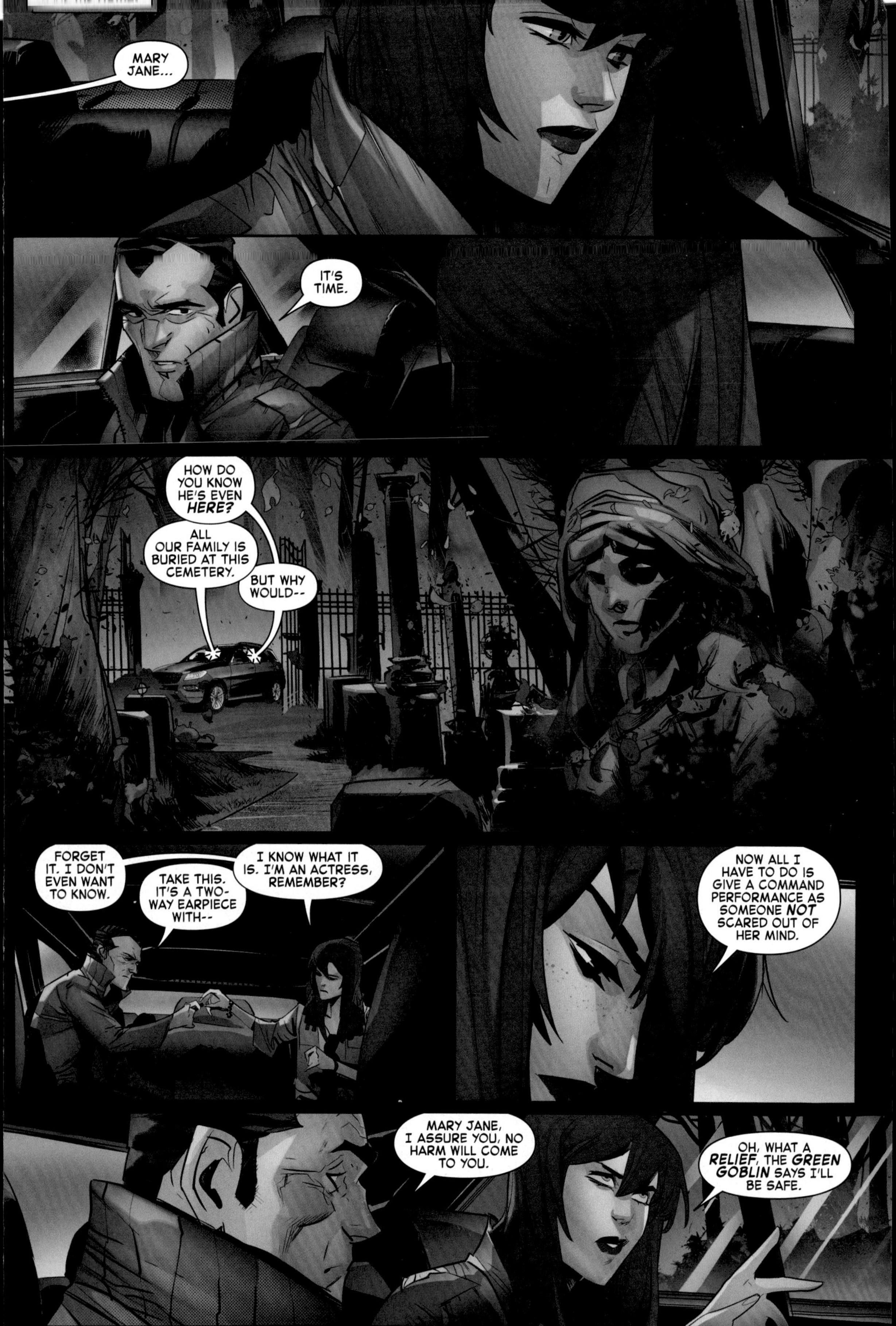

MARY JANE...
IT'S TIME.
HOW DO YOU KNOW HE'S EVEN *HERE?*
ALL OUR FAMILY IS BURIED AT THIS CEMETERY.
BUT WHY WOULD--
TAKE THIS. IT'S A TWO-WAY EARPIECE WITH--
I KNOW WHAT IT IS. I'M AN ACTRESS, REMEMBER?
FORGET IT. I DON'T EVEN WANT TO KNOW.
NOW ALL I HAVE TO DO IS GIVE A COMMAND PERFORMANCE AS SOMEONE *NOT* SCARED OUT OF HER MIND.
MARY JANE, I ASSURE YOU, NO HARM WILL COME TO YOU.
OH, WHAT A *RELIEF*, THE *GREEN GOBLIN* SAYS I'LL BE SAFE.

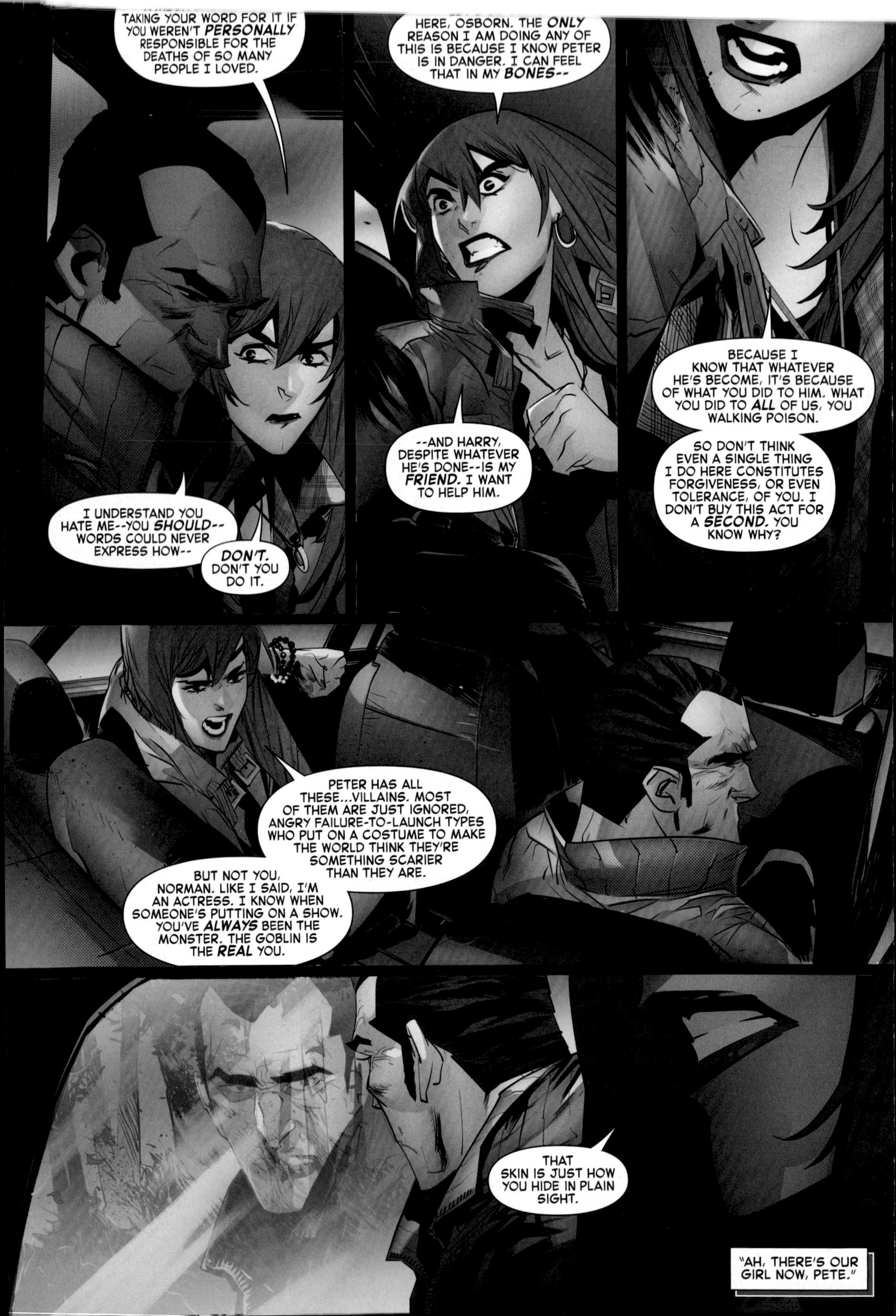
TAKING YOUR WORD FOR IT IF YOU WEREN'T PERSONALLY RESPONSIBLE FOR THE DEATHS OF SO MANY PEOPLE I LOVED.
I UNDERSTAND YOU HATE ME--YOU SHOULD--WORDS COULD NEVER EXPRESS HOW--
DON'T. DON'T YOU DO IT.
HERE, OSBORN. THE ONLY REASON I AM DOING ANY OF THIS IS BECAUSE I KNOW PETER IS IN DANGER. I CAN FEEL THAT IN MY BONES--
--AND HARRY, DESPITE WHATEVER HE'S DONE--IS MY FRIEND. I WANT TO HELP HIM.
BECAUSE I KNOW THAT WHATEVER HE'S BECOME, IT'S BECAUSE OF WHAT YOU DID TO HIM. WHAT YOU DID TO ALL OF US, YOU WALKING POISON.
SO DON'T THINK EVEN A SINGLE THING I DO HERE CONSTITUTES FORGIVENESS, OR EVEN TOLERANCE, OF YOU. I DON'T BUY THIS ACT FOR A SECOND. YOU KNOW WHY?
PETER HAS ALL THESE...VILLAINS. MOST OF THEM ARE JUST IGNORED, ANGRY FAILURE-TO-LAUNCH TYPES WHO PUT ON A COSTUME TO MAKE THE WORLD THINK THEY'RE SOMETHING SCARIER THAN THEY ARE.
BUT NOT YOU, NORMAN. LIKE I SAID, I'M AN ACTRESS. I KNOW WHEN SOMEONE'S PUTTING ON A SHOW. YOU'VE ALWAYS BEEN THE MONSTER. THE GOBLIN IS THE REAL YOU.
THAT SKIN IS JUST HOW YOU HIDE IN PLAIN SIGHT.
"AH, THERE'S OUR GIRL NOW, PETE."

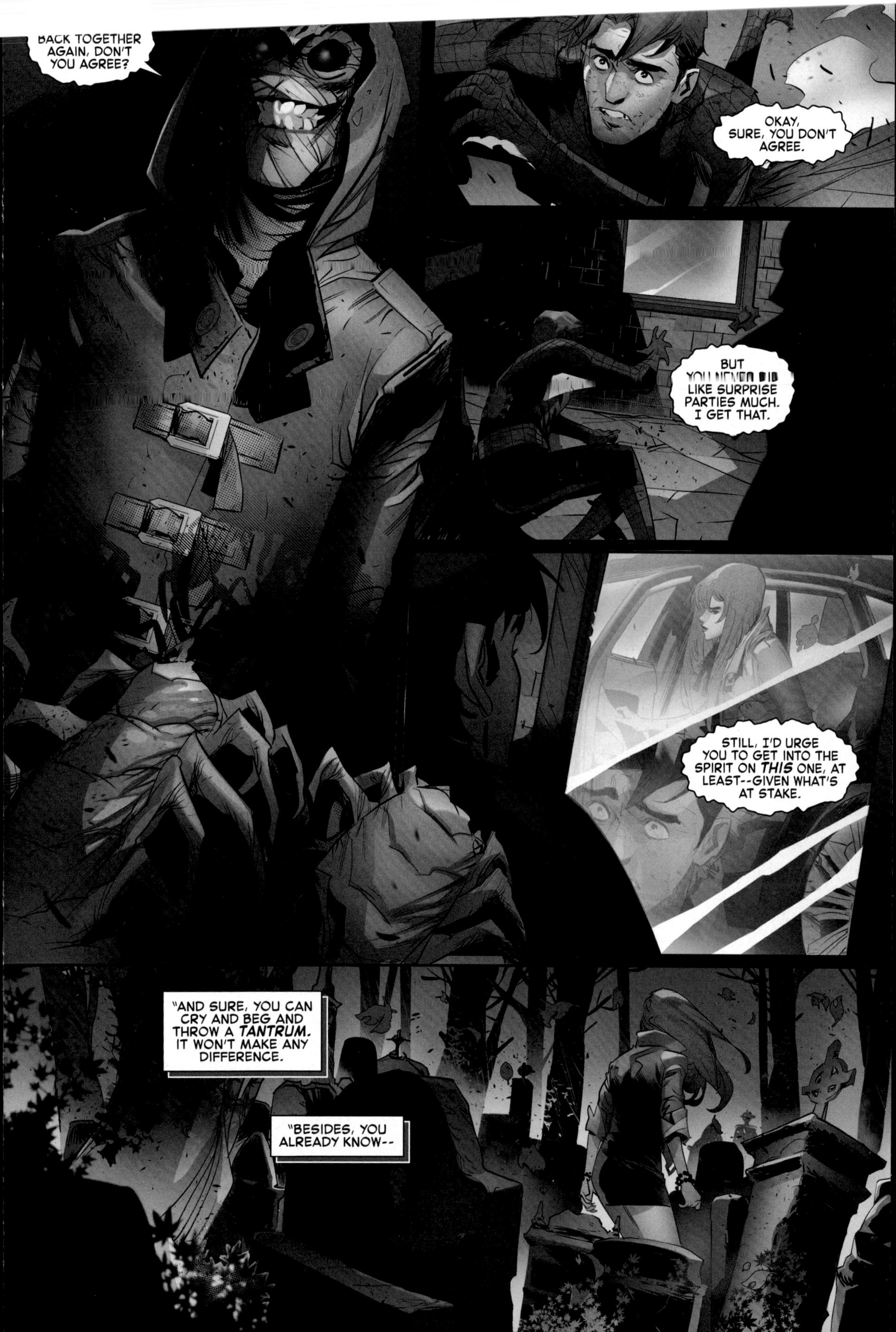
BACK TOGETHER AGAIN, DON'T YOU AGREE?
OKAY, SURE, YOU DON'T AGREE.
BUT YOU NEVER DID LIKE SURPRISE PARTIES MUCH. I GET THAT.
STILL, I'D URGE YOU TO GET INTO THE SPIRIT ON *THIS* ONE, AT LEAST--GIVEN WHAT'S AT STAKE.
"AND SURE, YOU CAN CRY AND BEG AND THROW A *TANTRUM.* IT WON'T MAKE ANY DIFFERENCE.
"BESIDES, YOU ALREADY KNOW--

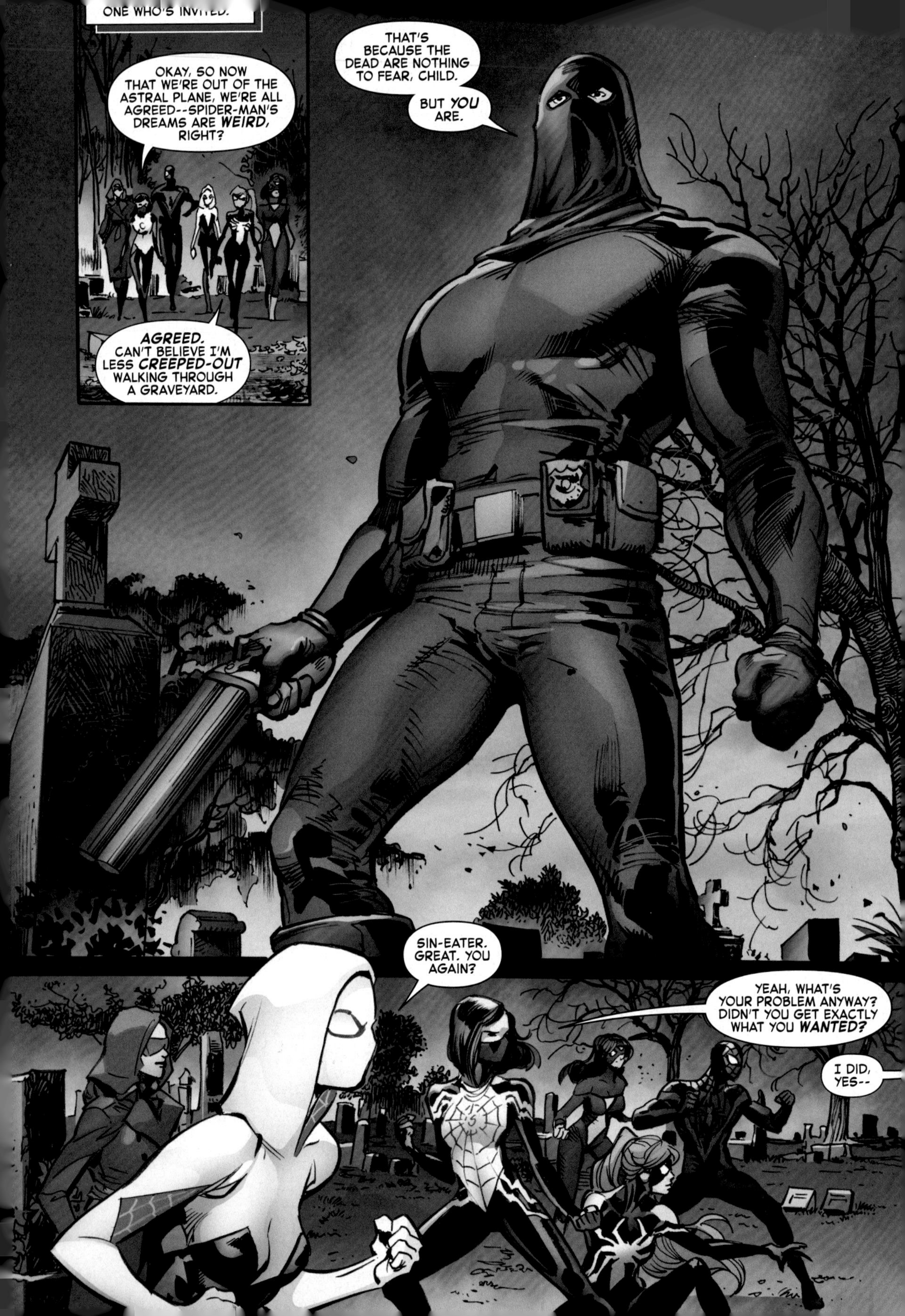
ONE WHO'S INVITED.
OKAY, SO NOW THAT WE'RE OUT OF THE ASTRAL PLANE, WE'RE ALL AGREED--SPIDER-MAN'S DREAMS ARE WEIRD, RIGHT?
AGREED. CAN'T BELIEVE I'M LESS CREEPED-OUT WALKING THROUGH A GRAVEYARD.
THAT'S BECAUSE THE DEAD ARE NOTHING TO FEAR, CHILD.
BUT YOU ARE.
SIN-EATER. GREAT. YOU AGAIN?
YEAH, WHAT'S YOUR PROBLEM ANYWAY? DIDN'T YOU GET EXACTLY WHAT YOU WANTED?
I DID, YES--

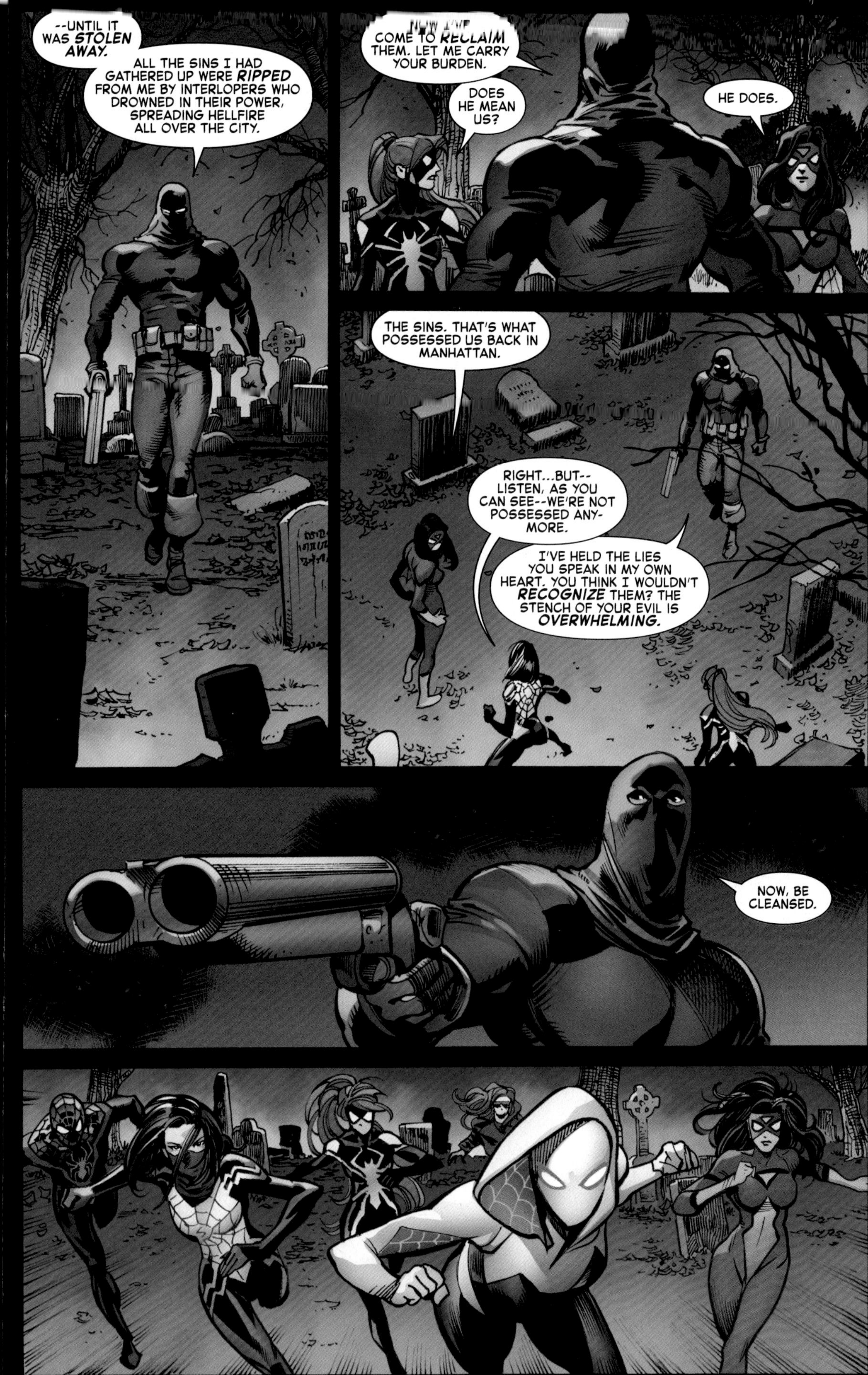
--UNTIL IT WAS STOLEN AWAY.
ALL THE SINS I HAD GATHERED UP WERE RIPPED FROM ME BY INTERLOPERS WHO DROWNED IN THEIR POWER, SPREADING HELLFIRE ALL OVER THE CITY.
COME TO RECLAIM THEM. LET ME CARRY YOUR BURDEN.
DOES HE MEAN US?
HE DOES.
THE SINS. THAT'S WHAT POSSESSED US BACK IN MANHATTAN.
RIGHT...BUT-- LISTEN, AS YOU CAN SEE--WE'RE NOT POSSESSED ANY-MORE.
I'VE HELD THE LIES YOU SPEAK IN MY OWN HEART. YOU THINK I WOULDN'T RECOGNIZE THEM? THE STENCH OF YOUR EVIL IS OVERWHELMING.
NOW, BE CLEANSED.

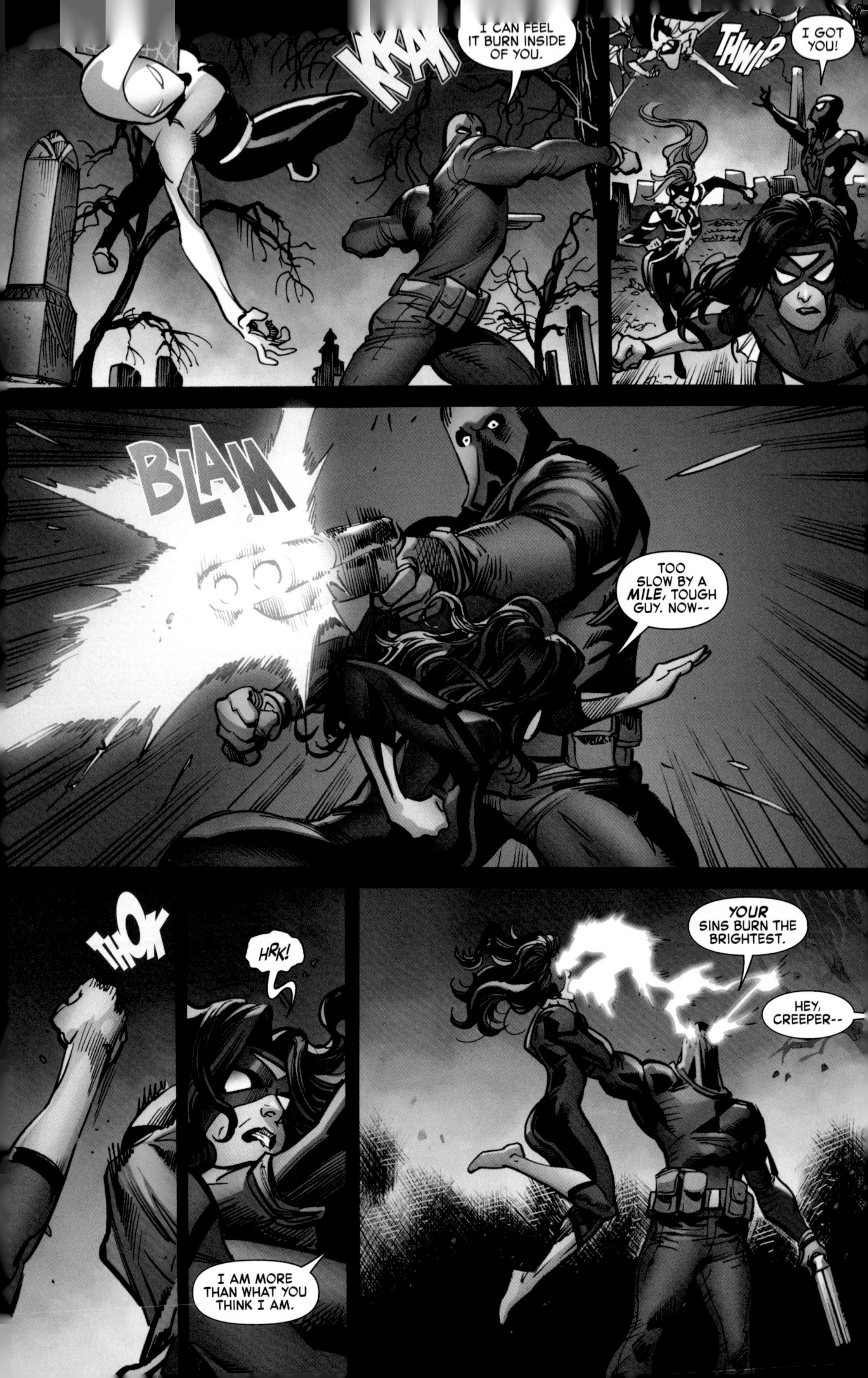
KRAK
I CAN FEEL IT BURN INSIDE OF YOU.
THWIP
I GOT YOU!
BLAM
TOO SLOW BY A *MILE*, TOUGH GUY. NOW--
THOK
HRK!
I AM MORE THAN WHAT YOU THINK I AM.
YOUR SINS BURN THE BRIGHTEST.
HEY, CREEPER--

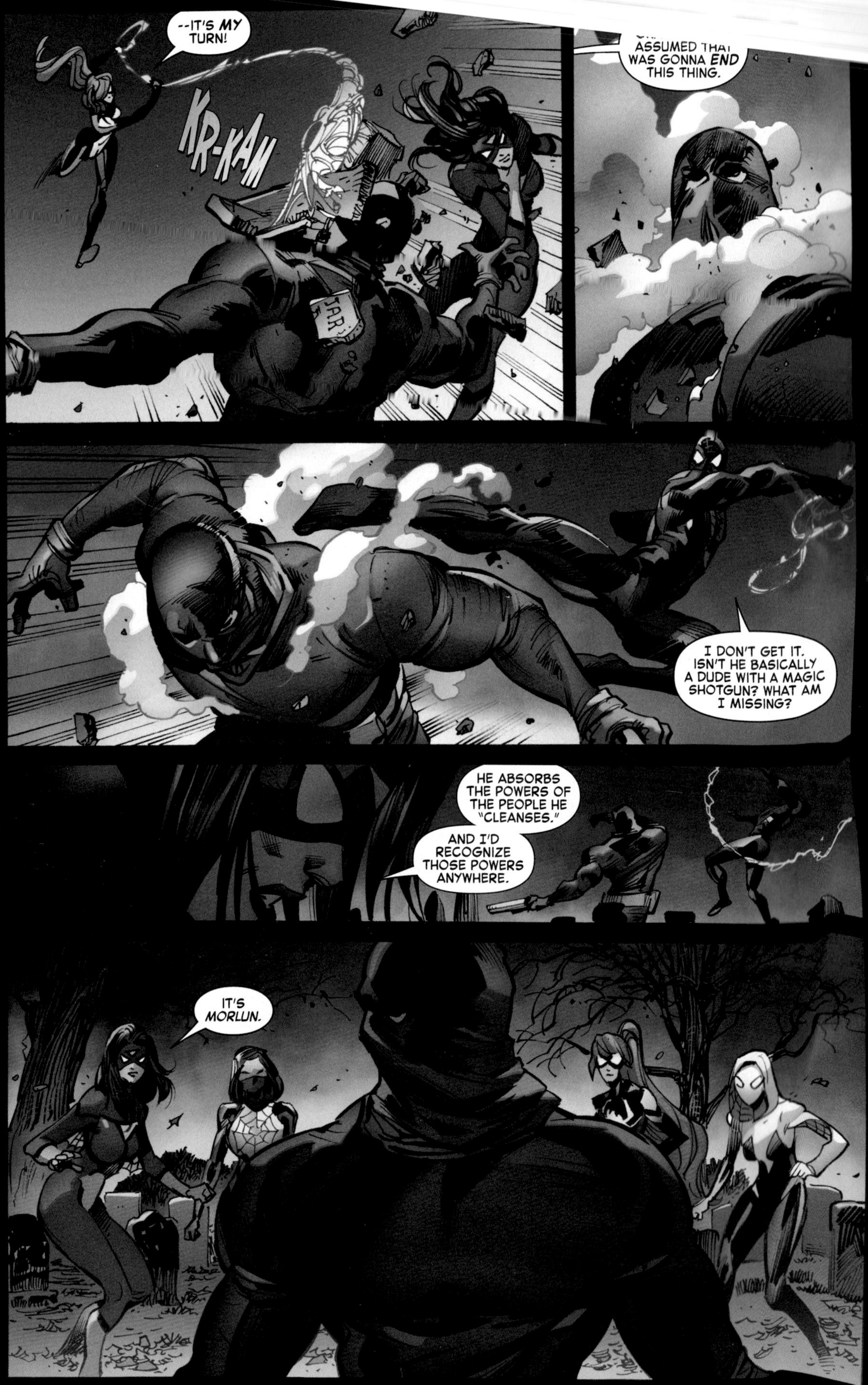
--IT'S MY TURN!
KR-KAM
ASSUMED THAT WAS GONNA END THIS THING.
J.A.R.
I DON'T GET IT. ISN'T HE BASICALLY A DUDE WITH A MAGIC SHOTGUN? WHAT AM I MISSING?
HE ABSORBS THE POWERS OF THE PEOPLE HE "CLEANSES."
AND I'D RECOGNIZE THOSE POWERS ANYWHERE.
IT'S MORLUN.

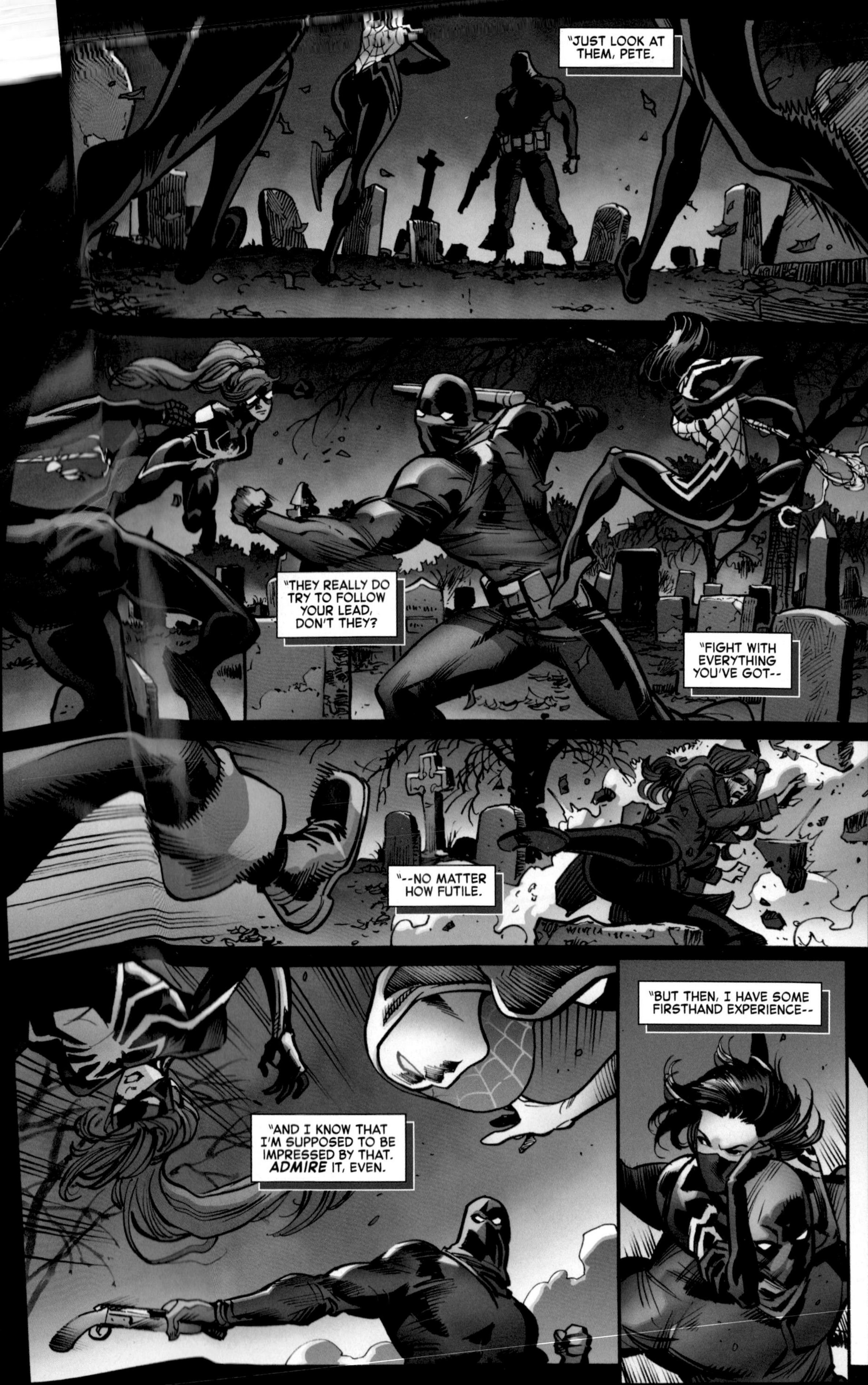
"JUST LOOK AT THEM, PETE.
"THEY REALLY DO TRY TO FOLLOW YOUR LEAD, DON'T THEY?
"FIGHT WITH EVERYTHING YOU'VE GOT--
"--NO MATTER HOW FUTILE.
"AND I KNOW THAT I'M SUPPOSED TO BE IMPRESSED BY THAT. *ADMIRE* IT, EVEN.
"BUT THEN, I HAVE SOME FIRSTHAND EXPERIENCE--

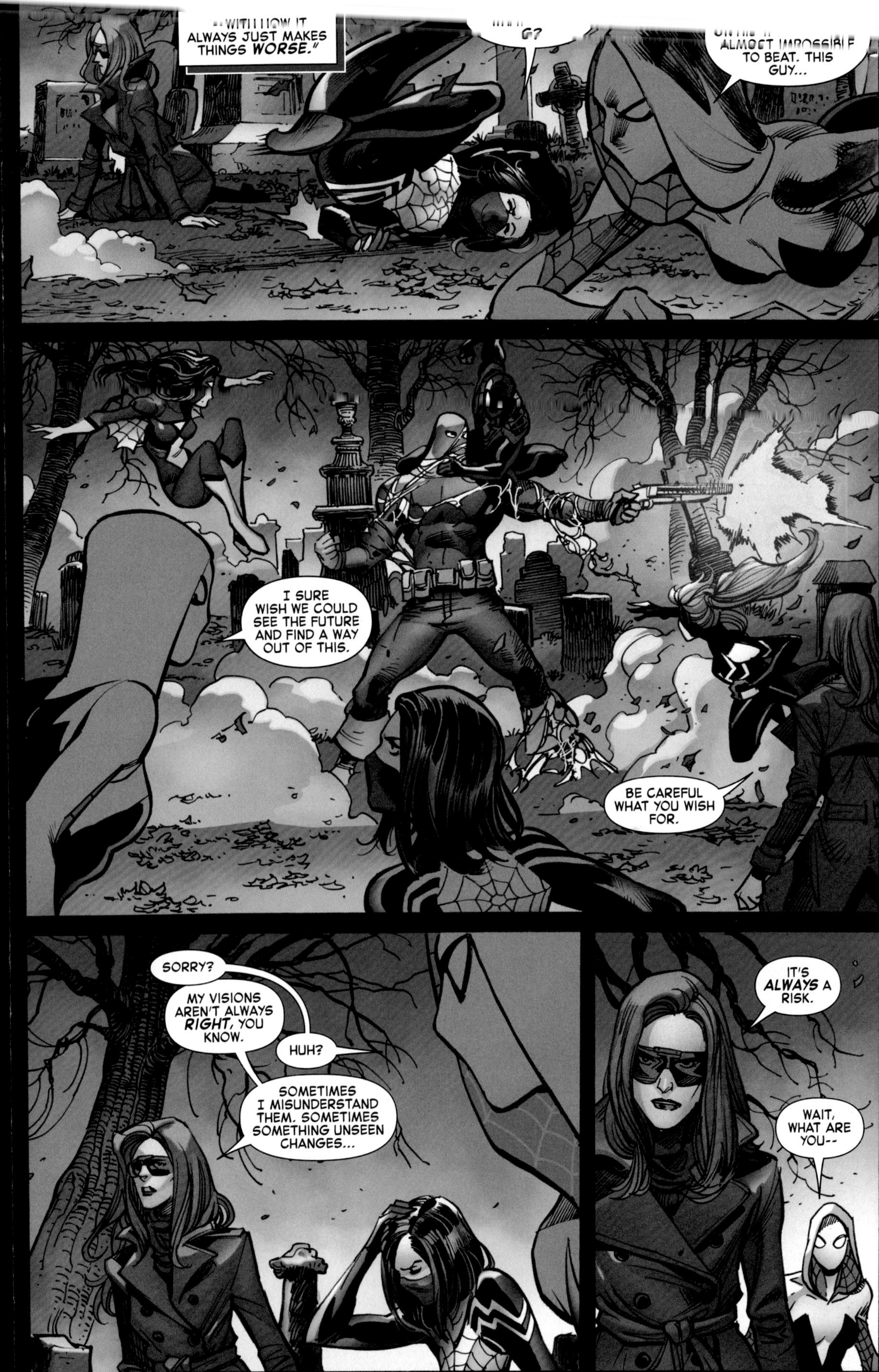

ALWAYS JUST MAKES THINGS WORSE."
ALMOST IMPOSSIBLE TO BEAT. THIS GUY...
I SURE WISH WE COULD SEE THE FUTURE AND FIND A WAY OUT OF THIS.
BE CAREFUL WHAT YOU WISH FOR.
SORRY?
MY VISIONS AREN'T ALWAYS RIGHT, YOU KNOW.
HUH?
SOMETIMES I MISUNDERSTAND THEM. SOMETIMES SOMETHING UNSEEN CHANGES...
IT'S ALWAYS A RISK.
WAIT, WHAT ARE YOU--

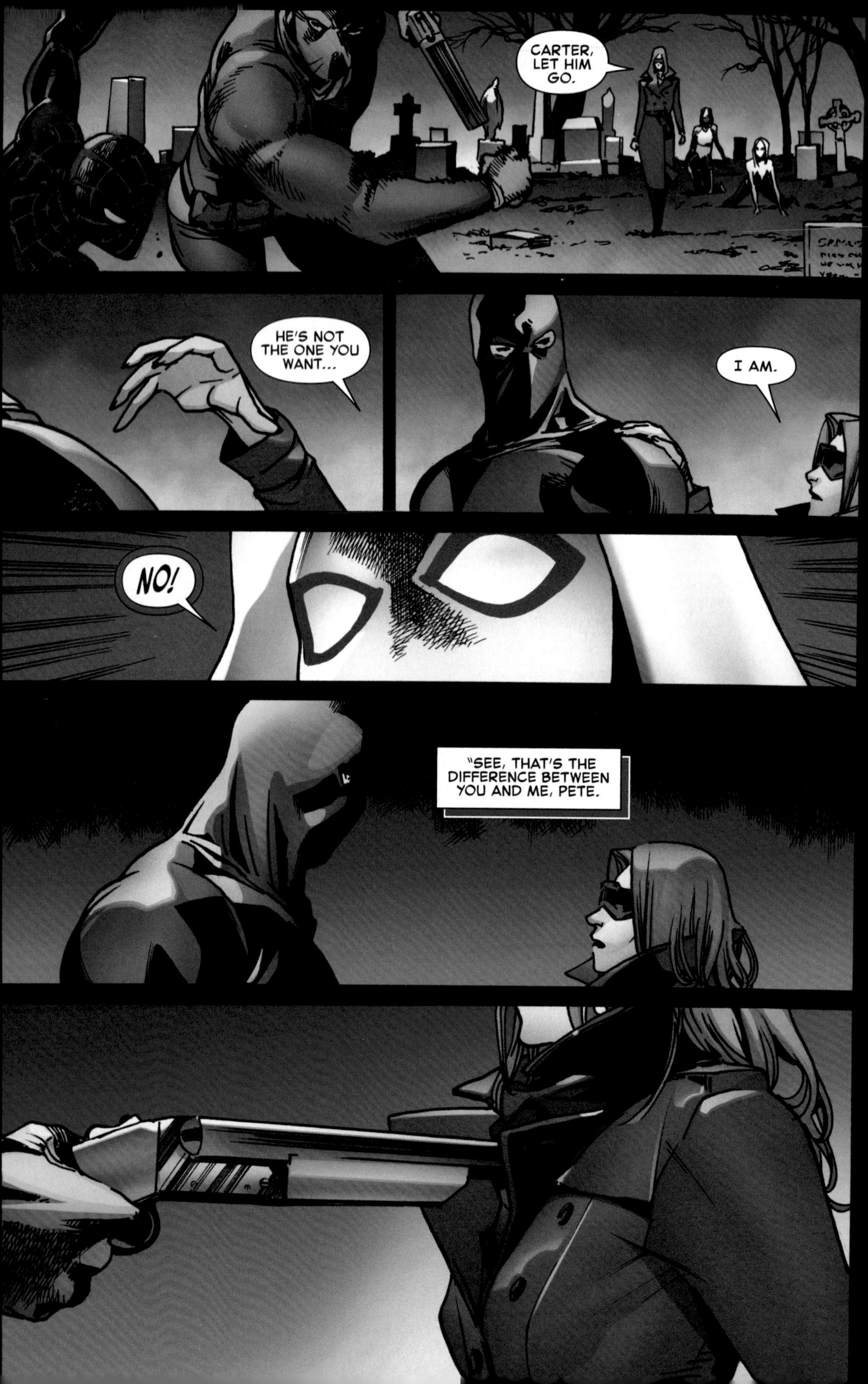
CARTER, LET HIM GO.
HE'S NOT THE ONE YOU WANT...
I AM.
NO!
"SEE, THAT'S THE DIFFERENCE BETWEEN YOU AND ME, PETE.

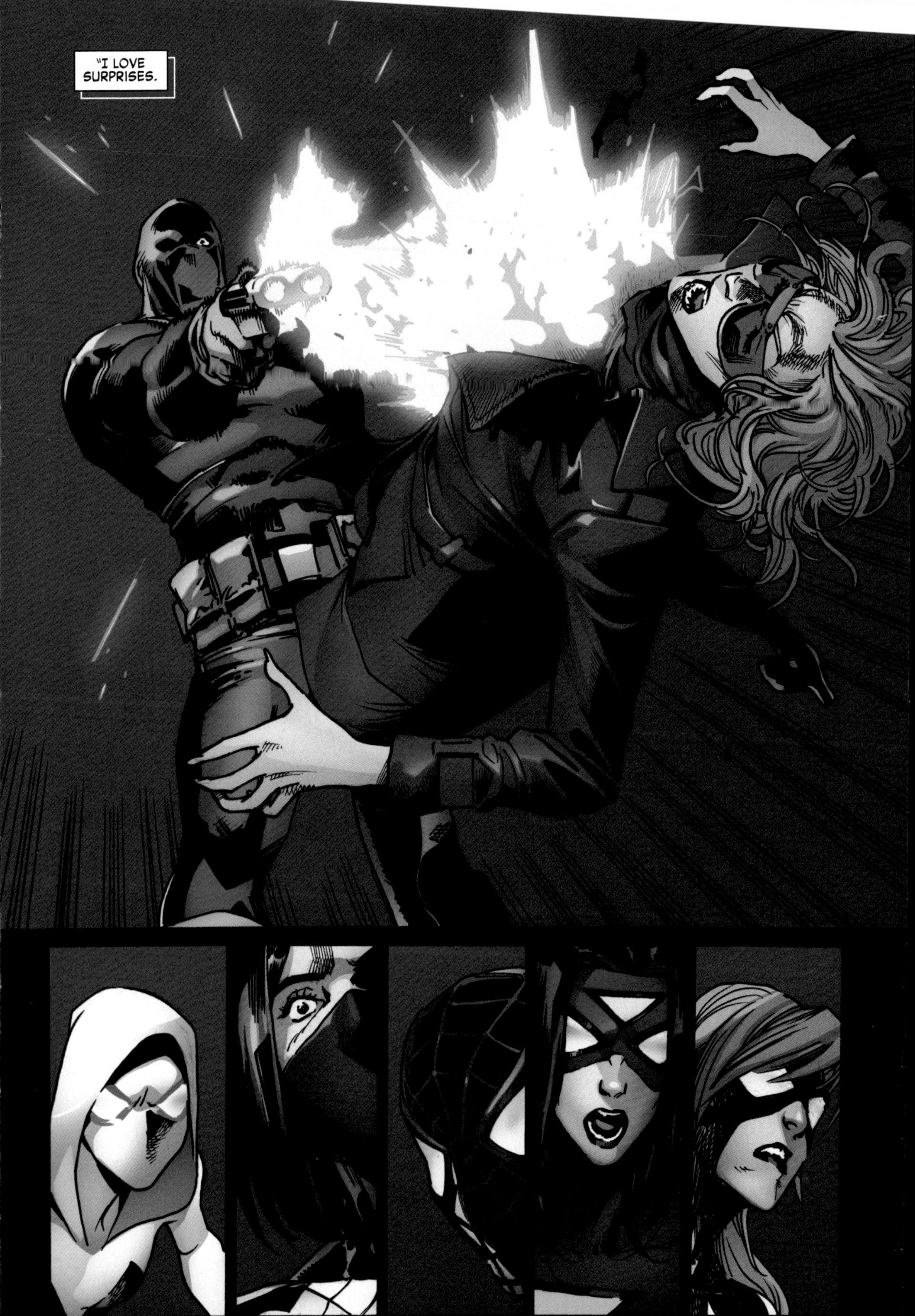
"I LOVE SURPRISES.

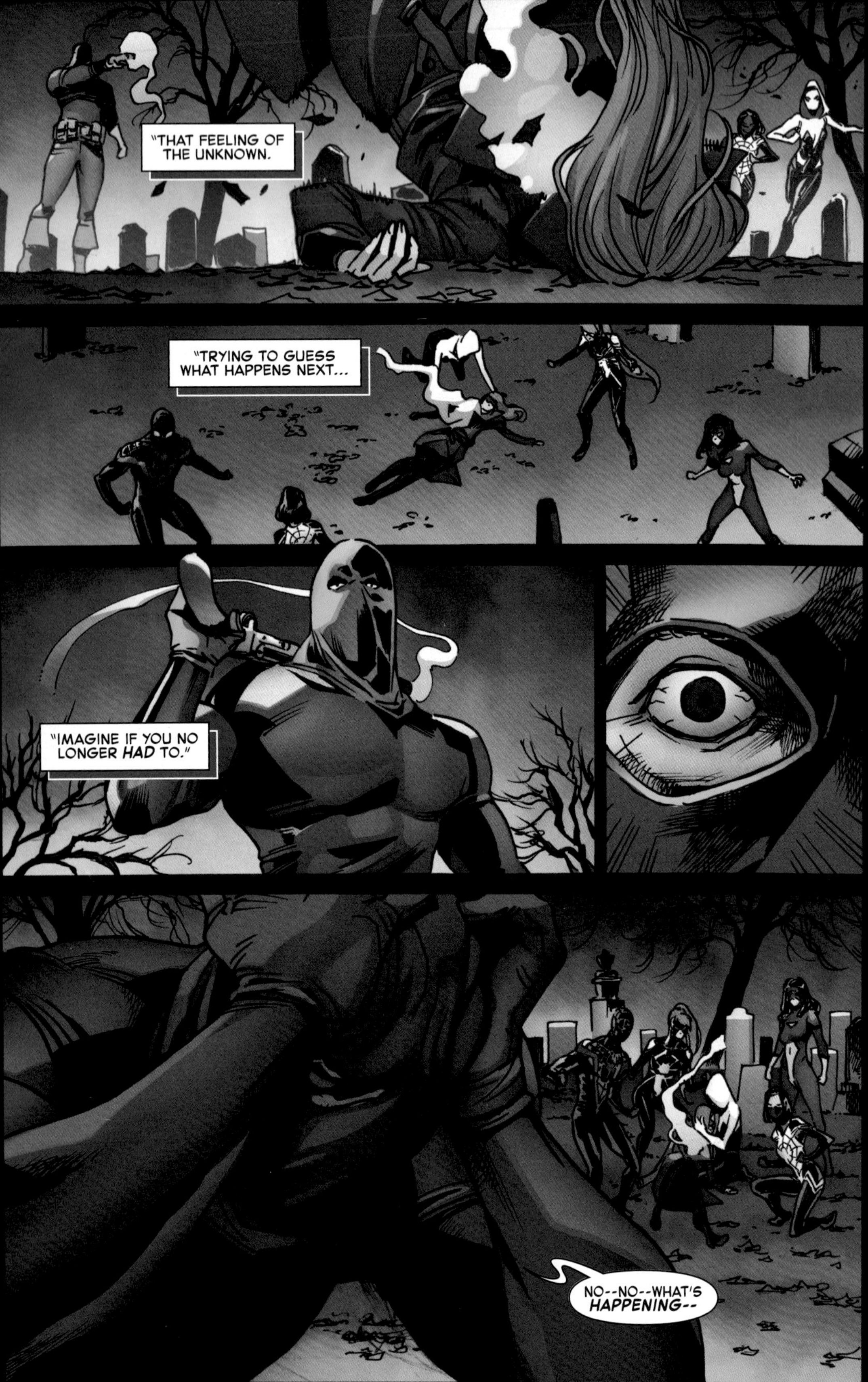
"THAT FEELING OF THE UNKNOWN.
"TRYING TO GUESS WHAT HAPPENS NEXT...
"IMAGINE IF YOU NO LONGER *HAD* TO."
NO--NO--WHAT'S *HAPPENING*--

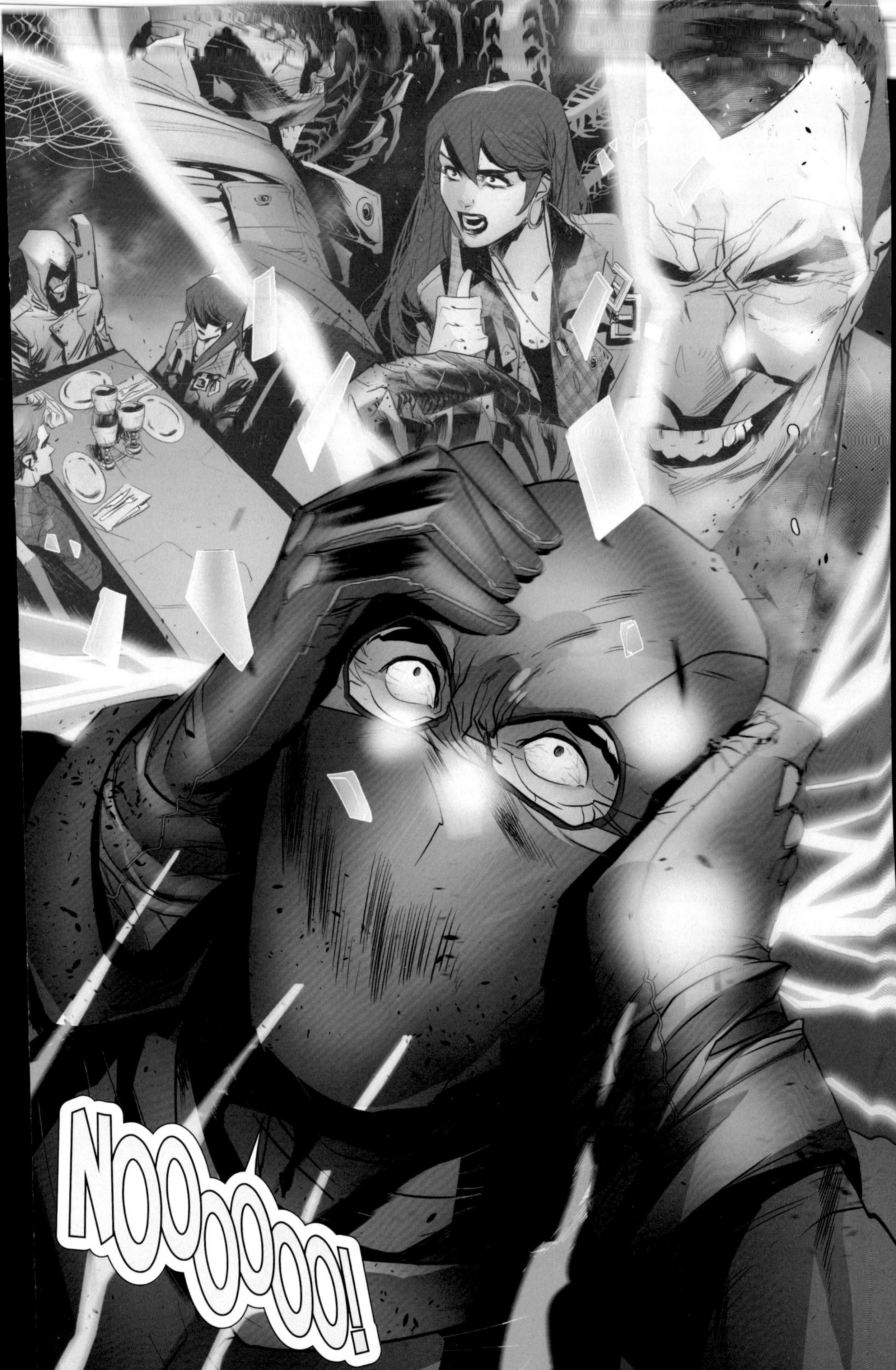
NOOOOOOO!

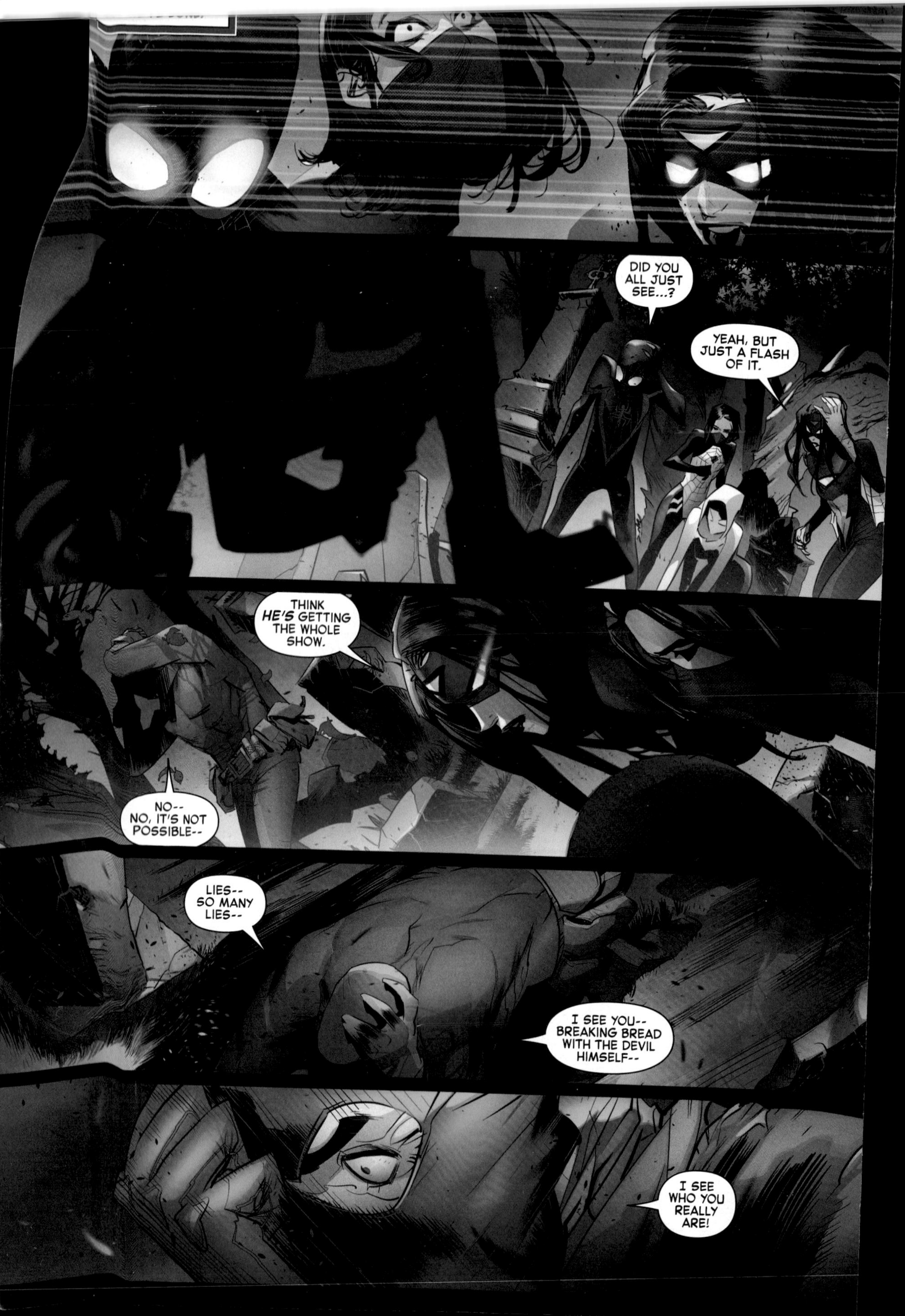
DID YOU ALL JUST SEE...?
YEAH, BUT JUST A FLASH OF IT.
THINK HE'S GETTING THE WHOLE SHOW.
NO-- NO, IT'S NOT POSSIBLE--
LIES-- SO MANY LIES--
I SEE YOU-- BREAKING BREAD WITH THE DEVIL HIMSELF--
I SEE WHO YOU REALLY ARE!

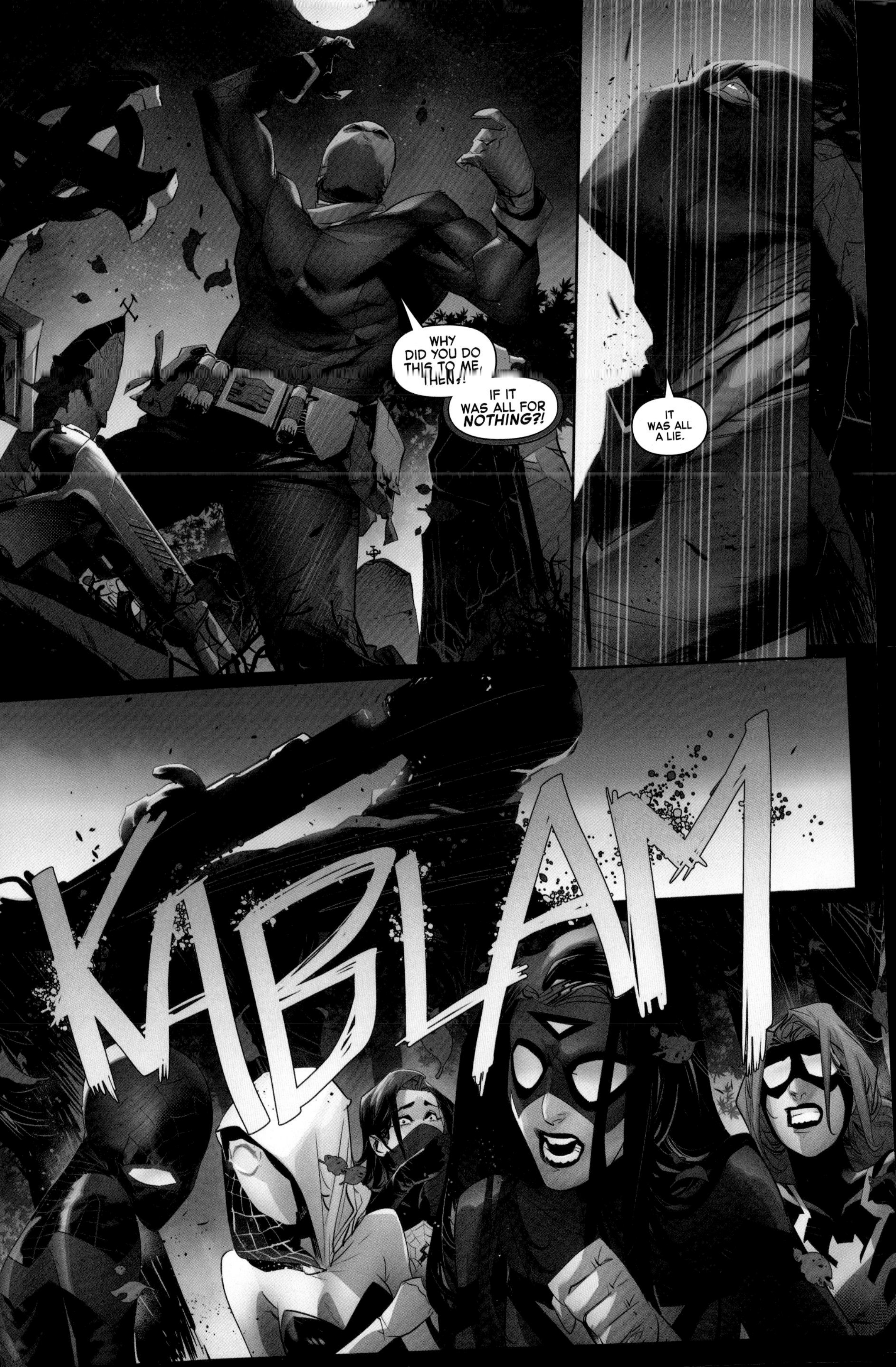

WHY DID YOU DO THIS TO ME, THEN?!
IF IT WAS ALL FOR NOTHING?!
IT WAS ALL A LIE.
KABLAM

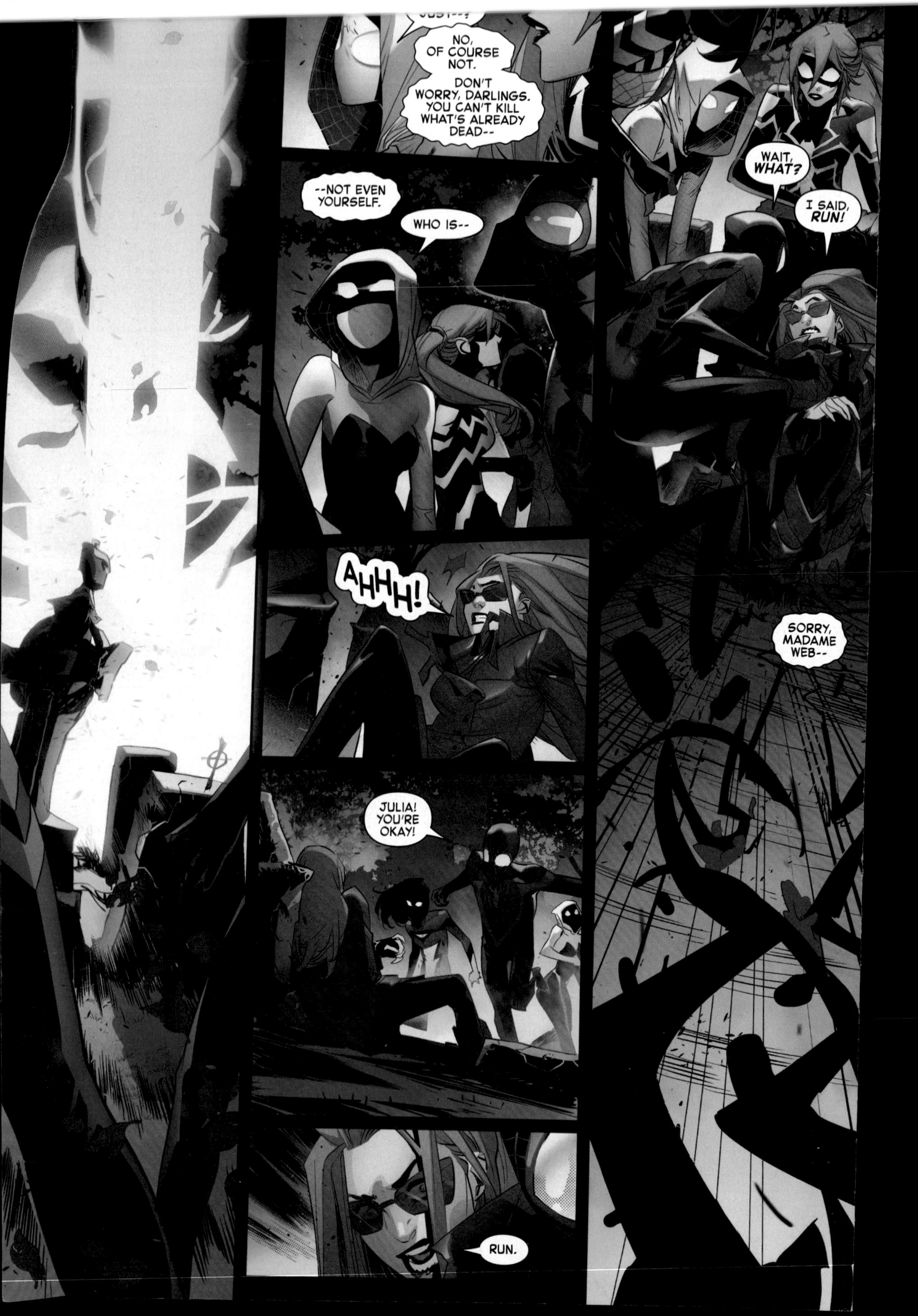
NO, OF COURSE NOT.
DON'T WORRY, DARLINGS. YOU CAN'T KILL WHAT'S ALREADY DEAD--
--NOT EVEN YOURSELF.
WHO IS--
AHHH!
JULIA! YOU'RE OKAY!
RUN.
WAIT, WHAT?
I SAID, RUN!
SORRY, MADAME WEB--

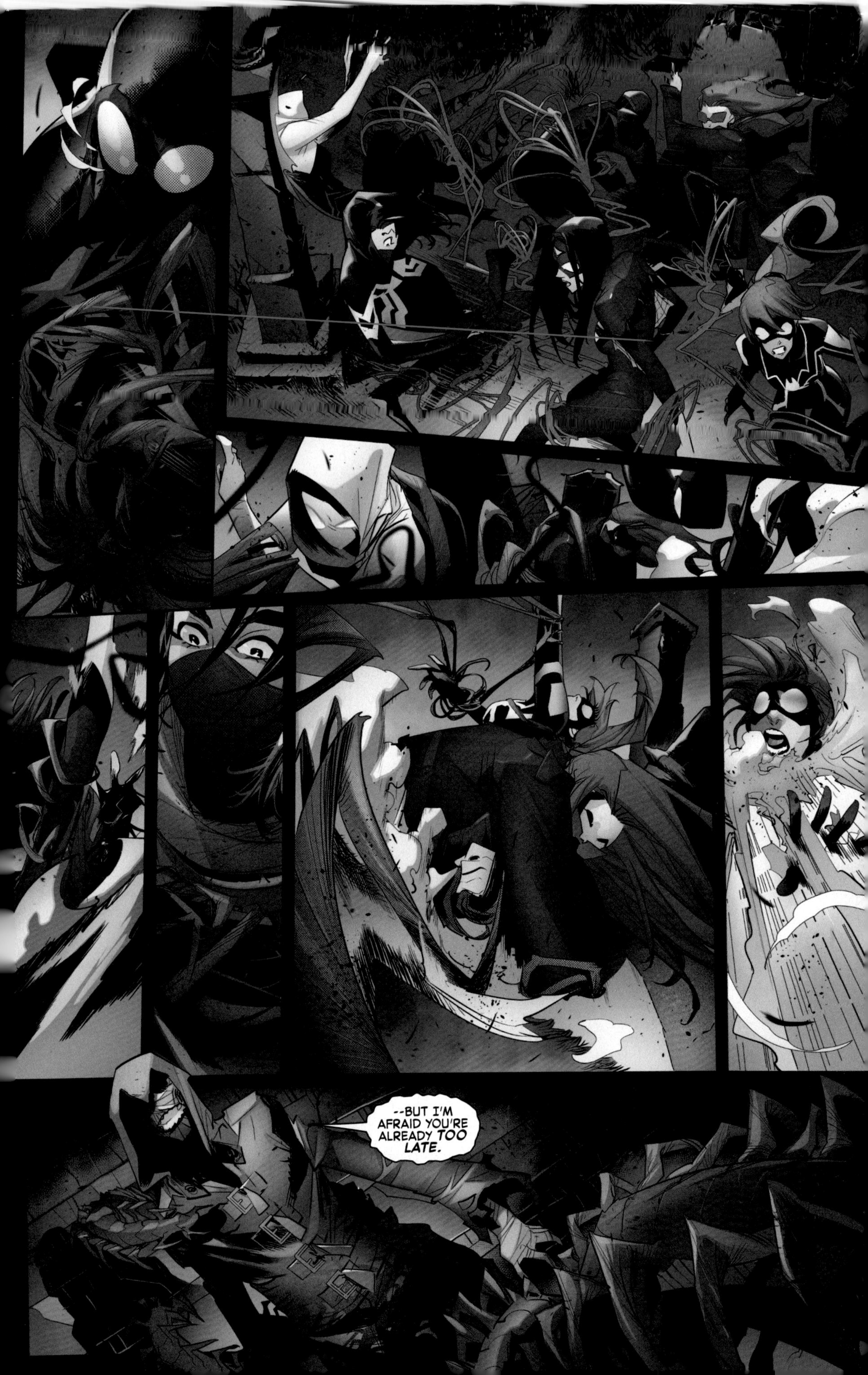
--BUT I'M AFRAID YOU'RE ALREADY TOO LATE.

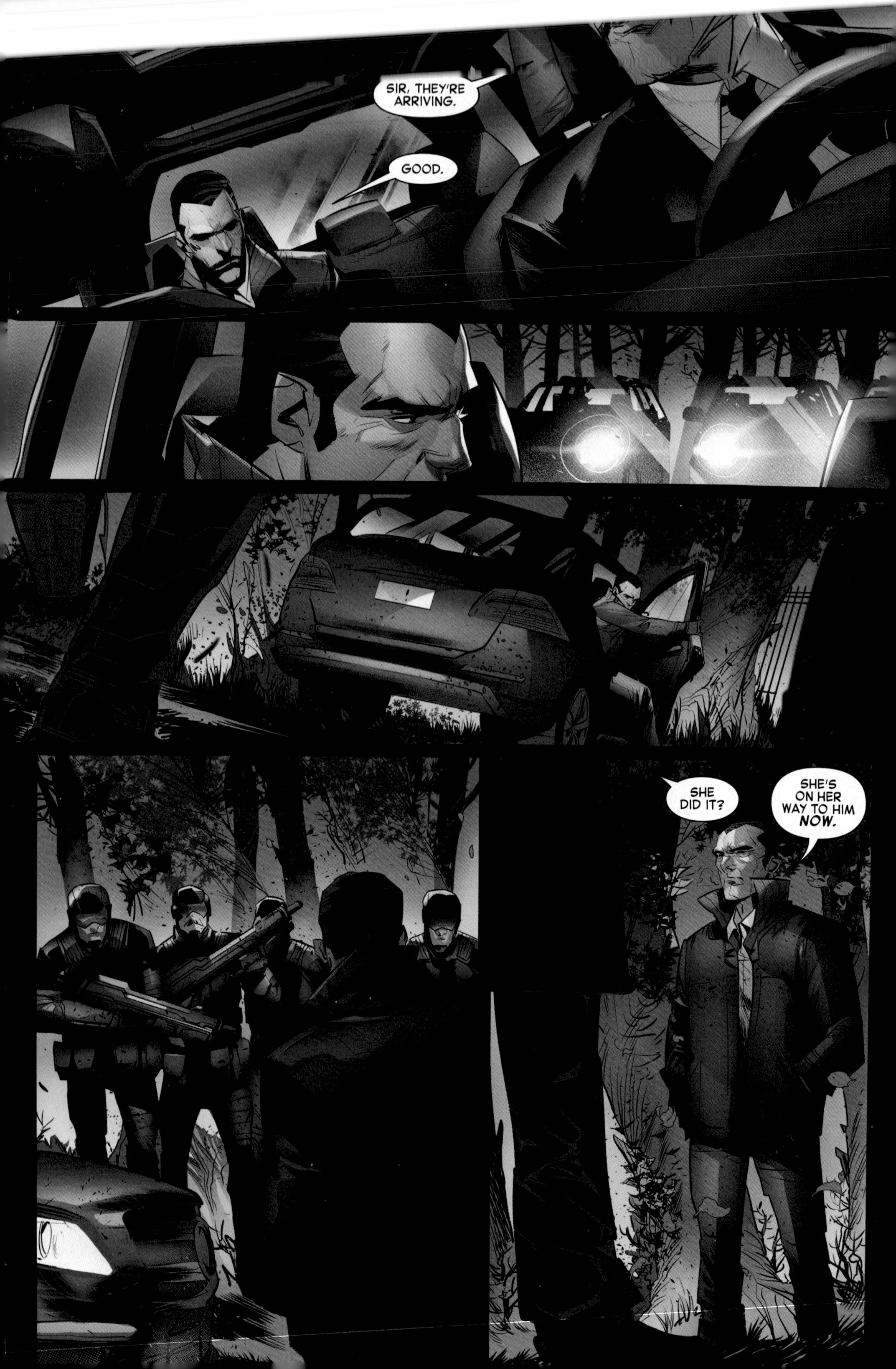
SIR, THEY'RE ARRIVING.
GOOD.
SHE DID IT?
SHE'S ON HER WAY TO HIM NOW.

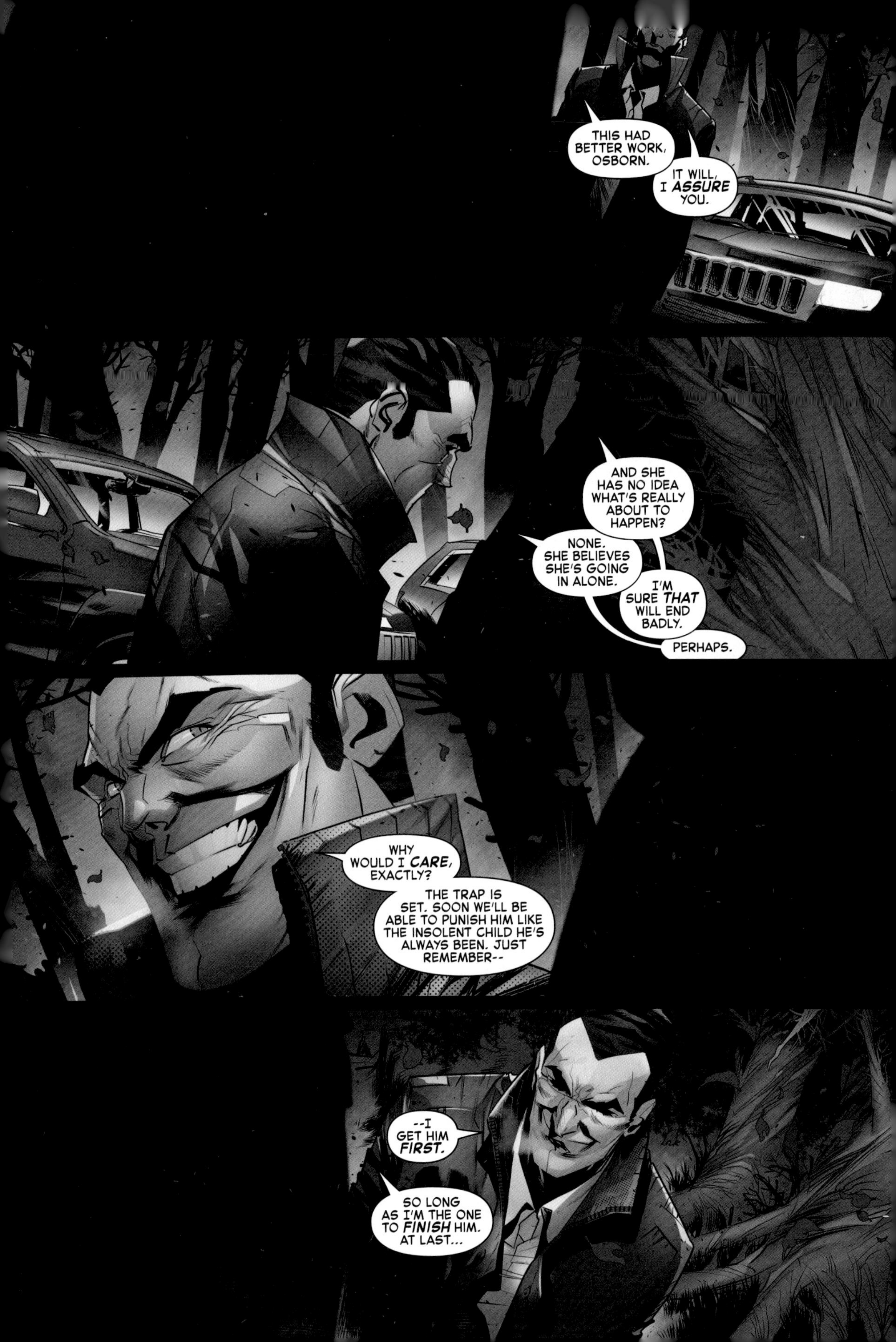
THIS HAD BETTER WORK, OSBORN.
IT WILL, I ASSURE YOU.
AND SHE HAS NO IDEA WHAT'S REALLY ABOUT TO HAPPEN?
NONE. SHE BELIEVES SHE'S GOING IN ALONE.
I'M SURE THAT WILL END BADLY.
PERHAPS.
WHY WOULD I CARE, EXACTLY?
THE TRAP IS SET. SOON WE'LL BE ABLE TO PUNISH HIM LIKE THE INSOLENT CHILD HE'S ALWAYS BEEN. JUST REMEMBER--
--I GET HIM FIRST.
SO LONG AS I'M THE ONE TO FINISH HIM. AT LAST...

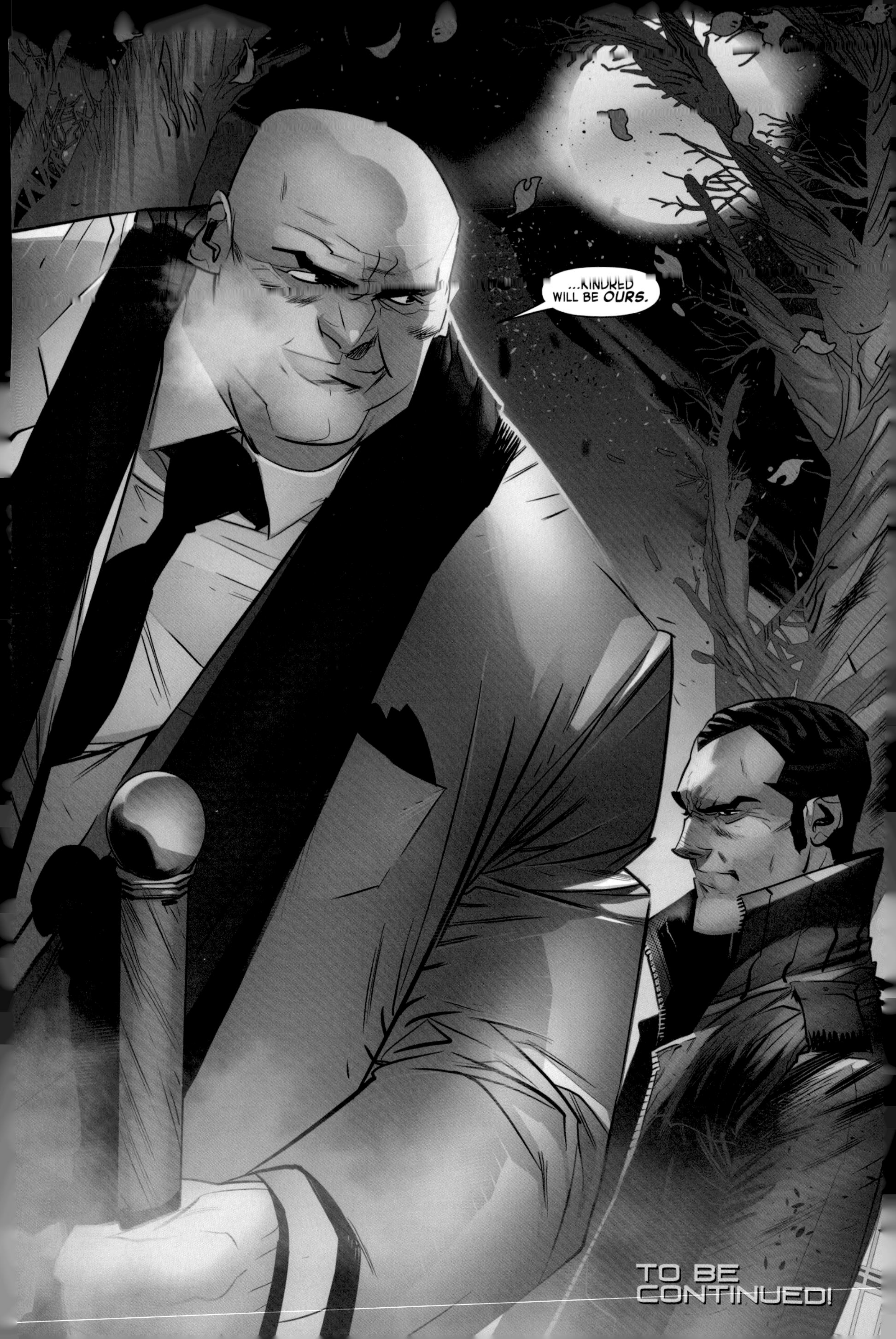
...KINDRED WILL BE OURS.
TO BE CONTINUED!

WEB-HEADS!

Before we get to the usual nonsense, we wanted to take a moment to talk about something serious. As you read in the pages of this issue, the Kindred-resurrected Sin-Eater turned his mystically powered shotgun on himself. Even though this is a story about a very strange and fantastical villain, suicide is a very real subject and not one to gloss over. We wanted to make sure that it was clear that we weren't glorifying or in any way endorsing Sin-Eater's method of solving his problems. Suicide is not the answer to any problem, no matter how huge that problem is. If you are struggling with thoughts of suicide or are worried about a friend or loved one, please reach out to a counselor or someone you trust, call your local helpline, or call the National Suicide Prevention Lifeline: 1-800-273-8255.

Anyway, this epic yarn is nearing its end! Spider-Man is face-to-face with Kindred and Mary Jane is on her way to both of them! The other Spiders have been taken by Kindred as well, and who knows what further plans that centipedal villain has in store for them. Add Kingpin and Norman Osborn to that mix and you know you've got a classic Spider-Man story in the making. Nick Spencer (with Matthew Rosenberg) has been working his butt off to make this the biggest and best story possible, and Patrick Gleason, Mark Bagley, Marcelo Ferreira, Federico Vicentini, and Takeshi Miyazawa have crafted some of the most mind-bending visuals in the history of comics, so we hope your minds have been suitably bent.

And wasn't it great to see those pages from PETER PARKER: THE SPECTACULAR SPIDER-MAN #200?! You can thank Nick Spencer for its wonderful inclusion here, but thank J.M. DeMatteis for writing it, Sal Buscema for drawing it, Joe Rosen for lettering it, Bob Sharen for coloring it and Rob Tokar for editing it! We're super grateful in the Spider-Office as it's one of our faves!

Join us next week for the last AMAZING SPIDER-MAN issue of this crazy year and the climax of LAST REMAINS!

Keep Swinging!

Nick Lowe
Astoria, NY
November 17, 2020

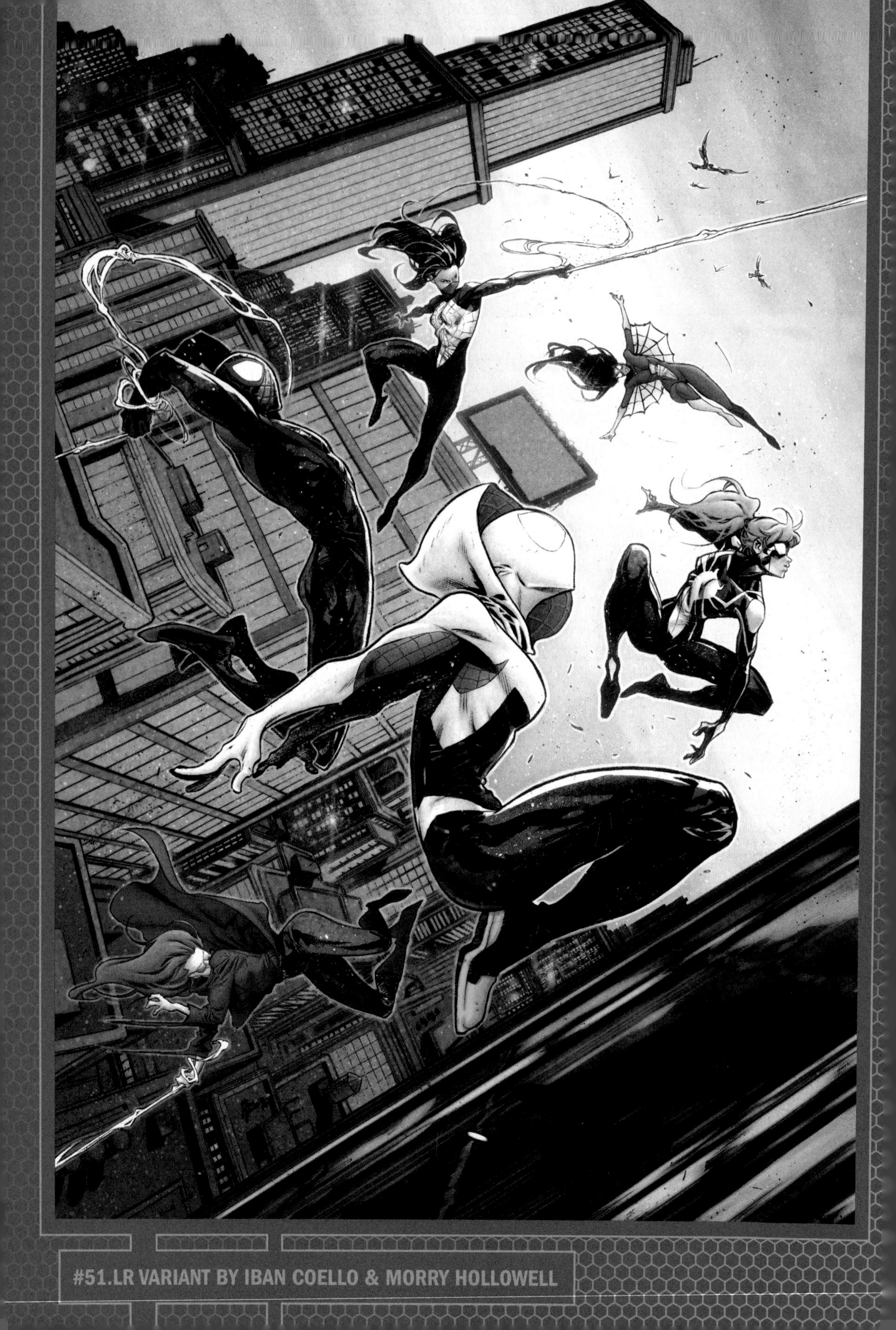

#51.LR VARIANT BY IBAN COELLO & MORRY HOLLOWELL

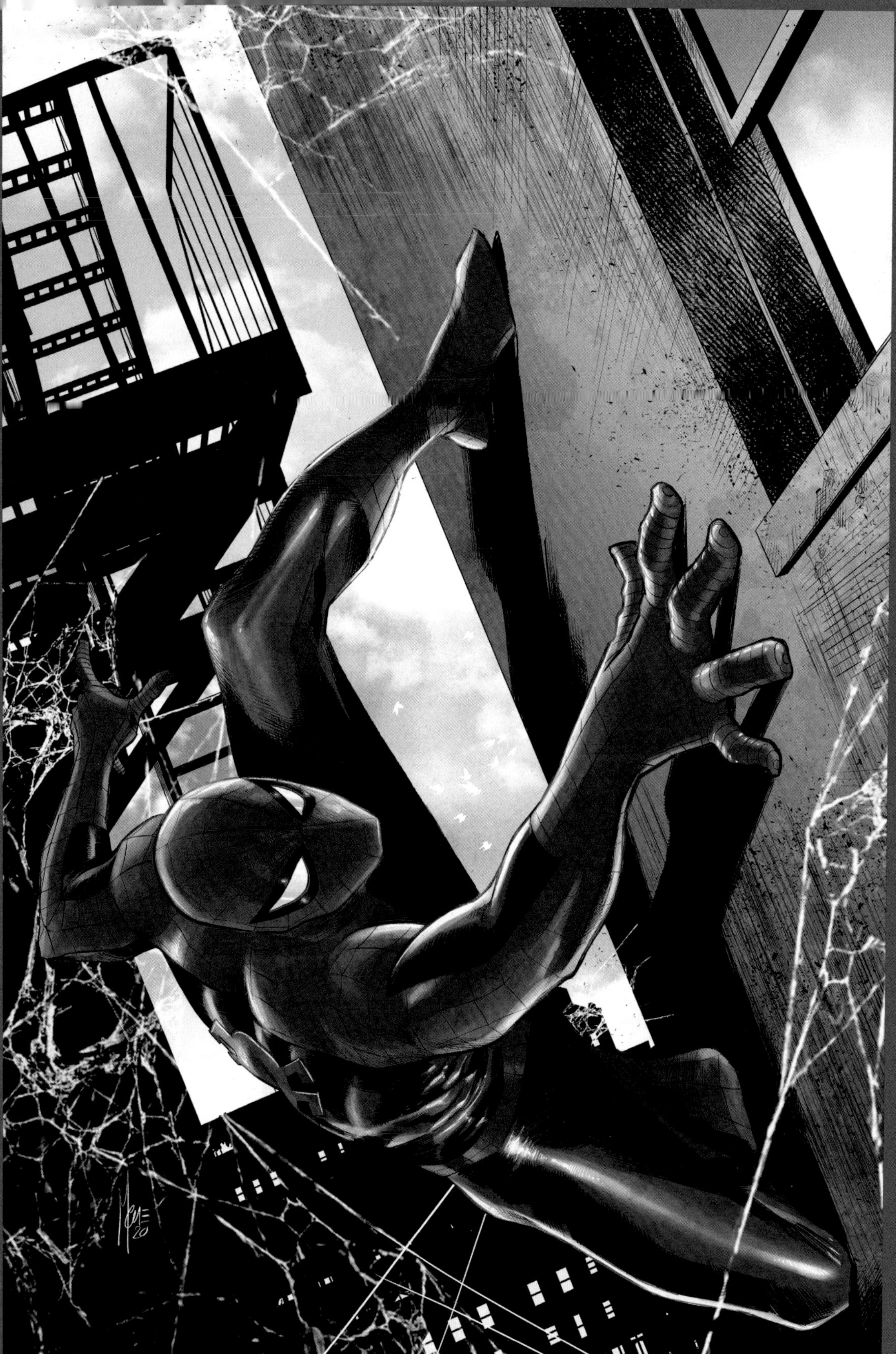

#52.LR VARIANT BY MARCO CHECCHETTO

#53.LR VARIANT BY
KHOI PHAM

#54.LR VARIANT BY
MARK BAGLEY, JOHN DELL & JASON KEITH